STORM OVER THE
CAUCASUS
IN THE WAKE OF INDEPENDENCE

CAUCASUS WORLD
SERIES EDITOR NICHOLAS AWDE

STORM OVER THE
CAUCASUS
IN THE WAKE OF INDEPENDENCE

Charles van der Leeuw

CURZON
CAUCASUS WORLD

CAUCASUS WORLD

First published in the UK in 1999
by Curzon Press
15 The Quadrant, Richmond
Surrey TW9 1BP
England

Typeset and designed by Nicholas Awde/Desert♥Hearts
Covers & maps by Nick Awde

Printed and bound in Great Britain by
Bookcraft, Midsomer Norton, Avon

British Library Cataloguing in Publication Data
A catalogue record for this book is available from the British Library

ISBN 0 7007 1116 3

Contents

C'est le destin des héros de se ruiner à conquérir des pays qu'il perdent soudain, ou à soumettre des nations qu'ils sont obligés eux-mêmes de détruire: comme cet insensé qui se consumoit à acheter des statues, qu'il jetoit dans la mer, et des glaces, qu'il brisoit aussitôt.

—*Montesquieu, 'Lettres persanes'*

PEOPLES OF THE CAUCASUS
— AT A GLANCE —

Acknowledgements

I am most grateful to the governments of Georgia, Azerbaijan and Armenia for their readiness to admit me to all necessary sources of information and make me welcome in their respective countries; to the newsdesk of AVRO Radio in the Netherlands, the editors of *Knack* magazine (Brussels), the *Haagse Courant* (Den Haag) and the magazines *ROM* and *Transfer* (Den Haag) for granting me the necessary assignments to make ends meet; and to the Clingendael Institute (Den Haag) and the Akhundov State Library (Baku) who generously granted research and other working facilities.

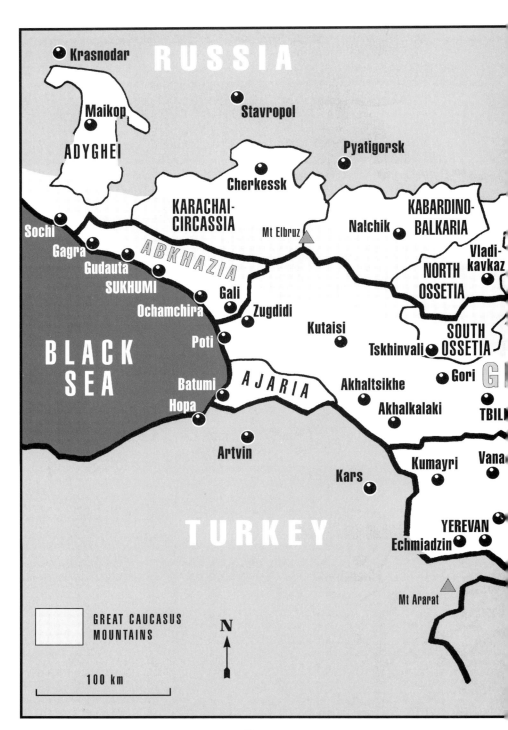

THE CAUCASUS

KALMYKIA

CHECHENIA

GROZNY

Kizlyar

Makhachkala

DAGHESTAN

Derbent

Khachmas

CASPIAN SEA

GIA

uri

Kazakh

Sheki

Mingechaur

Kuba

Sumgayt

Ganja

AZERBAIJAN

BAKU

NAGORNO-KARABAKH

Ali-Bayramli

Stepanakert

ENIA

hchivan

NAKHCHIVAN

Lenkoran

Astara

IRAN

Introduction

Why a book on the Caucasus? The most obvious answer has to be the lamentable lack of up-to-date information on the region despite the fact that since the collapse of the Soviet Union it has become one of the most intriguing and dangerous arenas of armed and political conflict in the world. Even material on the region's historic background is hard to find for those who unprepared to carry out extensive academic research.

As this book is meant to fill both gaps, it necessarily consists of elements the details of which tend to vary. First of all, the work is intended to be an update on the historical and geopolitical backrop that has helped create conditions in Transcaucasia as they exist today. Secondly, in order to make events 'come to life', I have turned to my experiences as a media correspondent in the region.

Transcaucasia is the name of the ever turbulent triangle situated on the crossroads in the very heart of Eurasia. It lies at the feet of one of the world's most forbidding mountain ranges — the Caucasus — which, unlike any other, has captivated imaginations since the dawn of humanity itself.

The region was given its name Transcaucasia by the Russians; before their coming, it was known as Ciscaucasia to the Persian, Greek, Roman and other conquerors who used to occupy the area. To the ancient civilisations the Caucasus represented the barrier that separated the world as they knew it from the "endless waste untrodden by human feet," as Aeschylus put it. The sentinals of the barrier were the Scyths, depicted in the Classics as the very symbol of cruelty and mercilessness.

According to more than one religious tradition, the Caucasus was the cradle of humanity. The name finds its origin in Greek mythology. It is the place where Zeus is said to have won victory over his father Kronos during that cosmic, cataclysmic battle for power which allowed order to gain over chaos. However, Kronos managed to escape, still carrying in his belly Zeus's brothers and sisters, whom he had earlier devoured. A shepherd boy named Kaukazos tried to stop him on the way, upon which Kronos put him cruelly to death. But the delay allowed Zeus to catch up with his foe and kill him in his turn. In honour of the brave young shepherd he named the mountain ridge after him.

The story could well have happened yesterday: the great leader pins a medal on the chests of his cannon-fodder, then comfortably settles down on his newly-conquered throne. But the Caucasus's location as the scene of ancient, heroic tragedy by no means ends here. It is the place where Prometheus, the mythological father of industrial espionage, endures his eternal punishment for stealing fire from heaven in order to console humanity in its suffering from cold and hunger. Modern thinkers turned Prometheus into a symbol of liberty and solidarity and he reappears in this capacity in significant works from Hobbes to Nietzsche: the theme of human progress not being limited to jealous elites but rightfully at the disposal of anyone who seeks to profit on it. This is a theme which unfortunately has been subject to political deformation in recent times and, as we shall see, the scene of Prometheus' destiny is no exception to this tendency.

In later ages another Hellenic tragic hero, Jason, was to tread in Prometheus' footsteps in the same area, namely the kingdom of Colchis, present north-west Georgia/Abkhazia. His quest was to steal the Golden Fleece, probably in reality the secret of forging gold, and then make his fortune with it in Greece. Thanks to the help of Medea, a local princess, Jason was successful. Unlike Prometheus, Jason has gone down in history as a playboy and adventurer — but, like Prometheus, he came to a bad end. Medea, who had accompanied him on the journey home, cruelly turned on her lover after his affair with a Corinthian princess. The Caucasus too was the fiefdom of the Amazons, the semi-mythical women-warriors against whom Alexander the Great is said to have waged battle on his campaign to the east — the only battle he ever lost, it is said.

The Caucasus returns regularly not only in Greek but also in Judaic traditions, although it is given different names. It has been identified with the 'Land of the Giants' where Cain sought refuge after the murder of his brother. In this context a fascinating parallel with Greek and Sumerian legends appears: according to Old Testament tradition, Cain is the traditional inventor of metal forging.

Finally, the Caucasus is said to have been the place where Noah, after his voyage on the Ark, set down on the Armenian holy mountain of Ararat. The Georgians claim it was in their lands that he cultivated the vine for the first time. Although this story has been reinforced by the Georgians throughout their long history by a disproportionately large consumption of wine, it remains contested by the people of Lebanon, who claim Noah found his new home in the Bekaa Valley.

Besides iron, the symbol of strength and ingenuity but also violence and hatred, and gold, the symbol of wealth and power but also greed, terror and self-indulgence, there is one more natural resource which has generated both wealth and war, and of which Transcaucasia is one of the oldest and still richest sources — oil.

Introduction

The symbol of Azerbaijan and the cause of so many struggles for power — black gold — completes the allegory that Transcaucasia has become over the course of history: the meeting place of the four winds where nations alternately shake hands then slaughter one another. Here is living proof that the gifts of the earth and the inventions of Man generate two opposing conclusions: downfall and destruction, if people allow themselves to be led blindly along by what they mistake for their destiny; and progress and wealth if they let themselves be enlightened and allow human spirit and reason to shape events. This is a dichotomy that still persists, unfortunately, and one in which enlightenment is forced to make way for blindness time and time again.

CHARLES VAN DER LEEUW
Baku, 1997

1

Land of fire, city of winds

Anyone driving to the city of Baku for the first time from the airport, sees mainly dislocation: derelict factories and storehouses, disorderly slums along the road and desolate concrete deserts on the horizon. Here and there water comes up to road level — one of the consequences of the ever rising sea-level of the Caspian. Once in the city, things appear less desolate than they first seemed. People go shopping, enjoy their refreshments on a terrace or stroll in the park that separates the sea-boulevard from the water. Even in those days when the war was still going on in all its horror without so much as a cease-fire in sight, there was nothing in Baku to suggest this apart from a few banners calling on people to donate blood and regular patrols of military police looking for youngsters trying to dodge military service.

"Karabakh . . . ? Oh, yes, a pity and all that, isn't it? All those terrible things happening there, what a waste. But what can you do?"

The buffet in the reception hall of the former Intourist hotel, the Azerbaijan, standing on the former Lenin Square (now Unity Square) still looks very much as it did in the old days. But people have changed significantly. The barman Jeyhun — or 'Jackie' as everyone calls him — is a professional of the new breed who always has a smile and a joke ready to cheer his customers up.

The regulars form an eclectic lot. There is Nazim, a doctor and member of the food inspection board. Every day he comes here to test the quality of the vodka: "Charley . . . you, my friend! Cheers!" Then there is the off-duty army major who likes toasting the Red Army: "The most feared army in the world, sir, and look now how these dogs of politicians have dropped it into the gutter!" As with most of the company, he is difficult to engage in any meaningful conversation long before sunset comes.

In those early days, a number of Algerian and other North African 'students' completed the scene. They had come here in the days of the

Soviet regime and, having been educated in the 'realm of the godless', could hardly expect to walk the streets safely in Algeria today. A number of these had managed to settle down in Azerbaijan while their compatriots returned home. As the war cooled down, even this remnant slowly vanished from the hotel buffet as the number of journalists to whom they offered their services as guides and translators dwindled.

Alexandre Dumas, who visited Baku on his trip through the Caucasus in the 1850s, divided the city into a *ville-blanche* and a *ville-noire*. The 'Black City' is the old Oriental part that lurks within the restored ancient wall, a labyrinth of alleys and gateways that breathes still some of the thousand-and-one-night atmosphere. Here is where stand most of the ancient monuments, including the Khan's Palace, dating from the 15th century AD, the Caravanserai, a number of 'Turkish' baths. There's also a curious structure called the Maiden Tower, which archeologists claim is the remainder of a massive defence structure dating from the ninth century or perhaps even earlier.

A more popular explanation for the origin of the building's name is the tale of a princess who lived the late Middle Ages and who asked her father, the king, to build a watch-tower so she could keep watch for her lover who had gone off to battle across the sea. Although the family disapproved of the marriage, the king relented and had the tower built for his daughter. The princess, on seeing her lover's ship approach the harbour carrying a black ensign, thought that he had perished and hurled herself from the tower. But in truth he was alive, and after learning his betrothed's fate he followed her example and died too.

In fact, today the 'Black City' is far less black than the 'White' one that surrounds it with its belle-epoque facades scorched with car fumes and chimney smog. Most of the gaps in the cityscape have been caused by fire or demolition. Baku was largely spared the fate of many other cities during both World Wars, except for sporadic artillery attacks in 1918 — in fact, the city has remained largely undamaged for nearly two hundred years.

Blacker than black, however, is the area surrounding the city, where thick layers of oil sludge have made the soil terminally barren. These moon-landscapes are separated from the central part of the city by massive concrete residential areas from the times of Brezhnev and Gorbachev. The only thing that brings a spark of life into these parts of Baku is the many thousands of stalls and shops where people try to sell anything they can lay their hands on.

The retail trade, disorganised and non-marketed as it is, is one of the most visible symptoms of post-Soviet societies as exist today. Since salaries have dropped to levels varying from a few dozen dollars to almost nothing, people keep their jobs only for the sake of prestige — "to be somebody" — while other members of the family make ends meet with the paltry and ignoble income that petty trade in sweets, cigarettes, drinks, food and small household articles provides. And so, aside from those unfortunate pensioners without relatives to rely on and many of the war refugees, few people in Transcaucasia are really threatened with utter starvation.

There is at least one other feature that strikes the attention of the first-time visitor to Baku — it is one of the world's windiest cities. Not for nothing does Baku mean 'City of Winds' in Ancient Persian. During the winter a freezing wind blows down from the mountains in the north which keeps the capital cold and damp until early May. Then, within a few weeks, the wind promptly turns east and is transformed into a dusty and glowing hot mistral from the deserts of Turkmenistan.

Within a surface area of some 35,000 square miles, Azerbaijan boasts nine out the the world's twelve main climatic categories, including the Mediterranean climate on the peninsula of Apsheron on which Baku is situated, the mountain climate in the Caucasus, the wet sea climate north of the Caucasus, the wet plains climate north of the River Kura and the dry one south of it, the desert climate of Qobustan south-west of Apsheron, and the wet sub-tropical climate of Talysh to the south between the Caspian Sea and the Iranian border.

The territory is as varied in the composition of its inhabitants too. Only a small fraction of the estimated 35 million 'ethnic' Azeri Turks live in the republic of Azerbaijan — about six million in a total population of 7.5 million. Over 20 million live in northern Iran and north-western Afghanistan, while over five million have migrated to the Russian Federation and other former republics of the Soviet Union, Turkey and Iraq, and about three-quarters of a million to Europe and North America.

The most important Azeri 'tribes' within the borders of Azerbaijan are the Padari in the east, the Ayrumi in the west, the Shahveveni in the plains of Mughan and Lower Karabakh in the south of the country and the Karapapakh in the south-western enclave of Nakhchivan. The most important minorities in Azerbaijan are Russian and Ukrainian immigrants and their descendants, the Talysh, speakers of an Indo-European language, to the south-east, and a number of Caucasian peoples, most of whom live scattered across villages in the north and west.

The Lezgians are the largest Caucasian people in Azerbaijan. There are 200,000 in the north-east of Azerbaijan and Baku, against 300,000 across the border in Daghestan, a Russian federal republic which contains 32 different ethnic minorities and no majority at all. The Lezgians have 'cultural autonomy' in Azerbaijan, but any political aspiration is radically ruled out. The Lezgian Sadval party, which until the mid-1990s called for an 'independent' Lezgistan along both banks of the River Samur, which forms the border, is legal in Daghestan yet still remains outlawed in Azerbaijan even after the offending separatist paragraphs were removed from the party's manifesto.

There are also the Armenians. Only a few thousand now linger on in Azerbaijan, most as a result of mixed marriages. How many Armenians have remained, returned or settled in the occupied territories, is marked as 'classified information' in Yerevan . . .

It is almost certain that the name Azerbaijan is a derivation of Atropates, the last Persian satrap under Darius III who sided with Alexander the Great against his sovereign. In later ages, the name was to change along with the development of Classical Persian into Aturpatakan, which subsequently became Ajarbajagan in medieval Persian to end up as Azerbaijan by the time of the Renaissance.

But Azerbaijan is much older than its Persian lords of old. In fact, the oldest organised state on the banks of the River Arax dates from the ninth century BC and was known as the principality of Zamoa. Subsequently, the area fell under the dominion of the Assyrians and the Medes to await the Persian conquerors. Not long after Alexander's death, Atropatena was incorporated into the Seleucid Empire and extended to the north. After another Persian conquest under the Arshakids, the northern part broke away and a feudal kingdom by the name of Albania was formed — a kingdom which has nothing in common with the Adriatic Albania but its name.

Early in the first century BC the kingdom of Armenia extended its sway over all the lands south of the Kura and held it until the Roman conquest of the whole of Transcaucasia in 69 BC. During the second century AD the Parthians took the place of the Romans. After the subsequent collapse of the Parthian Empire, Azerbaijan was split into Atropatena to the south under Persian rule and Albania north of the River Arax as an independent federal kingdom.

In the early fourth century Albania adopted Christianity as state religion while Atropatena came under the domination of Sassanid Neo-Zoroastrism, or Mazdeism. At the coming of the Arabs in the seventh century, Islam was introduced gradually, but politically the north and the south developed independently under for the caliphate's overlordship. Up to this day, several political parties in Azerbaijan have a 'reunification' paragraph in their programmes in respect to 'South Azerbaijan', although attempts in the area to split from Iran in 1920 and 1945 to join their cousins to the north failed.

Though they may be 'ethnically' Turks, Azeris enjoy a culture which is an amalgam of Caucasian (the Albanians of old are considered to originate from the Greater or High Caucasus), Persian and Turkic elements. Until well into the 20th century, Persian and not Azeri was spoken in large parts of the countryside. Until the independence of 1918, the Persian alphabet was used for the Azeri language. After that, the Latin script was introduced after Atatürk's literacy drive in Turkey. In 1938, Stalin ordered the Cyrillic alphabet to be imposed on all languages throughout the USSR. There were some exceptions, including Armenian and Georgian (Stalin's mother tongue), but not Azeri. Today, since 1993, the Latin alphabet is being re-introduced steadily but surely.

According to most ethnologists, the main ancestors of the present-day Azeris were the Central Asian Oghuz whose leaders, the Seljuqs, ruled Persia, Mesopotamia and Transcaucasia during the 11th and the first half of the 12th centuries. The second half of the 11th century saw the Oghuz at their most glorious in Azerbaijan under the Il-Tengiz, better known as the Atabeks. Under Atabek supremacy, a range of principalities such as Arran, Nakhchivan, Karabakh, Sheki and Shirvan developed an exceptionally high level of political, scientific, economic and cultural development.

Little has been preserved of the architecture from that time. In the course of time medieval cities such as Ganja, Barda (Partav), Shemakha, Shirvan and Belagan have been hit by devastating earthquakes — and what nature left undamaged, human intervention with the aid of fire and later guns has razed the rest to the ground. Apart from Sheki, Nakhchivan and the city of Baku and its immediate environs where some of the features still breathe the atmosphere of the days of the Silk Route, one has to look hard for reminders of the glory that was old Azerbaijan. Most places today look like any in the former Soviet Union and are distinguished mainly by dull concrete blocks and the gleaming aluminium roofs of the farms and dachas.

It is essentially the nation's immense rich literary heritage, mercifully spared by Stalin's cultural revolution, which has comforted the hearts of the Azeri intellectual in those dark days. Even today the names of Meskheti, Khagani, Nassimi and Fizuli and Nizami are on everybody's lips.

What Shakespeare means for any Briton, Descartes for any Frenchman, Dante for any Italian, Cervantes for any Spaniard and Confucius for any Chinese, Nizami is for any Azeri. He lived from 1141 to 1209 and, apart from a large collection of shorter poetry, his *Khamsa*, a five-volume feast of lengthy poems, remains the flower of Azeri literature. The *Khamsa* consists of the 'House of Mysteries', 'Khosrow and Shirin', 'Leyla and Majnun' (the Eastern version of Romeo and Juliet — Fizuli's own version in later times was to be adapted by the Azeri composer Uzeyr Haddjibekov to become the world's first Islamic opera), the 'Seven Beauties' and an epic poem dedicated to Alexander the Great, the 'Iskander-nameh'.

Two main themes prevail throughout the Azeri classics: the passion of human love and the call for spiritual and intellectual freedom. In numerous works, including 'Leyla and Majnun', these two themes are heavily intertwined. Poets such as Nizami, Fizuli and others offered love ruled out by a patriarchal social order as an act of resistance against the said order's contempt for individual conscience.

This is reflected in the mentality of the people themselves. Every visitor will recall the Azeri's typical reaction to any attempt at pressurization: they merely shrug, not as a sign of contempt but rather the expression of sincere amazement at the other's animosity — "So what?"

It is precisely this same contemplative attitude that makes the Azeri regard with both curiosity and distance such phenomena as nationalism in Turkey or the religious zeal displayed by their Iranian neighbours to the south. In fact, Azeris have been Shi'i Muslims ever since 1501 when Shah Ismail I of Persia, founder of the Safavid dynasty which originated from Azerbaijan and whose realm included it, proclaimed Shi'i Islam as state religion throughout his empire. But this does not mean that at any stage, including today, that Azerbaijan was ever in danger of becoming a 'Little Iran'. Caucasians who decline from a glass of vodka are a rare species and the Azeris are no exception to this. Homosexuality is accepted as a social phenomenon, and the only place where women wear veils is on the stage of a traditional dance theatre. It couldn't be simpler: religious rituals remain within the mosque's walls and politics stay outside them.

What it all boils down to is that Azerbaijan is possibly the only place in the world where Shi'ism as it was first conceived may still be found intact. The principal difference with Sunni Islam is the Shi'i refusal to blindly accept the authority of the *ulema*, the 'council of the wise' whose task it is to see to it that the letter of the Qur'an — God's final and indisputable message to mankind till the Day of Judgement — is followed. The saying that "God continues to speak to he who is ready to hear Him" — attributed to Imam Ali — is a blasphemy in the eyes of any conservative Sunni. According to Shi'ism, man's own judgement for any of his personal decisions is answerable to the heavenly power only and not to any earthly one, and this should be followed at every stage of one's earthly life, even if it means going against social consensus. Such a declaration of the supremacy of every man's personal conscience is a dismaying thought for Sunnis everywhere — with the notable exception of those Sunnis in the Eastern Caucasus, who share many of the attitudes of their Azeri neighbours.

During the 1920s and 1930s, the Soviets tried — with occasional success but largely in vain — not so much to outlaw Islam in Azerbaijan but reduce it to a curiosity of folklore. In contrast with the Christian clergy, the Islamic leaders were granted party membership on the basis of their status — presumably one of the Soviets' motives being a strategic alliance with Atatürk's new Turkey. The celebration of Ramadan and Ashura — the ten day Shi'i ceremony in commemoration of the death of Imam Hussein — remained official sanctioned, even though the latter included public rituals of self-flagellation, popularly referred to as *'shaksey-vaksey'* after the chant to the rhythm of the whip of "Shah-Husseyn! Vah-Husseyn!"

But in the immediate years following the independence of 1991, the impact of Islam on daily life remained limited in Azerbaijan. Though in spring 1995 in Baku the *shaksey-vaksey* attracted hundreds of participants and tens of thousands of spectators, it did not stop the onlookers from sitting down afterwards for a glass or two of alcoholic refreshment. Now the historical symbol of the Azeri tendency for tolerance and spiritual self-determination has become embodied in Babek, leader of the ninth century rebellion. Novels, dramas, movies, a ballet and even an opera have been dedicated to the rebel hero, and his significance for Azerbaijan may be compared to that Joan of Arc for France, William Tell for Switzerland or even Robin Hood for England.

Originally Babek was the spiritual leader of an Islamic mystical sect, the Khorammites, and it was only after the Caliph of Damascus ordered Babek's sect to be exterminated to the last man that he joined a revolt already in full swing. The Khorammites sought a form of synthesis between the Brahmin doctrine of self-exaltation and the Qur'an by trying to explain the Holy Book as a secret code of symbolic meaning — a principle used also by the Alavis in later days. The Khorammites denied any authority of the clergy over worldly matters, thus undermining directly the position of the Caliph — in those days the most powerful individual in the world, with the possible exception of Charlemagne and the Emperor of China, and not therefore inclined to bow to any provocation.

The bloody persecutions perpetrated against the Khorammites drove Babek and his peers into the arms of Javidan, the leader of an armed uprising who commanded a guerrilla force centred in Upper Karabakh and who enjoyed the hardly covert support of the princes of Sheki and Shirvan and a number of other feudal lords. After Javidan's death in 816, Babek took over command of the rebel force and ten years on found himself virtual ruler over a vast piece of land on the south banks of the River Kura — in 829, he even captured the city of Isfahan.

At that point, the feudal rulers back on the other side of the river decided that Babek had over-reached himself. Money and troops stopped flowing from the north and Babek's former patrons looked the other way when in 833 and 835 he suffered fatal defeats against expeditions by the Caliphate from Baghdad. After losing Bazz, his final stronghold, to the Caliph's army in 837, Babek escaped to Sheki, where his former protector put him in jail and handed him over to the Arabs. Shortly afterwards, he was ignominiously decapitated in Baghdad.

While Babek's presence has certainly not diminished in Azerbaijan, certainly most of the once omnipresent Soviet symbols have already disappeared from the streets. In the capital, however, there are two notable exceptions. The first is a monument to Nariman Narimanov, Azerbaijan's first Bolshevik leader after the occupation in 1920, but whose hands were stained with the blood of tens of thousands Azeri citizens until he himself perished in Stalin's purges of 1937-38. His statue once dominated the centre of Baku from the top of a nearby hilltop, but even though the statue still stands, it found itself overshadowed in 1997 by the construction of a huge apartment block immediately behind it. The second monument to be spared is that dedicated to the Twenty Six Commissars — Bolsheviks massacred in the desert near Baku in 1919 standing in a square near the centre and, ironically enough, right under the Turkish embassy's balcony. Their continuing presence is the all more ironic since their leader was an Armenian by the name of Stepan Shaumian.

The main reason that both monuments remain untoppled is the fact that the main perpetrator of their evil deeds has since long been identified: the Great Bear of Russia. The pretext under which Peter the Great occupied the entire east coast of the Caspian in 1722 is still in high fashion today, namely that of security. Not that it was the first time — in 1032, long before the Mongol wave of terror in the area, King Yaroslav of Kiev, son of Saint Vladimir who had founded the Russian Orthodox Empire, despatched his brother Mstislav over the Caucasus Range with an impressive army with which he occupied most of Shirvan, including Baku, and even penetrated south of the Kura by occupying Barda.

The reason for the campaign remains unclear: it was only after the downfall of Constantinople in 1453 that the Russian sovereigns took on the title of Tsar, or Caesar, and swore to settle for no less than the throne of restored Byzantium. The 'Ros' stayed in Transcaucasia for less than a year. But not even ages of Mongol supremacy could prevent the Russians from continuing to look greedily to the Silk Route zone to their south where in those days more than half the trade caravans between Europe and the Far East stopped over. And throughout history up to this day, satisfaction of greed for any Russian powerbroker has meant one thing only: total submission.

The threat to Azerbaijan of Peter the Great's campaign was immensely more real than that of his 11th century predecessors had been. At that time, powerful principalities such as Shirvan and Sheki stood firm; moreover, the Seljuqs who had united the region under their banner thanks to their ever-expanding human resources of Turkmen soldier-tribesmen, held both Byzantium and Persia at bay with their iron grip on the communities and had no trouble at all in dealing with invaders from the north. But in 1722, the situation was quite different since the Azeri lords had multiplied in number and dwindled in force, involved as they were in internal struggles and endless feuds. Complaints by Russian traders about disorder on land and pirate attacks at sea finally gave Peter his chance to make his move and occupy both Derbent and Baku, including much of its hinterland. An expedition to the Persian coast, however, failed.

It was less Azeri resistance than the coming of a new powerful ruler over Persia, called Nadir, who invaded Azerbaijan in 1735 that forced the Russians to withdraw. Nadir was to rule with an iron fist and in 1747 got himself murdered, followed by the break-up of his empire. For the Azeri feudal lords, once more left to their own devices, it meant only the continuation of their previous version of the War of the Roses.

First, Hajj Saleb, lord of Sheki, manoeuvred himself into a position to take over the country at the expense of his peers. After his murder, Fath Ali-Khan, lord of Quba, attempted the same thing and was on the point of succeeding when the newly crowned Shah of Persia Aga-Muhammad invaded the country from the south in the early 1789s. At this, the lords of Derbent and Karabakh, following the king of Georgia's example (see later) called on the Russian Empress Catherine II for help. It was only shortly before her death in 1796 that Catherine was to send troops over the Caucasus, an action which came too late and in insufficient number. Her successor Paul I then saw himself forced to withdraw the troops because of alarming events in Europe. The return of the Russians five years later was not exactly what the king who had called on them had quite in mind; they had come to stay, whereas the royal family would soon be forced to leave.

After some hesitation, presumably in order to reach a consensus with the British, who by that time exerted firm control over Iran, the Russian army ran through Azerbaijan like a steamroller. Ganja and the sultanate of Ilisu fell in 1804, Sheki, Shirvan and Karabakh in 1805, and Quba in 1806. In 1828, after a war with Persia over Azerbaijan, the Russians gained Talysh-Mughan, Nakhchivan and Yerevan in a peace treaty by which the River Arax was officially recognised as the international border between the two empires.

The fall of Baku was particularly colourful. As the Russian army marched on the city, their commander-in-chief General Tsitsianov (a bankrupt Georgian nobleman who as a compensation had been offered rapid promotion through the ranks of the imperial army) rode ahead to demand the keys of the city from the hands of its ruler. He was relying on the chivalry of his opponent despite warnings from his Armenian lieutenants that heads of ambassadors tended to be knocked off easily in this part of the world.

According to Alexandre Dumas, on hearing this, the general is said to have shouted: "They would never dare . . . !" — quoting Julius Caesar. But the quote would prove to be in the correct context at least as the khan came in person to meet the general at the gates of his city, sword in hand. But instead of humbly offering it to the conqueror, he promptly lopped his head off with it. Such was the consternation among the Russian chiefs of staff that they decided to leave Baku aside until reinforcements had arrived — which took nearly a year. Meanwhile, the khan had escaped to Iran, but the revenge the Russians wreaked on those who remained was terrible. For ten days, the city was bombarded into the ground, at which the Russian soldiers then entered the place in a drunken orgy of rape, pillage and murder. An inconceivable and irreplaceable treasure of architecture and other cultural objects was lost forever.

The first decades of Russian dominion over Azerbaijan were a time of purely colonial rule which reduced the entire Azeri nation to the status of third-rate citizens in their own land. All property fell to the Russian Crown which promptly divided it up as a reward for those officers who had distinguished themselves during the campaigns against Napoleon. Some of the *beks* (the Azeri feudal land-owners), deprived of their land and thereby their sole source of income, managed to continue their luxurious lifestyle of old by entering into their new lords' service as caretakers, in charge of estates now belonging to the Russian gentry. As for the farmers who had worked on the land for countless generations, they now became the serfs of the new owners, while the townsfolk saw all their civil rights abolished, including the right to trade. Absolute power over property, life and death had been gathered into the hands of the Russian military governor.

The radical political oppression was to last for almost forty years. During this time, several uprisings occurred such as several in Ganja throughout the 1820s, in Quba in 1830 and in Talysh in 1831. Not many details about them are known since there was a wall constructed around the ever-expanding Russian Empire and Russian citizens were not permitted to travel abroad except on state missions. It is certain, however, that every uprising was drenched in blood and that numerous mass deportations of Azeri communities took place. The general rule was that if there was any conflict between villagers and/or farmers on one side and the land-owning class on the other, the 'hard-core' leadership of the former was executed and the area's population 'displaced' — which meant a one-way ticket to Kazakhstan in Central Asia or Siberia. Only in 1841, under Viceroy Baron P. V. Hahn — said to have been of a somewhat more humane character and a great admirer of the 'Tatar' culture — was land returned to its previous owners, except for a number of 'strategic territories' for which, however, there was financial compensation.

Under Alexander II, the Azeris were granted the same civil rights as all other inhabitants of the Empire — be it at a snail's pace: whereas serfdom was abolished in Russia proper in 1861, Azerbaijan had to wait until 1869. But even then, farmers remained in the same state of misery they had been ever since the Russian occupation. In Baku, the illiterate countrymen proved hard to adapt to modern labour discipline in comparison to the Russian, Turkish and Iranian cheap labour force, crowds of which had poored into the city at the eruption of the oil rush. By the turn of the century, Azeris would still number less than ten per cent of Baku's labour force.

It was against all these odds that nonetheless an intellectual Azeri middle class emerged — partly in Tbilisi, which was the Caucasus region's intellectual and cultural capital during the 19th century as well as its political one, and in Baku too as the development of the oil industry mushroomed. They laid the basis for Azerbaijan as it is today, by reasoning that Azeri nationalism could hardly be based on glory of old alone.

The bottom-line reasoning of this intellectual middle class was far from groundless. In contrast to Armenia and Georgia, Azerbaijan throughout its long history has never known a strong royal house to protect the community against the whims of feudal lords. In the absence of flag-carrying monarchs, local princes were interrupted only by foreign invasions at times in their everlasting internal feuds. Even the Mikhranids who used to rule over what was then Caspian Albania from the third to the eighth centuries had merely consolidated the territory's boundaries, and no Azeri empire has ever put the region under its bounds in the entire history of the Caucasus. In order to turn this 'historic tragedy' to their advantage, the young intellectuals reasoned, Azerbaijan had to take the lead in establishing a modern, democratic state, where democratic principles rather than royalty should put the aspirations of all society's layers in balance and preserve the nation's unity.

These are briefly the ideas of people like Mammeddin Rasulzadeh, leader of the Mussavat-party and self-made tycoon Zeynalabdul Taghiyev and his Liberal Party, whose respective stars rose in Baku in the aftermath of the events of 1905-6 (see later chapters). Unfortunately, the development of their thoughts, expressed in their periodicals and public statements, did not pass unnoticed in those two somewhat less than democratic neighbours: Turkey and Russia.

Turkish influence was already substantial in the early 20th century as Rasulzadeh had heavily relied on the Sublime Porte's support. After a failed attempt to provoke a revolt in Iranian Azerbaijan in 1905, he fled to Turkey and from there focused on Russian Azerbaijan in order to make his dream come true. But Turkish support for the Mussavat came under pressure in 1908 as Enver Pasha's Ittihad movement put an end to the fossilised regime of the Ottoman Sultanate. Back in Baku, the Azeri branch of the Ittihad won the support of Nariman Narimanov's Hummet party, founded in 1904 and cheerfully supported Enver's ambition of a 'roll-forward Eastwards' which was supposed to end up in the establishment of a Greater Turkish Empire encompassing all the ancestral land of the Turks and stretching from the Bosphorus in the west to the Chinese Wall in the east.

In an attempt to counter his rivals' ambitions, Rasulsadeh responded with a vast propaganda campaign for the re-establishment of 'Greater Azerbaijan' stretching from West Afghanistan to the Caucasus. The fact that the Mussavat was to win back Enver Pasha's support in the end was largely thanks to the Hummet party's 'switch to the Left' after the outbreak of the First World War which ended in Narimanov taking sides with the Bolsheviks.

The Left in Azerbaijan found its origin in the belle epoque with the foundation of the Mollah Nasreddin group, named after its founder's pen-name. Even pseudo-revolutionary straightforward political activities were risky business in those days, and it was therefore that the group operated as a literary salon and through the publication of a satirical magazine by the same name. Initially, the company was extremely mixed and its platform was filled with salon Socialists, barricade Communists, sworn anarchists and other strange birds. As time went by, however, its witty character of the earlier hours graudally made place for doctrinary Marxism and eventually the group was marginalised by a new, this time underground and ready-to-go Bolshevik under the heavy influence of the very geopolitical megaforce that ruled already over Azerbaijan — Russia.

Well hidden in the slums of the Pyervomayskaya district, near the heart of Baku, stands an old barracks. It was here, in the early years of the 20th century, that four gentlemen used to meet whose very names were to stand for terror in years to come. Two were Armenians by the names of Kamp Ter-Petrossian and Anastas Mikoyan. The other two were Georgians, one was Kote Tsintsadze and the other 'Koba' Jughashvili, later to become better known as Joseph Stalin.

Between 1905 and 1907, in the middle of ethnic bloodshed on the streets of Baku (see below), these four came to prominence through their publications in the legal leftist paper *Gudok* ('Signal') and the underground *Bakyinsky Proletariy*. Anyone looking at old copies of both periodicals will be surprised at how such an uproar at the time could be caused by such air-filled leaflets that contained no news whatsoever and seemed intent only on boring their readership with bawling rhetoric that told them nothing new.

But other acts, carried out especially by Mikoyan who was in charge of the 'operative' section of the gang, were of a far more spectacular character than the movement's manifestations in speech and writing — acts such as bombings and hold-ups on banks and trains, including the highjacking of the Motor Ship Nicholas I in which they managed to lay their hands on a million gold roubles. Cash acquired this way enabled the Communist movement to purchase massive stockpiles of arms and ammunition and at the same time build up the necessary funds to pay strikers when the hour came.

It came, or so it was believed, on June 7th 1907. A call for a general strike received mass support in Baku, mainly because on this occasion Bolshevik die-hards, Mensheviks, social-revolutionaries, the Hummet and even Armenian Dashnak nationalists were all ready to back the action. The Dashnaks had signed up since they had previously joined the Second International (the revisionist movement that denounced doctrinary Marxism, resulting in the formation of the Menshevik socialist-democratic parties) in a tactical move (see below). The reason for such a bizarre coalition, although it proved to be occasional, was that in those days party ideologies contributed to party images and identities to a very limited extent only. It was indeed hard to tell the difference between a moderate Hummetist and a radical Mussavatist or between a radical Menshevik and a moderate Bolshevik. Moreover, personalities regularly switched from one party to another, as did parties in respect to one another in terms of alliances.

At the time, none of these arguments were taken into account and it was widely believed that the common front was solid enough and that capitalism was faltering in Baku. Back in Geneva, Lenin and his companions were ready to step in and overthrow the world order altogether, starting in Baku where, as they were convinced, the torch of the proletariat's triumph would be lit in order to carry it around the rest of the world.

In reality, the bad news was to break through soon enough. After a week or so, the proletariat cheerfully resumed work after having concluded an agreement with the employers which included a slight wage increase and a few measures to keep the prices of consumer goods and real estate under control. As for the proletariat's failed dictatorship on the spot, they went behind bars — even if their sentences were strangely mild. Thus, Stalin got ten years of exile and even after an escape attempt he was only sentenced once more to serve out the rest of his term. It seems as though the authorities never fully realised the true dimensions of the danger the 'proletarian' movement represented to the actual physical existence of the Russian imperial system and all that it stood for.

Nonetheless, the Communist movement saw the break-up of the Baku strike as the worst setback in its existence to date. Lenin expressed his despair by publicly stating that he had lost every hope of seeing the Proletarian Revolution happen while he lived and that he would devote the rest of his days to writing an exhaustive treatise on the history of mankind as a social animal.

Although Mikoyan after his release had managed to restore the underground movement's infrastructure, enthusiasm for it had dwindled in Baku, and Lenin and co. now turned their tired focus on Moscow and St Petersburg in a bid to try and trigger off fresh revolts there. In this way, in Azerbaijan in 1915, shortly after the Turks had entered the First World War on the side of the German-Austrian alliance, it was not not the Bolsheviks but the nationalists who were to step into the power vacuum in the Southern Caucasus to realise their dream of a new and sovereign Azerbaijan. That same year, in Ganja, an armed group calling itself Difay, composed mainly of Mussavat militants and supported by Constantinople, emerged from its hide-out to occupy public buildings, in the process proclaiming the republic of Azerbaijan. Ironically, according to reports, they were only able to do so thanks to support by local Dashnak cells whose anti-Russian feelings for once had prevailed over their natural mistrust of Azeri nationalism. Whatever the case, the step was taken prematurely and within a week fresh Russian troops were moved in and the insurgency drenched in blood as soldiers opened random fire at anyone they considered suspect.

The First Revolution in Russia in early 1917 brought about the creation of the Transcaucasian Federation, consisting of Georgia, Armenia and Azerbaijan, in the elected parliament of which the Mensheviks had a relative majority. The nascent republic lasted only a year and imploded under its government's inability to prevent armed conflicts between the participants (see below).

In Baku, May 28th has become once more a public holiday after the collapse of the USSR. This was the day on which in 1918 the first independent republic of Azerbaijan was solemnly proclaimed — in a suite at the Orient Hotel in Tbilisi. The initiative was masterminded by the Mussavat party, much to the chagrin of Narimanov who left at once for

Baku and openly joined the man who had been his 'secret love' for a long time — Mikoyan, who had usurped power several months earlier by installing the 'Commune of Baku'. The following day, they together proclaimed the 'Socialist Republic of Transcaucasia' with Baku as its capital.

In order to establish an image of legitimacy, the local assembly of people's representatives was given the status of 'revolutionary people's assembly' and, to the surprise of most, the body's over-all majority confirmed this. This was more than the Mussavat could bear. On March 30th 1918, popular uprisings had started throughout the city which seemed to have been well-prepared.

But not well enough. Having taken entire areas inhabited by Azeri and Iranian civilians after hours of field artillery bombardment, revolutionary guards took positions around the Mussavat movement's strongholds and shot at everything that moved, killing thousands in a single day. In the ensuing days, over twenty thousand Azeris were murdered in a thorough campaign by mainly Armenian armed gangs who systematically went from street to street and from house to house to do their butcher's job. Only on April 4th did the nightmare come finally to a standstill.

By that time, most of the Mussavat's surviving leadership had fled, mainly to nearby villages in order to hold out for better times. Mikoyan, however, was heavily criticised for the brutal way in which the revolt had been suppressed and was replaced by his fellow Armenian Shaumian, a close friend of Lenin whose relations with Stalin were less hearty than Mikoyan's. The revolt had also put an end to the short-lived romance between Mussavats and Dashnaks, as the latter had taken sides with the Bolsheviks and had been the main perpetrator of the mass murders.

As a result of the crisis, both the Socialist Revolutionaries and the Hummet party split into three factions, illustrating once more of how little significance ideological parties were in those days. Of each party, one faction continued to support Mikoyan, a second joined forces with Shaumian while the remainder joined the Mussavat party, which had gone underground in Baku while mobilising the countryside. In this way the so-called Savage Division was created, consisting mainly of survivors of the bloodshed in early April and eager to take revenge.

In the meantime, a provisional government led by a Mussavat leader by the name of Fathali Khan-Khoiski had taken control in Ganja and had soon controlled virtually all the country except for Baku. Massive recruiting had resulted in an army of 14,000 men, topped off by 7,000 Turkish elite troops commanded by Enver Pasha's brother Nuri Pasha, latterly despatched from Turkey.

In the early summer, Shaumian despatched a noisy but ill-trained rag-tag army inland with orders to march on Ganja. The expedition ended halfway in disaster, at which Shaumian's government was brought down by the Dashnaks and the Socialist Revolutionaries — with less than discreet support from Mikoyan in his hide-out — who proclaimed the so-called Central Caspian Dictatorship. Once in power, they did something Shaumian had always refused, under pressure from Lenin: they called upon the British for help, whose fleet had been poised to sail from Iran for several months. On August 3rd, the British landed in the port of Baku, in order to save the day against the advancing Turks.

The intervention of 1918 is one of the most pathetic chapters in the entire history of British colonialism. It consisted of a handful of troops conducted by a general by the name of L. C. Dunsterville, a conceited egoist whose sense of reality was somewhat troubled to say the least. His flagship was called the Kruger and on its mast flew an upside-down Russian ensign which turned it into Serbian colours. In his memoirs, *Dunsterforce*, the failed liberator was to describe himself as "a British general on the Caspian, the only sea unploughed before by British keels, on board a ship named after a South-African president and enemy, sailing from a Persian port, under the Serbian flag, to relieve from the Turks a body of Armenians in a Russian town." His words well illustrate the Anglo-Saxon mentality of those days — which appears to have changed little since — that throughout the whole quotation (in doubtful English moreover), the word 'Azerbaijan' does not once appear.

The British landing was only the beginning of a series of complete fiascos. The day before, Shaumian and 25 of his peers — which meant all of the government's commissars except for Mikoyan, who as usual used his own means to vanish from the surface of the earth — had fled to Krasnovodsk, apparently unaware of the fact that the Socialist Revolutionaries had taken over through a putsch there as well some time earlier, and so ran straight into their arms. A few days later, the fallen communards of Baku were executed in the nearby desert — according to some, in the presence of British officers.

In Baku, the English were not able to organise the defence of the city since its local leaders refused to accept the idea of an attack on it and dreamt instead of a new march on Ganja. Reports on Turkish troops marching on Baku were stigmatised as 'enemy propaganda' and the 'dictatorship' saw enemies everywhere except where they really were. In an attempt to attack the Savage Division in the Qobustan Desert, Dunsterville's men, accompanied by an unruly regiment of Armenian exiles from Turkey who were as uncertain of their bearings as the British, got lost and narrowly escaped total annihilation. On the eve of the occupation of Baku by Nuri Pasha's troops, the British sailed out of the port in the dead of night with their ships' lights put out, bound for Persia.

In C. Gerretson's *Geschiedenis der Koninklijke* ('History of the Royal

Dutch') the taking of Baku is described as follows:

"On September 14th early in the morning the attack started. The government made it known through the workers' councils that the situation was extremely dangerous. The English pulled out in the night. What could not be taken away, was destroyed in the best way they could. As soon as word about it got out next morning, a general 'sauve qui peut!' was the result. The city lay under Turkish fire, which caused much damage in the 'Black City' as well; the tanks belonging to Mazout [Rothschild's company] caught fire. The city's fate was sealed: at 8:00 hrs, Turkish troops entered the city from all sides. Their advance guard consisted of Tatar volunteers from villages that had been ransacked by the Armenians, and among them were numerous Russian officers. The fighting was brief; after an hour, only in some remote corners the rattling of gunfire still resounded from forgotten Bolshevik outposts which fought themselves to death to the last man. Now, revenge was sweet, and the wholescale massacre of Armenians began which lasted from the 15th until the 18th of September. Only on September 18th did regular Turkish troops enter and the Turkish army command manage to get things in hand, at least in the city centre."

According to Armenian tradition, this "wholescale massacre" is said to have cost the lives of 9,000 Armenians — as we shall see, these events are still heavily focused on by the Armenian side in the Karabakh conflict while those of early April 1918 are usually played down or simply left out. On the other hand, Azeris show a tendency to describe what happened after the taking of Baku as a "tragedy" while for the massacres perpetrated by Mikoyan and co. substantially more dramatic terminology is used.

On October 30th 1918, Turkey capitulated and engaged to withdraw all its forces from Transcaucasia after the armistice of Mudros. In Baku, on November 17th, the British took their place once more. This time, they were in the company of a marauding army consisting of Russian counter-revolutionary adventurers commanded by a self-made 'general' by the name of Lazar Bicherakhov. This ragtag, nomadic 'army' did little more than roam around, murdering and ransacking, in the city and its surrounding areas. In order to complete the general state of disorder, the omnipresent Mikoyan, operating from his shadowy hide-out, managed to trigger off an all-out strike.

The British commander, General Thomson, who had proclaimed himself governor-general of Azerbaijan on behalf of the British government, had initially promised the Mussavat government "every possible respect for the sovereignty of the republic." As early as November 24th, he had to admit in public what he had known all the time, namely that behind everybody's back all of Transcaucasia had been handed over by Lloyd George to the Russian counter-revolutionary leader General Denikin, reassuring him that if all went well the British government would in no way object to the "principle" that Transcaucasia was "basically Russian territory."

Thomson's conduct in Baku was in no way less duplicitous than that of his predecessor. As he exhausted himself with pious declarations towards the government, he refused to return the money which he claimed had been stolen from the (now empty) public treasury by Bicherakhov but a substantial part of which had ended up in London in reality. He also refused to intervene on behalf of the government in respect to European defaulters who kept refusing to pay taxes and royalties they owed the government over the whole period since 1917. In spring 1919, as the government, driven by dire need of cash, attempted to conclude an oil contract with US Standard Oil, Thomson bluntly threatened with "intervention" on behalf of the European concession-holders.

During the autumn of 1919, Denikin's positions in the Caucasus fell like dominoes to the Bolsheviks. Only the coming of winter prevented the Red Army from breaking through. Meanwhile, the British left through the back door for the second time. In early spring, Chechenia and Daghestan were overrun. On April 28th, the Red Flag was waving from the tops of every public building in Baku.

On the eve of the occupation, Khan-Khoiski had tried to get the British garrison back to Baku, including a British guarantee for Azerbaijan's sovereignty, in exchange for a new and extremely favorable oil contract. It could have worked, since Lenin had remained reluctant to provoke an open military confrontation with Britain. But, as it was, the British had made their choice long before in favour of the Bolsheviks, out of "purely business considerations" naturally — considerations, cherished mostly by politicians and diplomats who claimed to play the role of the world's peace-bringing angels in the name of democracy and humanity. So often it is the worst actors who get the best parts.

Although Soviet rule was to set the scene of world politics for the next seventy years, there was initially little change for Azerbaijan. Krassin made it clear to his Western counterparts right from the outset that the establishment of the new proletarian paradise-on-earth meant little more to the outside world than business as usual. For Azerbaijan, this meant no business as usual.

2
From gulag to independence

There are only a few people alive who remember the terror of the 1920s — and even fewer who are willing to talk about it even if they were able to do so. It has been estimated that under Narimanov, between 1920 and 1925, between 100,000 and 120,000 Azeri citizens were 'dispatched' as it was so quaintly put. Under Narimanov's successor, Sultan Mejid Effendiev, things could hardly get worse — but they did.

In 1930, as Effendiev was given orders by Stalin to carry out the latter's decree on collectivisation of the rural sector, widespread resistance broke out once more. Once more Russian troops moved in, this time assisted by aircraft, which has to say something about the scale of the resistance. Twenty thousand rural families were wiped out, while an equivalent number managed to cross the Iranian border with a far larger number given a one-way ticket to Kazakhstan and Siberia.

Effendiev, Hamid Sultanov and other leaders were to become victims in their turn during the purges between 1937 and 1939, when, after the example of the 'White-Coat Conspiracy' in Moscow, another fake anti-Stalin conspiracy was set up and subsequently 'discovered' in Baku. Stagemaster of the bloody scenes that followed was Mir-Jafer Bagirov, a former convict (jailed for preceisely what is not clear) whose mental capacities were subject to the severest doubts by even his friends.

Hussein Bagirov is today the rector of the Western University, one of the private institutes for higher education in Baku — and a descendant of the leader of the reign of terror of the 1930s.

"I don't want to think about these things," is his usual remark. "I never knew him but I suspect he was a real bastard. But there is one thing I should say in his favour — which is also the reason why in later days he's been judged relatively mildly — it does look as if he used his influence in 1944 to prevent Stalin from deporting the Azeris en masse to the deserts of Kazakhstan, as he did with the Chechens and the others."

The plan was aleady drawn up, designed by Mikoyan who afterwards simply wanted to incorporate Azerbaijan into Armenia. But Bagirov was to suffer the same fate as that of Beria after Stalin's demise. Mikoyan, however, was to survive as he had survived everything and everyone else, including Stalin, one of the few original companions of the dictator. During the Second World War, the Muslim nations were used by Stalin as cannon-fodder. Over a hundred thousand Azeris failed to return from the front. The rest of the population including elderly, women and children were mobilised for forced labour. The war was to leave in its wake a brutalised society.

"Of course, officially there was no unemployment," one elder recalls, "but poverty was in sharp contrast to what one would expect from a Socialist paradise-on-earth. Salaries were no longer paid. People were employed by the government but got their earnings from a second job on the black-labour market in their spare time.

"In the meantime, children wandered about the streets to make their living through begging, stealing and prostituting themselves. Violence was everywhere — fights and murders were part of the daily routine. Not surprisingly, the police were never anywhere to be seen. Newspapers were filled with incomprehensible rants about ideological matters no one could even remotely grasp.

"When Stalin was finally dead and gone, Baku had become this savage place where people lived like predatory animals while the local elite plunged itself in the good life and hardly ever showed its face in public without heavily armed bodyguards. Many people weren't allowed to even leave Apsheron, but they say in the countryside things were even worse."

In the countryside, however, people talk differently.

"That's not true, there *was* food for everyone. Alright, so it's true that state authority had all but disappeared by 1950, and all the government and other authority buildings had no one in them, but the official power vacuum was filled by our traditional family ties. In central and south Azerbaijan we even gave shelter and food to the large numbers of starving children sent from Baku by their parents to seek their fortune wherever they could — and those local authorities that were still functioning even helped us do that. You know, whether or not they were part of the offical Communist apparatus, Azerbaijan has always been full of people who, whatever the situation was, always managed to keep their hearts in the right place." These words were spoken by a chemical engineer, whose salary as a university lecturer was less than $30 a month by summer 1995 — at which he left for Istanbul. In passing, the country's modern brain-drain is said to have affected over half the entire educated classes.

*

They say that the French and the Greeks have their hearts on their left side and their wallets on their right. The Azeri fits the same cliche to a large extent. Hidden behind this human compassion used to lurk the most alarming indifference and incredible capacity for extortion, which was to get completely out of hand in later days under the centre-right leadership of Abulfaz Elchibey. Then it had to be constrained by the same man who earlier had been assigned to put things in order in Azerbaijan by Brezhnev, shortly after the latter's ascension to the throne. This was Heydar Aliev.

Heydar Ali Rezaoglu Aliev was born on May 10th 1923 in Nakhchivan. According to some, his parents had come from Tabriz fleeing the aftermath of the failed uprising of 1917, according to others his family had lived in Nakhchivan for at least three generations.

In his official biography it states that Aliev gained degrees in history and political science. His real career started when he was 22 years old when after the Second World War he was sent by the KGB to Pakistan, Turkey and Iran, after having worked during the war in the Middle East for SMERSH, the organisation which has subsequently become known all over the West in caricature-like form as Stalin's 'Organisation for Revenge and Murder' through Ian Fleming's James Bond novels. Whatever the case, Aliev's later biographers preferred to keep a rather thick smokescreen over this episode in his life.

By the 1970s, Aliev was considered useful enough to take charge of Azerbaijan's growing problems. But although he succeeded in containing the most visible excesses of corruption and nepotism there, he was hardly in a position to tackle the real cause of the problem — the Kremlin's iron grip on Azerbaijan's economy. In 1990, the 7.13 million Azeri citizens made up 2.5 per cent of the USSR's population who lived on 0.35 per cent of its territory. Gross national income was at 66 billion roubles or 1.25 per cent of the all-Union GNP. Not that this meant anything: the rouble had remained non-convertible although its value in respect to hard currency had dropped from two dollars in the early 1980s to less than 15 cents. The real plunge had yet to begin and was to drag the Transcaucasian republics down in freefall until spring 1995 when the bottom of the pit was hit as the rate hit a frightening 5,000 roubles a dollar.

Manipulating statistics and tendentiously interpreting them is an art unsurpassedly mastered by Soviet and ex-Soviet bureaucrats. It was thus that in the early 1980s the ninth five-year plan singled out Azerbaijan for praise as the Soviet republic where 'prosperity-growth' was progressing faster than in any other Soviet republic. In order to illustrate this, it was explained that over the last ten years cotton, cereal and grape production had more than doubled. For this achievement the republic was awarded the Order of Lenin.

What it failed to do was make money on it. For the sad truth is that the USSR ransacked Azerbaijan in the most shameless way. In 1980 bread, meat and other provisions were rationed, and the number of homeless in Baku was put at over 100,000. The number of jobless was 250,000-plus. Ninety per cent of cotton production, 92 per cent of tobacco, 93 per cent of wool and as much as synthetic materials went out of the country as the raw materials or half-fabricates headed for Moscow. Prices were kept artificially low, while those of the end-products returned according to the rules of the barter system were exorbitant. In the same way, the Russians considered themselves wealthy in respect to the other assets of the other republics, simply by systematically undervaluing their own assets outside the Russian Federation and overvaluing those of the others within the Russian Federation. In this way, after the USSR's downfall, the Russians were to claim $1.4 billion from Azerbaijan as compensatory payment for 'liabilities'.

Officially, the history of the 'Third Republic' of Azerbaijan (the first being the republic of 1918-1920 and the second the Soviet republic of 1937) begins on August 30th 1991 in the aftermath of the failed coup in Moscow — to which Mutalibov had so shamelessly paid tribute — as the Supreme Soviet of Azerbaijan voted for a resolution in which independence was proclaimed. Mutalibov was later to explain his attitude as "realism," drawing a rather painful parallel: had not in 1918 the country "forcibly" become independent at the collapse of the Transcaucasian Federation?

In order to stress his position, Mutalibov had himself elected president three weeks later — entirely in post-colonial style since he was the sole candidate. Even if the new old-styled head of state appointed a fifty member-strong 'National Council', half of which consisted of old loyalists and the other half of opposition representatives (essentially adherents of the yet unofficial Popular Front), this organism had only an 'advisory' function whereas the old parliament remained in place without much more say in things than it used to have.

Meanwhile, the situation in Karabakh (see below) had got completely out of hand and the president's position became untenable. On March 6th, Parliament forced Mutalibov to step down. He was replaced by one of his shady courtiers, Yaqub Mamedov, who was to be acting president until free and pluriform presidential elections were held, scheduled for June 7th. In spite of its internal discords, the Popular Front managed to present a common candidate, the teacher and man of letters Abulfaz Elchibey, from Ordubad in the east of Nakhchivan. During the 1970s he was already involved in dissident movements which had cost him two years behind bars under Aliev.

The Popular Front had no clear political programme except for a few slogans like privatisation, restored religious freedom and a multiparty system — none of which however had been elaborated in any concrete terms. In respect of one point only were they absolutely straightforward: the army would get priority over anything else and the Armenians would be put in their place by the toughest means possible.

After the fall of Shusha into Armenian hands on May 9th, Mutalibov astonished friend and foe alike by simple re-entering the presidential palace and taking Mamedov's seat behind his desk as if nothing had happened. To the Supreme Soviet of Azerbaijan he humbly offered his "apologies" for his former mistakes, a plea that was promptly lapped up by the Soviet, much to the people's consternation. The June 7th elections were suspended indefinitely and a state of emergency was proclaimed.

It was more than the public was prepared to swallow. The same day, the Popular Front called for an all-out strike and opposition-minded troops in Karabakh abandoned their posts and, along with their arms, marched on Baku.

The House of Parliament is situated, together with the Anba Hotel, the national television complex and the defence ministry, on a hilltop overlooking Baku. Anyone occupying that hilltop has in view all there really is to the city of Baku, starting with the presidential palace, a square pompous marble colossus that disfigures the edge of the elegant city centre and stands just under the Anba hilltop.

That was precisely what the military and paramilitary units loyal to the Popular Front did on arrival in Baku on May 15th. In the morning Mutalibov received an ultimatum: if he hadn't vacated the presidential palace by the end of the afternoon they would come and get him. Meanwhile, the Popular Front had all roads to the palace blocked. Both army and police kept themselves at a distance which said about all there was to tell. Even the presidential guard understood after a few skirmishes that further resistance would not be in their interest.

That afternoon, Mutalibov surrendered in exchange for free conduct to the airport, from where he and a handful of old comrades flew to Moscow — for the second time in ten weeks but this time for good. The position of acting head of state was taken by Mussavat leader Issa Gambarov who cancelled the state of emergency again and resumed preparations for elections on June 7th.

When the day came, the ballots were much as predicted. Yaqub Mamedov, who had stayed behind and refused to give up, had put himself forward as a candidate but gained less than ten per cent of the votes. Nizami Suleymanov, of the centre-left United Democratic Intelligentsia, did better with 27.5 per cent. Participation was 73 per cent and Elchibey ended up with a clear 55.1 per cent victory. Later, the UDI accused the Popular Front and especially its member-organisation led by Iskander Hamidov, the Azeri branch of the Turkish extreme-rightist movement Boz Gurd ('Grey Wolves'), of widespread vote-rigging and intimidation during the elections — to which the accused furiously replied: "If that were true you wouldn't have got a single vote!"

Hamidov was granted the key post of interior minister in the new government. Gambarov became Speaker of Parliament and thereby also vice-president. Rahim Gaziev, defence minister under Mutalibov, Yaqub Mamedov and again under Mutalibov during his short-lived attempt to claw back power, was returned to his post. His and Hamidov's appointments in particular would prove catastrophic and undermine the very basis for Elchibey's administration. Other factors marring the new regime's authority were the war in Karabakh which despite fierce offensives developed in a chaotic and, for the Azeris, shameful manner, and the hyperinflation caused by a plummeting rouble.

It was a time when purchasing power was delivered body blow after body blow, yet the economic performance of the Popular Front was far from its worst. The introduction of the 'manaat', the new Azeri currency, slowed down the process of monetary depreciation, relief aided by a positive trend in the external trade balance which switched from $25 million in the red for 1991 to $400 million in the black for 1992. The reason was that Elchibey's finance minister, the economist Sahl Mamedov, had cut off virtually all trade relations with the bankrupt former Soviet republics in favour of relations with those countries who paid in hard currency. In the meantime, the government had suspended its canditature for membership of the newly created Commonwealth of Independent States (CIS).

In those days the hall of the Azerbaijan Hotel (the former Intourist), a centre humming with investors, entrepreneurs and trade representatives, all nosing around in search of profit with colonial proportions: cheap raw materials for their home countries and delivery contracts for the luxury goods the local market was was ready and primed for. Indeed, a number of these businessmen made good money in those years. But then, it tended to be the less scrupulous of their number while those with integrity faced hardship.

"You've got to have nerves of steel," one Turkish trade-house representative confided to me one day at the coffee bar. "Letters of credit are unheard of. They honestly expect you to turn up with a suitcase stuffed full of dollars, leave the money with them, and all this just for the privilege of hanging around, waiting to see whether you ever get your merchandise."

But despite a certain amount of euphoria, the days of the Popular Front were already numbered. Two events were crucial for what was to follow. In spring 1993, the president of Turkey, Turgut Özal, paid a visit to Baku. The media circus ran its show with the greatest of devotion. Mr Özal was not the only one who was bombarded with questions — the controversial Iskander Hamidov had to beat pushy journalists off. Which he did — in the most literal sense and under the very nose of his distinguished visitor. The result was one black eye, one bleeding nose and a smashed microphone. This proved too much for Elchibey who fired Hamidov the day after the disgraceful show.

However, the incident was a pretext rather than a cause. The real reason the president wanted to get rid of his impetuous cabinet member lay in the fact that Hamidov had gradually turned the so-called OPON troops, special interior security units which dated from the times of the KGB and meant for operations most of which could not bear daylight, into his private militia, thus creating a state-within-a-state. The OPON troops had the reputation of being ruthless fighters who had little need to observe the law and never did so, as a result of which they had notched up an impressive list of political murders to their name, all the while, in order to upgrade their meagre incomes, they had mastered an intensive practice of racketeering on an everyday basis.

The second event took place in January at Cirkhavend, one of the hotspots on the Karabakh front. It was there that a unit from the Ganja garrison under the command of a young volunteer, Lieutenant-Corporal Surat Husseynov, son of an immensely rich industrialist from Yevlakh who had made his fortune in the times of perestroika, was in command of an operation on the south bank of the River Kachin. The unit retook about forty villages and settlements which had been previously occupied by the Armenians. However the operation ended in shambles, its mission failed. Later, Husseynov was to claim that the reinforcements promised him from Baku had failed to show and so he had been forced to withdraw to the river's north bank. From that point on, he declared he would refuse to obey any further orders issuing from Baku.

On February 1st, President Elchibey fired Husseynov from active service for insubordination. The unsuccessful warlord, who had missed his chance before, refused to comply and entrenched himself with an estimated 7,000 armed followers in the garrison barracks in Ganja and the nearby former Red Army base. For a while, tension gripped the town as fears grew that soon an army would come over from Baku to restore order by force. But nothing happened and as time went by people began to get the impression that behind the scenes things had been settled and the row would fade away.

That proved to be a mistake.

*

Thursday, June 4th. The inhabitants of Ganja were starting their daily routine. Fuel was scarce and expensive in this part of oil-rich Azerbaijan as supplies from Baku were few and far between. Packed buses and trolleybuses rolled groaning along the streets and those with not far to go shuffled their way to work. In the nearby garrison, soldiers of the regiment were at breakfast in the mess hall. Others were on their way to the showers. Many were still asleep in their bunks.

Suddenly, explosions resounded disconcertingly nearby. Before anyone realised what was happening, tanks and armoured cars had swooped in on the area, randomly firing in every direction possible. Tank-grenades left two dormitories and the dining room shot into pieces.

For an hour, utter pandemonium prevailed. Some shouted that the Armenians had taken Ganja in a surprise attack. Hardly had the first panic passed than terror made way for confused surprise as it dawned that the attackers were not Armenians but OPON units, their own countrymen.

At this point the soldiers of the garrison finally took up their arms and start shooting at the military vehicles in the yard. The vehicles withdrew to the city centre, still firing randomly, this time at passers-by and at the windows and balconies of residential blocks. After the space of another hour, the invaders turned back to the direction of Terter from where they had come.

The next morning, Husseynov issued a press release in which he reported casualties of 68 dead and over 200 seriously wounded of which about a dozen were on in critical condition. He promised to see to it that the wrongdoers would be apprehended and punished although he had to hunt them down as far as Baku. Which is precisely what he was to do. The same day, a witchhunt in Ganja began against everything and anything that could be identified with the national authorities in Baku. Within the brief space of 24 hours the number of hostages ("detained suspects," to useHusseynov's words) was 500, and grew to 1,500 within the next three days. These 'suspects' included a government delegation from Baku consisting of three cabinet ministers and the attorney-general of Azerbaijan.

On the way to Ganja, myself and a German camera crew (the rest of the Western media-types flown in from Moscow never left Baku) encountered one roadblock after another. Some were manned by traffic police, others by military police. Nobody appeared to know what to do. The commander of Husseynov's first outpost, a rough man in his forties who had given himself the fighter's nickname of 'Saddam Hussein' greeted us in a jolly manner and ordered his men to form a guard of honour for us. These were the boys who were going to save the country from all its misery as soon as that sickening government had been removed, so he assured us. Hundreds had already switched from the national army to Husseynov's side, he adds. Meanwhile, our guard of honour had already dissolved again into a motley crew waving 'V for victory' signs and Kalashnikovs in the air. The commander promised to take us personally to Husseynov and arrange a highly exclusive interview for us.

On arriving, we first took a look at the blackened ruins of the barracks as if it were a sight-seeing tour. By the end of the day, a mass demonstration has gathered in the centre of Ganja. Husseynov himself had already left after a speech of no more than three minutes. After him, anyone who thought he had something to say was allowed to take the stage. There was no lack of speakers: in this provincial town there was hardly anybody who was not some committee's chairman or secretary. It is odd how the normally so phlegmatic Azeris are transformed into devoted, emotional orators the instance they get a microphone under their nose, orators who can easily incite their audience to lengthy cheers and more.

The next day, after making us wait for a long time, the leader of the insurgents finally received us in the garden of his 'tea-house'.

Leader of insurgents?

Pardon. "We are not insurgents," the commander stated flatly. "Anyone who calls us insurgents is committing an offence." Surat Husseynov did not exactly fit the figure of a leader of knights-in-arms, attired as he was in a fine dark brown suit made-to-measure after the latest Italian fashion. A short, slim man, he had somewhat unexpressive face.

So what are your demands?

"Resignation of the president and the government."

And what then?

"New elections for a new parliament and a new head of state."

Are you a candidate?

"No."

Have you any other political aspirations?

"No."

How do you see your own future career — a businessman perhaps?

"Perhaps, if it lets me help my country out of its economic deadlock.'"

Even as we spoke, Husseynov's troops, insurgents or otherwise, were on their way to Baku with tanks and heavy artillery. That Sunday the town of Shamkor was taken without so much of a shot. On our return to Baku next day, it was reported that Yevlakh and Geranboy had also fallen. After one day more, the vice-president and speaker of Parliament Issa Gambarov handed in his letter of resignation to the president. The same day, Elchibey had Heydar Aliev flown in from Nakhchivan to take Gambarov's place.

The coalition between Elchibey and Aliev was to hold until the evening of the following Thursday. Meanwhile, Husseynov's men had taken almost the whole country by storm. Officials loyal to the government in the occupied towns were removed. Most of them were put behind bars. A number of them were never again to be seen alive; the circumstances of their death have never been made clear. Later, the Popular Front would refer to "hundreds of political murders and disappearences."

On Thursday morning, Husseynov's tanks rolled down the roads leading to Baku. Some units shot their way into the suburbs in the afternoon and panic spread. A large-scale military confrontation, however, was not to occur.

On Friday morning, Aliev appeared on television. By then, everybody knew already what had happened: that night, around three, Elchibey and his family had left the capital and flown on board of his presidential plane to his native village of Keleky in Ordubad, eastern Nakhchivan. Aliev told his television viewers how the president had made a telephone call to him on his arrival in Nakhchivan with the request to take over all presidential functions as long as he was absent.

"And that is what I promised him," Aliev declared.

On Saturday, Aliev concluded a 'truce' with Husseynov who withdrew his troops as agreed to a radius of 25 miles outside of Baku. That afternoon, a tumultuous press conference took place. Baku in the meantime had been transformed into a media circus as hundreds of reporters and camera teams were flown in from Moscow — CNN had even chartered a plane for the purpose. Not that I spotted any of these image-shooters at the frontline.

At the briefing local television teams pushed themselves forward through the foreign ones without so much as saying sorry. A seemingly artificially smiling Aliev remains stoic under it all.

Is it going to be civil war?

"There is no civil war in Azerbaijan and there is not going to be one."

Where are the hostages?

"The hostage problem is a serious problem and will be duely solved."

Are you the new president?

"The president is Mr Abulfaz Elchibey and I am acting on his behalf and at his request. I myself have no ambition whatsoever to become head of state."

Shortly before, to be exact on the very day the massacre in Ganja took place, I had visited Aliev in Nakhchivan. On that occasion, he had assured me that he had no intention of returning to Baku "or play any other role in national politics — unless the people explicitly ask me to do so."

Politicians . . .

That evening, the numerous foreign television teams could be spotted around the Anba Hotel — after all, from there the view over Baku is quite stunning — so the correspondents could hold their fireside chats on the evening news for the folks back home.

The same day, word got out that in Lenkoran, by the Talysh coast to the south, the local garrison commander, Colonel Alikram Humbetov, had followed Husseynov's example and had announced that he intended no longer to obey Baku's orders. He threatened to proclaim the 'Republic of Talysh-Mughan' but his precise reasons for breaking with Baku remained unclear. A week later, Husseyn was no longer a rebel and conspirator against the state but prime minister and acting minister of defence and economic affairs at the same time. He was later to explain this "indulgence" by pointing out that the situation at the Karabakh front had made him accept the leadership. He added that there was also his "desire to spare the people of Baku from a bloodbath."

It seemed however as if the city's population had kept as cool as Siberia throughout these upheavals. On the street life went on as it has never stopped doing, and if people got angry it was not because of the political crisis or the threat of a hail of shells upon the city, but because their salaries had not been paid for several months while everything kept getting more and more expensive — bring back the good old days!

Heydar Aliev?

"Oh, yes, he's back again isn't he? Well, at least he knows how to put things into order. Give the good man a chance . . ."

That he would get — and seize.

That Sunday evening, viewers of Azeri television were to get an unexpected surprise as Elchibey appeared on the screen, eyes rolling, beard and hair tousled. In a simultaneously broadcast press conference he called for all "foreign powers" to "hurry to the aid of Azerbaijan's democracy." The foreign power the exiled head of state referred to in particular was beyond any doubt Turkey.

"Forget it," replied the Turkish ambassador to Baku Mr Karamanoglu the following day. "Azerbaijan is a sovereign state where it's up to the nation to hire and fire its own leaders. We can only wish that it will happen through democratic procedures."

By mid-July, after a hectic visit to the front in Agdam, I found myself traveling to Lenkoran where Colonel Alikram received me. He hardly gave the impression of being a rebellious firebrand. Lean as a rake, thick spectacles, a peculiarly muffled voice and gentle, genuine joviality, he in no way resembled the snappy and nervous Husseynov and even less the Iranian fifth-columnist which those in Baku have accused him of being. This last accusation had already been objected to by Leyla Yunussova, defence secretary of state under Elchibey until she resigned in protest against the government's mismanagement of the war: "Alikram — an Islamic fanatic?

Nonsense, I know him well, he's a lettered and well-educated man who would never allow those mullahs to abuse him!"

Once at the coffee table, the colonel looked at his watch and said: "Forgive me, but in half an hour I have to leave for Baku. No, not to talk with Aliev but I'll try to talk business with Surat Husseynov. Just look at things the way they are: Elchibey's been forced out of the game and Aliev is dying to jump in, which is far from an improvement on things. The man is a power-grabber and will always be one. There's not many people who rate him at the moment but mark my words, he's prepared himself well for all this.

"You can already see all those old pals of his who helped him out pop up like jack-in-the-boxes in high places. They're all in it together, busy turning Azerbaijan into exactly the type of totalitarian state it was until recently, and that's going to mean big trouble. We're quarreling over a lot of things in this country but at least there's one thing we all agree on: no more dictatorship. And that's why I'm prepared to talk to anyone except for Heydar Aliev. Please be my guest as long as I'm away. Tomorrow we'll talk further . . ."

That afternoon I killed time by taking a series of photographs in the area. The landscape of Talysh would be quite picturesque and welcoming were it not for the sad state of the flooded villages and estates along the coastline. Each time the Caspian Sea pushes a little further inland, whole villages and settlements are engulfed, only to be rebuilt a mile or so inland. It would be considerably cheaper to build a sea-wall to protect the land — and it certainly does not have to be of Dutch Delta quality since the Caspian is tideless.

"That's precisely what I'm getting at," Colonel Alkram exclaimed the next day. "We've been asking Baku for assistance with this type of thing for twenty years now. We're not allowed to do anything about it ourselves because if we do, we get instantly branded as subversive while all our requests stay unanswered. They've let us rot here for two hundred years now and it's high time that changed!" He brightened up — the colonel had news to share. "My talks in Baku didn't come to anything. I hereby have the honour to welcome you as the first foreign guest to the Republic of Talysh-Mughan!"

He turned stern and sad once more. "It won't be easy, you know. We produce plenty of food. But we barely have any industry and fuel, and we also lack other effective energy sources. We therefore hope to conclude barter deals with . . . certain countries here in the region so we can exchange fruit and vegetables for gasoline and fuel oil."

Iran?

"Don't get me wrong. We're going to stick to commerce and nothing else. Islamic fundamentalism is completely alien to the history and culture of Azerbaijan, and so it'll never get a firm grip on our country. There's only one way for Azerbaijan to survive and that's through a liberal-democratic model based on example of Western Europe. A federation after the German example? Now that's the direction I'm thinking along."

The colonel was not to be granted much more than a month to think. In mid-August I returned to Lenkoran. Near a crossroads from where the (only) road that connects the area with the rest of Azerbaijan starts, a few solitary pieces of artillery had been positioned in trenches, somewhat less than impressive. In the morning, Alikram received us in his office. What he had to say was basically the same as on the previous occasion: he still had no faith in Aliev whatsoever, and had his reservations about Husseynov. A sergeant entered shortly and whispered something in his leader's ear. The colonel turned to me.

"I'm sorry," he apologised, "but a demonstration is about to take place in front of the building. I think it would be best to leave shortly."

Within the hour, the incredible was to happen. The impressively large square was slowly filling with people who debated, loudly and at length. As always, in this part of the world, they inevitably do this loudly and at length — whether they agree or not on anything is not important. All of a sudden, security troops fired over the heads of those assembled, just for a few seconds. But this was evidently taken as a signal and not a warning, for in less than five minutes, projectiles were whizzing through the air, smashing the windows of Alikram's offices. As the colonel hurried out through the back door to the nearby military barracks, a chaotic band of civilians, farmers and policemen entered the building and started smashing up the furniture and fittings. Some spotted my camera and cheerfully made victory signs as amidst the chaos a woman in her mid-fifties, dressed in neat coat and skirt, shiny handbag on her arm, was carried onto the premises. This was Iruda Jamalova, lecturer and board-member of the local university, who now, it seemed, represented authority.

That afternoon, it appeared that the "spontaneous action taken by the people" was in fact a conspiracy drawn up in the well-established tradition of the KGB. Groups of agent-provocateurs roamed the city looking to settle scores with Alikram's supporters, an indeterminable number of whom lay motionlessly in the gutters.

By ten in the evening, a bunch of heavily-armed Rambos arrived at the hotel where I was staying. Shortly afterwards, they made off in the direction of the barracks where the colonel had entrenched himself. In the dead of night, an armed vehicle managed to blast its way out of the stronghold. Men fell dead and wounded. Only then did people realise that this was a ploy to distract attention, buying precious minutes for Colonel Alikram

Humbetov to make his getaway in an army helicopter. Search expeditions over the following weeks were to remain without any result.

Months later, Alikram was to pop up in Lenkoran once more with motives that were unclear — only to be arrested on the spot and taken to Baku where, locked up in the former KGB prison, he enjoyed the company of, among others, Rahim Ghaziev who was there awaiting his trial for "murder and conspiracy to murder."

A few months later again, the pair, together with a few others, managed to escape miraculously from the underground, heavily-guarded gulag-style detention centre. Alikram was detained again in 1995 after a controversial trial in which he had been condemned to death *in absentia* — a sentence that was reduced to 25 years in jail, since from 1990 on, no executions have been carried out in Azerbaijan. Ghaziev was also condemned to death for "high treason and neglect of duty," but in the autumn of 1996 he was still in hiding in Moscow.

After the Talysh experience in the late summer of 1993, the next journey was to Nakhchivan. At the airport a car without number-plates was waiting right next to the plane and took me on a Mad Max-style drive to Keleky. Although we drove at breakneck speed, it was after dark when we arrived.

And dark it was: Nakhchivan, encircled by Iran and Armenia bar a single direct border post with Turkey, suffers from a chronical lack of power. The village was shrouded in pitch darkness. In the garden by a house that had been provisionally set up as an office, the "tragi-comic figure" as Aliev had called him not long before, was sitting behind a table with two lanterns like a kind of guru lecturing a few dozen youngsters sitting on the lawn. The spooky shadows gave Elchibey the image of an evil sorcerer from a Russian fairy-tale.

It was half past one in the morning when the interview started — meanwhile, the electricity had come back on again. The day before, Aliev had telephoned from Baku asking his rival whether or not he was planning to return in order to take up his duties again.

Elchibey reported with relish: "I told him that I shall only return if Parliament gives me a guarantee that things will be settled without any further bloodshed. When he heard this, Aliev said that there was no need for that since I still had the presidential guard at my disposal. Now that's the exact proof that he's heading for a violent confrontation, or am I wrong?"

To my surprise, the former president appeared remarkably frank about the sequence of events that had led to the bloodbath in Ganja. "I observed at the time that the local command of the Ganja garrison was guilty of insubordination against the supreme army commander — that was me — and — in my name — the minister of defence. Tell me in which civilised state is that allowed to happen? So I did what any head of state in my position would have done: I ordered the defence minister to put an end to the situation using any means he deemed necessary to re-establish legal authority over and within the armed forces. That he failed to do. The result was a military coup. And the result of *that* is the situation in which we now find ourselves: dictatorship."

Alikram Humbetov's suggestion that the Azeri population would unanimously reject the "power-mad Aliev" was to be contradicted by reality at first — and at second and at third, for all it mattered. By the end of August, Aliev had organised a referendum in which the populace was asked whether or not they still considered Elchibey the legitimate head of state of Azerbaijan. According to the official results, participation was 93 per cent, 97 per cent of which voted "no" against Elchibey — which led to angry frustration among adherents of the Popular Front who spoke of vote-rigging and intimidation. Iskander Hamidov threatened strikes, demonstrations and other "peaceful actions." However, the strikes were not carried through and planned demonstrations one after another were called off at the final moment. Armed resistance was excluded by the leader of the Grey Wolves "unless Russian troops appear in Azerbaijan — *that* will mean war!"

After a few weeks of heated debate in Parliament it was agreed that presidential elections were to take place on the last Sunday of September. For a long while, Aliev was the sole contender, and the two counter-candidates called in at the very last minute obviously stood little chance. This was how Aliev was elected head of state with 90 per cent-plus of the votes at an reported participation level of more than 80 per cent.

On the night of October 1st, shortly after the elections, the police detained four terrorists in possession of machine-guns and hand-grenades, who were supposedly about to assassinate the new president early the next morning on his way to his office. Among the thugs were two Turks, Boz Gurds. However, it was to take one more year before Hamidov was to end up behind bars as well.

Except for one last frantic attempt to tip the balance at the war-front of Karabakh, little was to happen during the months that followed. Life in Baku returned to normal. But after a few months of hoping for the best, people started complaining once again about meagre wages and high prices, as the new president travelled around the world and conferred with such leaders as John Major, François Mitterrand, Deng Zhiaoping and Jean-Luc de Haene.

"He's a good diplomat," presidential adviser for foreign affairs Wafa

Gulizadeh, a shrewd political survivor who had weathered both Mutalibov's and Elchibey's respective downfalls, observed in those days. "And that's something you could never say of Abulfaz. I still remember how I had to grab him by the arm because he was too shy to be introduced to George Bush . . ."

After endless talking and even more endless hesitation, in October 1994 a new constitution finally was adopted, which included the commitment to hold general elections within a year according to multi-party principles. However, exciting events were yet to happen in the meantime.

On October 4th 1994, early in the morning, the centre of Baku presented an unusual sight to the astonished cityfolk walking to their jobs: soldiers and tanks in the streets. Coup d'etat? Well, it hardly looked like one, the military — OPON members by the look of their uniforms — seemed relaxed as they chatted with bypassers and, as usual, asking them for cigarettes. After an hour or so, they had disappeared from the city centre to occupy, as later became clear, the military barracks in Nefchilar.

Leader of the insurgents was a junior interior minister by the name of Rovshan Javadov. The previous weekend, he lost his temper with the prosecutor-general, Ali Omarov, who had just accused him and his pals of the murder on September 24th of the vice-speaker of Parliament, Efeydin Jalilov, who had been shot dead in the streets in broad daylight by unidentified assailants.

Javadov must have been angry indeed. On the night of October 3rd, he had the prosecutor taken from his bed by OPON troops who took him to the basement of the interior ministry, in the centre of Baku. By the end of the morning, Javadov, along with a few hundred OPON paramilitary and his hostage, had entrenched himself in the Nefchilar barracks. That day, a curfew was proclaimed — suspended by midnight as President Aliev made a dramatic appeal to the people, calling on them to flock to the presidential palace "to save the republic from going under." The real motive behind this appeal still remains an open question.

Subsequently, Javadov, Omarov and even Husseynov (making a rare appearance) took the stage. Each tried to outdo the others with patriotic slogans. But all were to be outdone in their turn. At long last, at 3.15am, the president appeared at the front of the presidential palace, surrounded by a crew of reporters and bodyguards. Cheers resounded all around as the head of state, a child borrowed from a bystander on his arm, addressed a 50,000-strong crowd.

The performance was both brilliant and rousing. Only those who wanted to know what exactly was going on were disappointed. But then, there were few those. In the emergency debate that followed next day, Parliament took the decision to fire Omarov, Javadov and Husseynov on the spot. The latter's parliamentary immunity was lifted at the same time — in Azerbaijan that means the police stand ready at the door with handcuffs.

Husseynov, however, had seen this coming and after his performance that night had already hopped straight onto the first plane to Moscow. In early March 1995 a second coup attempt was to follow, again led by Rovshan Javadov who had mysteriously managed to remain a free man, and his brother Mahir.

The move was made after a presidential decree to dismantle the OPON altogether, accused as they were of "racketeering, insubordination and links with organised crime." Again, the setting where the OPON warriors chose to entrench themselves was the Nefchilar barracks. But this time the death toll was not four as in October of the previous year, but around fifty — including the initiator, Javadov. It was easy to point the finger of guilt: the Kremlin, whose backstage served as a hide-out for Husseynov. The aim was evident: to prevent constitutional parliamentary elections from being held that year.

By the end of spring 1995, over fifty political parties had registered themselves for the elections. In a bid to avoid an Italian-style scenario, a five per cent electoral threshold was imposed. This was for good reason: according to opinion polls, no single party would win more than 20 per cent of the votes. In the lead were President Aliev's New Azerbaijan party, the Social-Democrats and the Communists (15 per cent apiece), the Democratic Congress (13 per cent and the National Independence Party (eight per cent). The Democratic Congress was an alliance whose principal players were Elchibey's Popular Front and Issa Gambarov's Mussavat party. They swallowed up existing minor parties as well as a number of MPs who had gained their seats in their own right. This enabled New Azerbaijan to gather enough support for the absolute majority it needed in the end, allowing only the Democratic Congress and the National Independence Party to take seats in the new Parliament.

The man behind both military insurrections was soon identified beyond doubt — and he clearly had the experience. According to the Baku-based news agency Turan, Husseynov was spotted during the second week of May 1995 in the Georgian district of Lagodekhi, which borders on Azerbaijan and is largely populated with ethnic Azeris. There he was supposedly attempting to set up a guerilla base, to be financed by Georgian, Azeri and (most of all) Russian drug-barons (see final chapter). Husseynov's right-hand man Aypara Aliev had been thrown into jail in Baku, along with some two hundred former OPON troops who had formed the hardcore of Javadov's petty army of cowboys. Aypara Aliev died in prison under dubious circumstances, while the others awaited jail terms varying from three to fourteen years. As for Husseynov, he was extradited from Russia and tried in Baku in 1997. As this book went to print, the verdict was yet to be reported.

Meanwhile, the Kremlin had sealed the border between Azerbaijan and Daghestan, accusing the Azeris of facilitating the smuggling of arms from Iran, Pakistan and Afghanistan to Chechenia. One of the key figures in the Azeri Connection with respect to the Chechen war was a certain Mahmudov, a wealthy businessman in Baku who the Russians saw as the mastermind behind the arms supply route between Central Asia and Chechenia. The way in which this information, normally considered classified, emerged was rather spectacular.

On April 24th 1995, police in Baku apprehended a Cobra unit, as the 'mission impossible'-style commandos of the Russian interior ministry are called. The infiltrators confessed they were under orders to kidnap Mahmudov and to turn him over in exchange for Mutalibov's extradition. The fact that the Cobras were caught red-handed meant less the end of the game of cat-and-mouse between Russia and Azerbaijan than the beginning of a new phase. Many of the pieces of the jigsaw have come to light since, but how the whole puzzle fits together has remained subject to speculation.

In November 1995, Fakhreddin Mamedov, the assassin of Azerbaijan's deputy prosecutor-general who was gunned down in July 1994, was arrested. At his trial, Mamedov claimed he had committed the murder on the orders of the Javadov brothers. During the same month, in an attempt to dismantle the network of the Mutalibov-Husseynov axis, the former Interpol chief Ilgar Safihanov and the former chief of staff and junior defence minister Isahan Veliyev were detained. Veliyev was arrested in Marneuli by the Georgian authorities and extradited to Azerbaijan.

At a later stage, the authorities were to connect these alleged henchmen of Husseynov to the murder by unknown assailants armed with machine-guns, in Kazakh on October 25th 1996, of the local security chief Sevla Gasimov, the head of the provincial authorities' internal office Firdusi Gasimov and the head of the local police in Dashzalakhi, Ziryaddin Ahmedov.

Kazakh, not far from the spot where the borders of Armenia, Azerbaijan and Georgia come together, on the surface appears an idyllic country town yet at the same time is reputed to be one of the hotspots in the 'Russian Connection' — and the three officials either knew or wanted to know too much. That connection turned up again in the investigation of the 1993 murder of public prosecutor Shamshir Aliev. At the time, the magistrate had been working on a number of cases brought against a notorious gang who had lived off kidnapping, racketeering and a string of other criminal activities. Some years later, a number of the gang members were to be recognised as having been involved in the two failed OPON coups.

Less spectacular and, according to human-rights monitors, highly suspect was the case against three army generals, only one of whom, Shahin Mussayev, was out of the country. He and the other two, Wahid Mussayev and Rafiq Agayev, had initially been charged with corruption and embezzlement of government property, but by the end of 1996 their charges were changed into conspiracy to bring about a military coup in the autumn of 1993. The row was to end with accusations printed in the local media that the upper echelons of Azeri politics were abusing the judicial system to settle old scores. Old Father Stalin may well have been cackling in his tomb . . .

President Aliev's government found itself threatened by far more conspiracies than the Russian Connection alone. In spring 1996, another row broke out between the governments of Iran and Azerbaijan, each of which hurled accusations of subversive activities towards the other. Iran voiced suspicions that "certain elements in Azeri politics," as they put it, were working to provoke a separatist war in the north-west of Iran, where over twelve million ethnic Azeris live, who are not even given the right to use their own language let alone enjoy political autonomy. In 'North' Azerbaijan this message of "reunification of the historic birth-ground of the Azeri nation" is actively propagated by a movement called Millistiqlal which has home bases in Baku and Lenkoran. The government tolerates the movement without actively supporting it.

Far more serious than these accusations of south-bound provocation, warnings of infiltration by Iranian Islamic fundamentalists were heeded in spring 1996, as hundreds of Iranians who maintained offices for religious propaganda in Baku, Lenkoran, Sabirabad and elsewhere in the country were arrested.

As they were sent packing across the border, many of their fellows in the various leaderships of the Azeri Islamic parties were thrown behind bars for lengthy periods. In early June, virtually the entire leadership of the semi-underground Islamic Party of Azerbaijan found themselves locked up. The party had already been dealt a severe blow with the arrest of its two main leaders Hajjalikram Aliev and Kablaha Guliev months earlier; the latter was "discovered dead" in his cell on May 2nd, according to a communique issued by the prison's directorate.

If there is one thing the history of Azerbaijan shows, as described in the brief overview of these first chapters, it is that the country's countless incorporations into neighbouring empires — Assyria, Persia, Rome, Persia again and again and then Russia — have failed to break the spirit of liberty that still fills the nation. There is, moreover, an extra characteristic that sets Azerbaijan apart from its two South Caucasian neighbours. The struggles of Georgia and Armenia against foreign-imposed authority has almost always been driven by princes, kings or other, no less authoritarian leaders, who inspired their followers with the flame of nationalism and loyalty. In contrast, Azeri resistance — such that of Atropates, Babek, Heydar and others in days of old — was always fundamentally inspired by feudal and patrician elites who had little desire for strong leadership but simply wished to be left alone. Modern independence movements such as Rasulzadeh's Mussavat and the PFA were very much of the same spirit, a fact that is well reflected today in the policies of the present Azeri head of state at the time of writing.

All this goes part-way to explaining the often vehemently reactionary attitude of Russia's political echelons towards the national aspirations of Azerbaijan. But the Russians are far from the only ones to exhibit such tendencies. Time and again the steady stream of evidence linking Turkey, Russia and Iran to acts of terror and other attempts to destabilise Azerbaijan make one suspect that the country's three powerful neighbours agree on little except that none wants to see the republic on the Caspian Sea develop into a regional power of any significance. Their reasons are probably related more to business than politics. After all, the nation's legendary, ever-promising oil reserves have tempted the high and mighty in world history — from Alexander the Great to Hitler.

3
Black gold, vile poison

Baku, June 1996. It was party time on the Tbilisi Prospekt, just over two miles from the city centre, in the sports complex — a monstrous piece of non-architecture which serves as exhibition space for the annual oil fair, here called the Oil and Gas Symposium. It was just like a real trade fair: each pavilion decorated more colourfully than its neighbour. Almost all the gang's here: Exxon, Agip, Chevron, BP, Amoco, Pennzoil, Ramco, Statoil, Elf-Aquitaine, Shell.

Two 'sisters', however, were conspicuous by their absence. No open explanation existed for the absence of Texaco, although some claimed that the old feud with Pennzoil over the controversial purchase of Getty's oil empire lay behind its non-appearance, while others suggested that, in an unspoken gentlemen's agreement, Texaco had abstained from its claim to a piece of the Azeri cake in favour of Amoco. Two explanations for Total's absence buzzed about on the grape-vine: they were either not to get in Elf-Aquitaine's way or else the real reason lay in the Rich affair . . .

Back in the late 1980s, a deal was being worked out by which companies could contract themselves to clean up the heavily polluted soils on Apsheron in return for all the recyclable slicks, oil-containing waste and other useful residues without further commission. Estimates put the potential value of materials to be recouped at about $500 million, the necessary investment substantially less at around $300 million.

The tender was won by a joint-venture between Total and Richco, a Swiss-based group of companies owned by an enigmatic businessman of Belgian origin, Marc Rich. Rich was faithful to his name by being one of the world's wealthiest men, whose gross turnover in 1992 was valued at $30 billion. Total was to deliver the necessary technology and Rich the cash.

However, a string of scandals arising from a colourful variety of financial indiscretions linked to Rich started making front page news across the world, leading many to conjecture that his investment in Azerbaijan was little more than a no-frills money laundering operation intended to process profits of previous deals made elsewhere. Moreover, the authorities had turned their attentions to Rich's representative in Baku, Krishna Pemsing, an Indian citizen who was suspected of planning to use the sites under his control to dump concentrated toxic industrial wastes brought in from abroad for hard cash payments, instead of cleaning up the environment. Clearly someone was only out for their own good here.

But the real surprise was that Total had gone in for the whole venture (deliberately?) blithely ignoring who their partner really was. When I pressed for an explanation just before the deal fell through, a spokeswoman would only repeat: "We're dealing with the company Richco. The man behind it is of no interest to us."

A diplomatic summary of this may be expressed in a single word: 'greed'. And in Azerbaijan, at least, greed stands for oil — the age-old legend come to life and stirring up adrenaline as it always did.

As mentioned earlier, Azerbaijan was named after its founder, the Persian satrap Atropates who abandoned his sovereign Darius III and joined forces with Alexander the Great. 'Atropates' means 'He who is protected by Fire' and the governor was lord and master over the oil and gasfields in the area of Baku. The natural gas that wells up in the oilfields was the source of Zarathustra's inspiration, and he stayed in the area for a long time developing his fire philosophy.

Oil in antiquity was known for its healing effects; this was the 'white nepht' which spurted out of the ground in refined form. The more inflammable 'black nepht' was used, among other things, as a weapon — a sack filled with it and covered with glowing pitch and a burning fuse attached could make a ship burn like a torch in a matter of minutes. For this invention in particular, Alexander showed extreme gratitude to his host. The weapon has gone into the history books as 'Greek fire', and in later times the Byzantines were to use it against the Arabs with devastating effect.

With the coming of the Arabs to Azerbaijan, oil's value as an export merchandise increased, as a result of which production also expanded. After initially being granted oil exploitation rights by the first Arab governors (see previous chapter), the governor of Derbent was stripped of them after it came to light that he was simply putting all the revenues into his own pocket instead of spending it for the community's benefit. These rights passed to the Al-Sayyid family, descendants of the Prophet, at the end of the eighth century, who claimed descent from the Prophet Muhammad. The industry was sufficiently developed for the Arab geographer Al-Mas'udi to write in 915: "Many ships sail to Baku since it is there that a well is situated of white oil ('nepht') and God is my witness that there is nowhere any white oil to be found of better quality than here. The city is situated in the principality of Shirvan; in the oilfields many holes in the soil can be seen where natural gas wells from the earth which makes fire burn without end."

Marco Polo himself makes mention of a "fountain from which oil wells up abundantly, in quantities with which one could store a hundred shiploads at the same time. This oil is useless for consumption, but it burns well and is also a remedy against camel-mange." Polo situates the oilwell "on the border between Georgia and Armenia" but admits not to have seen it himself and only to have heard about it on the way.

The oldest detailed written description of the oilfields of Baku comes from the German scientist Engelbert Kaempfer, who visited the area in 1684. He relates how in some places the oil flows spontaneously out of the ground, whereas in other places people dig shallow holes from which oil is extracted by hand, and deeper ones from which the oil is pulled up in buckets. The oil was then transported in bags of sheep-leather across to Persia and Central Asia.

The same method was still in use as the Russians occupied Azerbaijan in the early 19th century. In 1806 the ruler of Baku, Hassan Khuli-Khan, had just lopped off the head of the commander-in-chief of the Russian invasion forces, the Georgian Prince Tsitsianov, he did not wait for the final strike of the Russian army but fled to Iran in a fishing-boat after he had had most of the oilwells closed and covered. Only a few open wells remained in use during the first thirty years of Russian occupation for the local consumption of lamp oil, which was refined in small factories on the spot. One of these factories belonged to the father of Sergius Witte, who was to write Russian history by bringing legislation and state organisation up to contemporary standards.

It was only by the end of the thirties of the same century that the governor of Baku sent a number of samples of the 'burning water' to St Petersburg with the request to have its usefulness tested. After extensive study, the imperial scientists sent a report to the czar which concluded that petroleum "stinks and is not suitable for any useful purpose except the lubrication of wagon-wheels." In the light of this information, the oil-bearing sites were leased to an Armenian businessman whose venture had soon plunged him into bankruptcy.

It would take until the end of the 1860s that a team of American explorers arrived on the scene and discovered oil on Apsheron at a depth of a hundred feet underground. Until then, it was always assumed that oil was present only in those sites where it came to the surface by itself. Inspired by Rockefeller's successes in Pennsylvania, Czar Alexander II at first granted the oil-bearing sites to his ministers and other favourites. After three years that failed to produce any initiative worth mentioning, he took back the intended treasures and had them auctioned in Tbilisi. A few people had begun to take notice, and among the colourful auction crowd of Russian patricians, Georgian *erestavis*, Azeri *beks* and Armenian speculators, there were two Swedish brothers by the names of Robert and Louis Nobel. Such lack of attention was not to last for too long now.

The siblings of Alfred, the inventor of dynamite, were the only members of those present who meant business with their purchase. As early as 1875 their first refinery in Baku was already up and running, in the meantime having purchased all the train wagons available on the Volgograd-Moscow-Riga line as well as the Baku-Volgograd pipeline, they became virtual owners of the market, leaving all local producers far behind them. As it was, most of the latter preferred to sell their crude oil to the Nobels instead of embarking on laborious attempts to compete with them.

On one hand, the seventies and eighties of the 19th century transformed the legend represented by Baku and its surrounding area since ancient times into a modern industrial venture. On the other hand, the activities of the Nobel family and later the Rothschilds have been harshly and unjustly labelled as savage capitalism. But while the Russian and Armenian oil industrialists hideously exploited their workers, most of whom were recruited from the Azeri hinterland and from Iran, and drenched the slightest hint of resistance in blood with the aid of Cossack brigades, the Nobels and the Rothschilds built up well-equipped housing facilities for their staff and established enterprise councils for joint consultation.

Local entrepreneurs, under the leadership of the Russian Lianosov, the Azeri Mirzoyev and the Armenian Mantashev, who with their exuberant lifestyles provoked the workers in their misery wherever they could, tried from the very beginning to oust these loathed Westerners through political scheming. But they were forever cut short by the excellent relations the Nobels maintained at the imperial court in St Petersburg. Moreover, Transcaucasian entrepreneurs lacked the two trump cards their Western rivals seemed to possess without limit: credit and capital.

The Nobels boosted the export of oil to Europe and the South Asian European colonies through the construction of the new railway to Batumi, financed by themselves, in 1882, shortly after the Black Sea port was handed over by the Turks to the Russians. However, within the space of only a few years, soaring production had already surpassed the railway's capacity. The Nobels, who up till now had enjoyed a monopoly on oil exports abroad, were soon to face competition in the shape of the immensely wealthy Rothschild family.

In co-operation with mainly British maritime transport companies, the Rothschilds had started the process of making Baku oil producers entirely dependent on them from a fairly early stage. By 1890, competition had become so fierce that the price of petroleum had tumbled to less than 20 kopeks per pud (1 pud = 16.2 kg) — less than half the previous year's average level. In 1892, it sank as low as seven kopeks, and so, at a cost price of nine kopeks, smaller producers were sent into bankrupcy — most into forced take-overs by the Rothschilds.

The city of Baku had not been spared either. A failed harvest right across the country in 1891 brought about widespread famine that lasted until late 1982. The following year, a plague epidemic broke out in the ever-expanding slums where under-nourishment and lack of hygiene had made the population physically defenceless, followed in 1894 by a cholera epidemic. The final blow for Azeri oil production seemed to be dealt by Rockefeller who in the same year launched a price war from New York by flooding the market with vast quantities of oil at levels far below cost price — an act that put a definitive end to the last remaining oil exploiters on the Caspian shore and the independent trade houses in Batumi. From that point on, it was a handful of Western companies that set the rules for Caucasian oil exports.

As early as 1889 the Rothschilds had developed themselves into the second ranking oil exporters after Nobel only. The most important product was still petroleum ('lamp oil') whereas most of its residue, the heavy fuel oil, was dumped into the environment. The crude oil extracted in and around Baku contained only 30 per cent lamp oil and 70 per cent fuel oil, in sharp contrast to the USA where proportions were 80-20 in favour of lamp oil.

However, this seemingly unfavourable condition proved to be the key to the 'Russian' oil industry's miraculous survival, largely the work of Sergius Witte, who in 1893 was appointed head of the imperial mega-ministry of transport, finance, trade and industry. One of the first measures this Balt of Dutch origin took was to switch the empire's industry and transport from charcoal to fuel oil. On the markets in Baku and Batumi this meant a true revolution, and before the year ended the price of fuel oil had surpassed that of lamp oil. It was to lead the industry to an heights it had never known, and would never know again. In 1900, Azeri oil production had overtaken American output by 600 million pud against 421 million, which made Baku the undisputed world leader. The prospect of a pipeline to Batumi, financed by the Rothschilds, made the gold shining on the horizon ever brighter.

The Rothschilds had not been idle and had expanded their supply market substantially by signing an exclusive delivery contract with a new rising star in the oil firmament, the British-based Shell company of Marcus

Samuel. The threat this posed Nobel was so ominous that it would have been hard to predict what would have happened had not another world giant in the oil business stepped into the breach between them: the Royal Dutch.

Access to Russian oil and oil products had been forced by the end of the nineties by British companies on the initiative of Alfred Stuart, an oil trader who in 1896 used an oil concession he had bought from an Armenian exiled in London to create the European Petroleum Company in Baku, the first British oil enterprise on Azeri soil. The example was soon to be followd by other British investors.

It was thus that the British broke through the monopolies till then exercised by the Rothschild and the Nobels, by offering smaller local producers the opportunity to sell their output against spot market prices. The largest British purchaser consisted of two sister companies, Baku Russian Petroleum Company and Russian Petroleum & Liquid Fuel Company, both controlled by Gladstone in a commercial capacity.

It would not take long, however, before new concentrations between initial Western rivals loomed. In 1899 the 'Koninklijke' — the Royal Dutch — had imposed itself in one fell swoop from incidental purchaser to rival to both Nobel and the Shell-Rothschild partnership through largescale trade agreements with Gladstone. In 1907, after the spectacular buy-out of Shell by the Royal Dutch, Rothschild proved too weak to compete any longer. In 1908, negotiations started which were to result in the buy-out by the newly merged Royal Dutch Shell of Rothschild's Transcaucasian 'jewels in the crown', the exploitation and export company Bnito (the Russian acronym for the Rothschild oil trade company)and the fuel oil company Mazout. After four years of cat and mouse talks, the transaction took place on January 1st 1912, leaving the bulk of the market to the 'Koninklijke' with Nobel remaining as its sole competitor.

Both 'monopolists', as they were resentfully dubbed by local small businesses, were to inherit assets that were literally scorched and blackened shadows of the glory predicted in earlier years. As a result of the ethno-political turbulence of 1905-6, installations lay in ruins. In 1910, one more market crisis erupted on the world market which caused prices to go through the floor. Even if during the following years numerous new wells were drilled and production showed a slight increase, sound planning as there had been in the early days of the Nobels was out of the question. The ever-tightening grip of the fiscal authorities, the government's unpredictable behaviour, as well as more and more frequent strikes and other expressions of social unrest were the main harbingers of the general atmosphere of *fin de règne*.

At the outbreak of the First World War, factories on Apsheron stood rusting away and the general mental and physical *imbroglio* was evident everywhere one looked. It was an apocalypic landscape the traces of which would be far from erased even eighty years later.

The general image of chaos and impredictability changed radically with the coming of the Soviets. Everything was nationalised, even where there had been negotiations on co-operation with, among others, the 'Koninklijke' and the British oil industry. This was the very reason Lloyd George and his Dutch counterpart Colijn had proved themselves ready to conclude a 'secret pact' with Krassin, the new regime's leading light in foreign affairs, which resulted in the promise of the two prime ministers to sell out Armenia, Azerbaijan and Georgia in violation of international agreements. The Royal Dutch/Shell, for their part, found themselves stuck with a pile of worthless paper, the interests of Lianosov, Mantashev and other local oil barons in Baku which they had purchased for a song.

One thing, however, remained the same under the dictatorship of the proletariat: Azerbaijan continued to be drained of oil with the Azeris receiving much back in return for it. From 1928 to 1940 production rose from 7.7 million to 22.2 million tons. But this share in the framework of total Soviet production gradually fell. In 1928, Azerbaijan still accounted for 90 per cent of the Marxist world empire's output. In 1940, this had already been reduced to 71 per cent. After the war, net production started to decline as well, from 15 million tons in 1950 to barely 10 million tons in 1990. Corruption, mismanagement and endless red tape had in the meantime reduced profitabilty to little more than zero.

Even though production of oil was not the Soviets' strongest feature, it must be said that they were far from idle where exploration and technological development were concerned. After the Second World War, a sound job was made in making an inventory of oilfields on the Caspian Sea — as well as under it. So, in the early 1950s, the 'Oil Rocks' on the sea bed off the coast of Apsheron were put into operation. These artificial islands, connected by causeways, were still operative under Gorbachev and were even exploited during the 1980s as a tourist attraction.

At the time of independence, it had already been established that under the sea bed dozens of billions of dollars worth of oil were still waiting to be pumped up. It was then established too that with a war on their hands, the end of which was by no means in sight, and with a state economy which consisted of figures sinking ever deeper into the red, the necessary capital could not possibly be raised without appealing to the oil multinationals of the West.

The resulting 'contract of the century', first conceived under Mutalibov, was at stake in a string of bizarre intrigues in which politics and business were heavily intertwined. At the first stage, the offshore oilfields of Azeri, Shirag and Gunashly were considered. Their joint turnover at 1992-93 prices was valued almost $100 billion. A consortium was to be created in which foreign companies could take part in exchange for the necessary investments — something totalling between seven and eight billion dollars. It looked like a dream.

But then the musical chairs began. Amoco and British Petroleum were first in line to sign up. At a later stage American Pennzoil (which was later to sell an important part of its shares it held in the newly formed consortium AIOC [Azerbaijan International Operating Company] to a Japanese multinational), Norwegian Statoil (which went in tandem with BP), and the Scottish company Ramco joined in the chorus. All together more than enough to guarantee comfortable coverage of the investment's needs. Revenues were to be shared between the Azeri national oil company SOCAR and its foreign partners on a 50-50 basis.

The trouble started under Elchibey's administration. As the war over Karabakh got out of hand and Georgia was struck by all-out civil war, the oil bosses started worrying about how to get the oil wealth out of the country if things were to go on as they were. The pipelines between Baku and Batumi had stopped functioning and the railway's capacity was unable to cope with demand. The pipeline through Daghestan and Chechenia was in dire need of repair. Chechenia had already broken with the Russian Federation by that time even if war had been avoided up till then. And finally, Elchibey's nationalist regime was little inclined to once more grant Russia its Azeri oil export monopoly of old.

At this stage, Turkey's Özal came up with a bright idea. His country would increase its economic assistance to Azerbaijan and provide substantial credit facilities if it agreed to a new pipeline ending up in Ceyhan on the Turkish Mediterranean coast. It looked, however, brighter than it was — at least in the short term. Turkish credits remained of modest size and had little to do with oil supplies. Moreover, with inflation at 150 per cent per annum and a civil war with the Kurds in the eastern part of its territory on its hands, Turkey was hardly in a better position than Russia to act as a solid credit partner. On top of that came the fact that not only was the proposed pipeline to run straight through the Kurdish war zone but had to go through either Armenia or Iran. Armenia was out of the question because of the war against Azerbaijan, while the Iranian option was vetoed by the political attitudes of Britain and America towards it.

The coming of Aliev brought some light in the darkness — at least for Azeri interests in the situation. He started, shortly after taking office, by calling the representatives of the Western oil companies together in July

1993. He spoke briefly but clearly: "Gentlemen, your investments are safe in Azerbaijan and revenues are guaranteed. As for sharing those revenues, we'll have to talk a little more since there's no question that you'll just be able to put half of it into your pockets . . ."

"Talking some more" was to take up one and a half years of laborious negotiations. The final result came down to the Azeri state being granted between 70 and 75 per cent of all revenues, taking profit shares and levies into account — which still meant that revenues of the oil companies quadrupled their investments.

In the meantime, however, SOCAR had come under significant pressure as a majority shareholder. In 1994, the new Turkish prime minister Tanzu Çiller stormed into Baku demanding ten per cent of SOCAR's shares for the Turkish national oil company, which she got, although at a later stage fresh injections of capital reduced the Turkish share to seven per cent. Shortly afterwards, Boris Yeltsin was to intervene on behalf of the newly privatised Russian oil company LUKoil in order to grant it ten per cent of SOCAR's shares as well. He got twenty.

Çiller appeared to be satisfied, but not Yeltsin. In the summer of 1994, the Kremlin came in with a fresh demand. The Caspian Sea, they put it, was part of international waters and so no one was entitled to exploit it without a 'treaty' having been first concluded. Here they referred to the North Sea treaty made between its coastal states with respect to oil exploitation.

Aliev declared that he was more than ready to talk about such an agreement, but he was in no way prepared to stop drilling until such an agreement had come about. This angered the Russian ambassador to Baku and he publicly threatened Azerbaijan with gunboat diplomacy. An opinion poll held in Moscow at the same time showed that 65 per cent of those interviewed were in favour of Russian military intervention to put Azerbaijan in its place.

But that was not to happen. What did was that LUKoil joined the lobby to join existing and new consortiums. They could do so, and did so, thanks to capital lavishly furnished by the American Richmond and other major Western investment companies. By using this formula, Richmond proved to be the only American concern that managed to find a loophole in Washington's Iranophobia; through LUKoil they were able to take a part of the minor offshore concession of Shah Deniz, which all other American investors had to skip because of the Iranian state oil company's presence. It was a public secret that, in the months previous to the agreement, Russian diplomats had been unusually active in Teheran.

The 'compromise' ultimately arranged by the oil magnates came down to a commitment to make 'provisional' use of both the 'Russian' and the 'Georgian' option. The latter proposed the repair and expansion of the pipeline facilities to Poti and Batumi from where — equally 'provisionally' — the oil would be transported to Rotterdam by sea-tanker. In order to keep up the pressure, the Turkish government was to allow Georgian oil shipments through the Bosphorus but not Russian ones.

In Russian there is a word for what one really means if one talks about an 'agreement'. That word is *diktat*. Russians like to look to the future — and so to forget the past. For their past stinks, both literally and figuratively speaking.

As mentioned before, the Russians implemented their policy of exhaustion in their 'colonies' from the early 19th century on without the slightest consideration for the consequences on the environment. This was true for agriculture: for instance, the forced conversion from wheat to cotton cultivation in the west of Azerbaijan under Stalin which exhausted the soil and on top of that enabled Moscow to feed or starve the Azeri population according to whim. This was even truer of industry, in particular those areas where the Soviets expanded existing oil installations and/or built new chemical factory complexes.

You see it the moment you step into Azerbaijan. The drive from the airport to the capital reveals the the hinterland of Baku in all its ruined glory. In 1993, almost half of Apsheron's territory consisted of barren moonscape where thousands of rusty drilling towers and 'nodding-donkeys' stick out of the ground like rotten teeth and where nothing grows among the black and brown slurry. Twenty four thousand hectares of soil in Azerbaijan (half of which is in Apsheron) has be dug up and decontaminated before it is too late. Almost every industrial installation needs to be modernised to prevent further damage to public health. But the cost is estimated at over \$15 billion.

Contamination of soil is not only a result of the oil industry but the other industrial sectors as well — the processing of copper and bauxite, over-use of agricultural pesticides and herbicides and the random dumping of industrial and domestic wastes. According to a government environment report in 1993 (the first of its kind in the country's history, since even at the height of Gorbachev's glasnost anything on pollution of the environment was classified) Azerbaijan was producing at the time 35 million tons of industrial waste of which, according to international standards, 85,000 tons should have been classified as concentrated toxic waste. On top of that, another 4,600 tons of concentrated chemical wastes were imported from abroad. A mere quarter of the sorry overall total was treated. Over two thirds were dumped into the environment without the slightest protective measure whatsoever. As for domestic waste, the situation was even worse as

97 per cent was dumped, two per cent incinerated and one per cent recycled.

In the final years of the USSR, Azeri agriculture consumed over 300,000 tons of synthetic fertiliser and 50,000 tons of pesticides and herbicides. But tests have shown that the nation's agricultural soil contained an average concentration of DDT — ten times the internationally accepted maximum, and in some places amounted to fifty-fold.

Surface waters proved to be in an even worse state than the soil. The Kura, the country's main river course, during the early 1990s contained ten times the permitted maximum of oil residues, 15 times that of phenol and 25 that of copper. Over 1990, 420 million cubic metres of industrial waste had been dumped in Azerbaijan's waters of which 280 million came from the oil and chemical industry. In the same year, six times the allowed maximum of oil residues and 14 times that of phenol were measured in Baku Bay.

The atmosphere was hardly in a better condition. The air in the population centres of Baku and Sumgayt showed annual readings of, among other materials, 60,000 tons of nitrous oxides, 75,000 tons of carbon dioxides, 90 000 tons of sulphur dioxides, and 1.7 million hydrocarbons.

The consequences in respect to public health have been clear for all to see over the generations, although their true proportions only first reached public knowledge as in 1996 the first statistics on the overall clinical picture in Baku and Sumgayt became issues. But even the heart-rending images of children born with two heads, without limbs, without kidneys, spleen or liver, with empty upper skulls and numerous other birth defects, failed to bring about a widespread environmental consciousness. There was the serious soil erosion which had already affected more than half the Azeri land surface. Salination through over-irrigation and the rising level of the Caspian Sea had taken their toll, and were responsible for the degradation of 50 per cent of all arable and pasture land. The constantly acute shortage of drinking water which had brought Baku to rationing it four hours a day . . . None of these were likely to break through the pervading lethargy which authorities and population alike appeared to share. Whereas the government opened declined to make any attempt at modernising agriculture, the public kept dumping their garbage on street corners, leaving their water taps running and failing to get broken mains repaired. *Laissez faire, laisser crever.*

Why so? The answer would always come something like: "You know, that's just the way it is." The "situation" was the excuse for all of the country's ills — including losing a war over something hardly anyone cared about: a remote backwater of the country known as Upper Karabakh.

*

The age-old quest for oil and the disregard it brought for the Azeri nation's well-being at the hands of foreign powers, fit in perfectly with the country's struggle for liberty as described in the previous chapters. One of the principal characteristics of oil which distinguishes it from almost all other commodities is the fact that its strategic value in times of conflict largely bypasses its commercial value on the free market in more peaceful times. Individuals kill one another for gold. Nations do it for fuel.

By the end of 1996, oil reserves under and around the Caspian were estimated at some 50 billion barrels. More than enough to earn a lot of money on , but not remotely sufficient to threaten the market position of OPEC's output in any way. It never looked as if the Caspian region could boost its joint production to more than ten million barrels of crude oil per day and then only if investments up to several dozens of billions of dollars are provided. On the other hand, OPEC could easily double its present output of some 25 mnbpd simply by opening a few more taps and without requiring a penny of extra investment. Worse: due to this and other factors the Caspian oil producers were forced to offer their crude oil on the free market at an average of at least $6 so as not to lose money, whereas the OPEC could maintain its break-even point even if the market price plunged to under $2.

All this, however, does not mean that the Russians have no reason to fear the rise of a 'Caspian OPEC' on which their own impact would be marginal. If this happened, they would be forced to pay for their fuel at market rates, something any non-radical Russian government could conceivably live with. But to have others keep their hands on the tap in case of need is more than Russian thought can bear, and Russian politicians have more than enough awareness of history to realise this would place them pretty much in a similar position as the Germans ended up with both world wars: huge technical and strategic advantages but no fuel to use them properly.

It is in this context that the often frantic and rather unscrupulous way Russia keeps feeding on the bloody and dramatic conflicts on its former outlands should be understood. This makes them no less horrendous for it, as we shall see in the next two chapters which deal with the reasonings and realities of the war in Karabakh.

4

Rotting on the plains

I t takes four hours for those international aid organisations who dispose of flashing 4-wheel drives to drive from Baku to Barda. However, those who have to manage with a hired Lada have to reckon with a seven hour drive. The first track follows the coast due south. On the left side, the sea surface sparkles, on the right side a grim volcanic rock desert looms up — a landscape resembling those seen in sci-fi movies. After an hour and a half the road turns inland, through the plains. From time to time one gets stuck in the middle of a herd of cows, sheep or goats. Along the road, young boys watch over the horns of their water buffalo, the impressive beasts up to their necks in the muddy ditches and ponds. Everywhere along the road, locals offer fruit, meat and home-made liquor. It is this seemingly contradictory combination of industry and inertia, of business fever and timeless apathy that has come to form one of the main characteristics of post-Soviet society. Anyhow, a war going on almost within shooting distance seems beyond imagination in these surroundings.

In 1992 Barda was not yet the final outpost of free Azerbaijan it was later to become. That honour was taken by Agdam, the same place where the International Red Cross had its main headquarters until the summer of 1992 when it became too dangerous — not only because of ever intensifying shellfire but, most of all, because of the gangs of armed bandits terrorising the area. As we visited Agdam in late autumn 1992, the steady pounding of the artillery could be heard every day, although the town itself was rarely hit.

Another dimension of the war with Armenia could be found in the plains between Barda and Agzhabedy, where the most disinherited part of the conflict's victims made their homes in dozens of "villages," as the settlements were called by the aid workers. In reality, they consisted of tents and holes in the ground covered with clay and scrapwood. By age-old tradition, they usually served as shelters for livestock driven by shepherds from Upper Karabakh to the plain during the winter when the mountains become too cold for the animals to feed on. Now animal life in the shelters had taken on human form.

The humans here belonged to the 'second wave' of refugees from Lachin and a number of locations in Karabakh itself during the first half of 1992 — the 'first wave' consisted of displaced persons in 1990 who are mainly from Armenia. The scenery surrounding their new home is sheer desolation. Nothing interrupts the straight line of the horizon for miles around. No sign of life, not even a tree or bush. Water comes from a pit, one or two of which each village possesses, electricity supplies are erratic to say the least, gas or butane supplies non-existent, let alone telephone connections. Worse, no sanitary provisions are at hand, as a result of which human and animal waste is piled stinking high on the edge of every settlement.

At the time of my first visit in November 1992, the refugees on the plain still had to endure their first winter. They had already been through a parched, roasting summer and the experience had left its mark literally on the children's skins in the form of ghastly red spots. They looked unnaturally pale and could be heard moaning and crying most of the time. One doesn't need to be told that living on a shitheap is bad for one's health — and a diet of starvation rations hardly relieves the suffering.

The cattle farmers who account for half the population of the refugee camps were not such strangers to the hardships of a half-nomadic existence. Moreover, a large number of them had managed to bring part of their livestock with them which enabled them to endure their present lifestyle better than the former civil servants and intellectuals who had fled along with them.

"The farmers had it lucky," said Adil, who used to teach French at secondary school in Lachin, "but look at me, I've lost everything! You should have seen my house: two storeys, a big veranda, a flower garden and orchard, a great lounge with antique furniture and carpets, stereo, video, two cars at the front . . . It's all gone now, smashed, stolen, who knows what!"

However lonely life may be on the plains, at night company less pleasant than visiting reporters and aid workers imposes itself in the form of bandits, most of whom come on horseback across the border from northern Iran in order to ransack the refugee camps. Mohammed was a young literary scientist by training who now walks around in a khaki suit with an old hunting rifle over his shoulder. Together with half a dozen other youngsters he has organised a security patrol but, as he wrily admitted, "the moment a gang of guys armed with Kalashnikovs comes galloping up there's not really much you can do to stop them."

Rotting on the plains

Ali and Mohammed were trying to put into words the nightmare that has haunted the camps' inhabitants ever since their flight and is likely to remain doing so for the rest of their lives: the terrible events in and around Lachin, May 16th 1992, when the Armenians stormed the district and occupied it. Unlike many war refugees elsewhere in the world who have learnt, after having lived for years in a world of violence and danger, to think according to 'war logic', testimonies from the people of Lachin consist mainly of an incoherent mass of images, impressions and flashes in which it is difficult to perceive any chronological order. Data, numbers and other 'hard' information may only be distilled after many dozens of interviews with people, each one of which is able to contribute only loose fragments.

From the stories, the following scene can be compiled. By the end of the night previous to the attack of May 16th, Lachin had come under unprecedented heavy artillery fire from two sides: Armenia and Karabakh. In the morning, tanks and armoured cars rolled into the town. Quarter by quarter, street by street, house by house, every building was entered and searched. Not only Azeri but also Armenian families accused of "treachery" were dragged out on the street and slaughtered in a variety grisly ways.

The following day, witnesses tell, everything seemed quiet. Those who had managed to escape came back into town to see what could be saved of their belongings. Not much, as it appeared, for awaiting them were the invaders of the previous day. Again, hundreds were killed and many more carried off in lorries. The precise number of casualties has never been known: estimates mount up to 700 civilians killed and at least the same number missing, never to be heard from again. Over the following weeks many families were forced to physically purchase their relatives — dead or alive — for substantial amounts of money, as the invaders brazenly threatened to "throw the bodies to the dogs."

It is hard to provide a clear answer to the question why acts of butchery like those in Lachin and Shusha (where shortly before similar scenes were reported) failed to trigger off the storm of outrage that burst after the Lebanese massacres of Sabra and Shatila in 1982, even if one takes into account the journalistic myth that Lebanon represented in those days and the part the always provocative Israeli played. It is curious that the world has steadfastly remained indifferent to the plight of the Southern Caucasus. Naturally the tradition of Soviet media consisted of a one-way flow of information with a maximum delay inbuilt. This disregard for the facts must take a large part of the responsibility for the 'blind spot' in the world news on events in the south of the former USSR in general.

Another important factor, however, is to be found in the articulate one-sidedness so carefully cultivated by the Western media at the expense of balanced information, for example, on war crimes in the Karabakh war. Ever since the Kuwait crisis in the 1990s, any semblance of balance in international news coverage has become lost — they blow up a single chain of events while at the same time systematically marginalising other matters which in themselves are no less serious. Even afterwards, when a clearer picture began to emerge about Karabakh, little of it attracted the world's attention in any meaningful way. For example, the only real eye-opener to do so — an account of the massacres of 1992 by Armenian military and paramilitary in Khojaly — did not appear until half a year later. Nevertheless, reports of this in the West did at least feature intriguing notes on the role played by the Russian armed forces, in particular the 366th Regiment of the former Red Army — then already re-baptised as the Confederal Combat Force of the Commonwealth of Independent States, which, despite its impressive name, consisted mainly of the same ill-motivated, undisciplined band of thugs as it had before.

Corruption and desertion were daily routine in the force. Arms and ammunition were sold or bartered in exchange for a case of vodka or a handful of drugs from the pharmacy. Wages were no longer paid — except to those who had volunteered to fight under command of the Armenians. The 366th's commander, Colonel Yuri Zarvigorov, had little say in what was and wasn't to be done. Real authority over most of the troops was firmly in the hands of an Armenian officer by the name of Yosef Oganian, who in his turn followed orders only from Yerevan and Stepanakert. Oganian was a fanatical Dashnak who later was to be marginalised by the former ASALA chief Monte Melkonian (see later) and the Armenian defence minister Vazgen Sarkissian.

It is generally accepted that the horrors of Khojaly, Shusha, Lachin and several dozens of other similar massacres on a lesser scale elsewhere in the area during the first half of 1992 were the handiwork of Oganian and his followers. On February 25th, by the end of the afternoon, the airstrip and villages and settlements around Khojaly were taken under artillery fire. By then civilian casualties were already said to have mounted to around 150. Next morning, Khojaly itself came under fire. By noon, tanks appeared in the streets followed by the type of atrocities that were to be repeated later in Shusha and Lachin.

On February 28th, Moscow ordered the 366th to withdraw. But its actual departure commenced a whole week later. On foot, hitchhiking or in stolen lorries and buses, the soldiers had to make their way through the firing line of hostile Azeri territory in order to reach the Russian Federation — leaving a long line of abandoned equipment behind them as well as comrades in arms who had joined up with the Armenian armed forces.

*

In the meantime the inhabitants of Khojaly found themselves plunged into the centre of hell. Here are just three examples, typical of the hundreds of testimonials from survivors:

Jamil Mamedov — "Tanks and armoured vehicles destroyed our houses and ran people over. Russian soldiers were followed by armed Armenians. I had managed to save my grandson, but I couldn't find my wife and my daughter. I took off my coat and wrapped the child in it so he wouldn't die from the cold. By dawn I realised that he wouldn't be able to survive the cold any longer and so I walked in the direction of the nearby Armenian village of Nakhchivanik. Armenian men with arms stopped us. I pleaded with them to take my money and let us through in the direction of Agdam, for the boy's sake. But they swore at me and knocked me down to the ground, then dragged me off to their commander. He ordered us to be locked up in a stable which had apparently earlier been used as a prison for Azeri women and children. They kept us there for four days without food or water. If it hadn't been for the help of a friendly family who secretly brought us bread and water during the night we would have died of starvation." After four days Mamedov was taken to Askeran with his grandchild to be exchanged for an Armenian taken prisoner by the other side. Before his release Mamedov was badly treated "by foreign mercenaries including a number of black men. They tore the nails out of my toes and kicked me in the face. Then they took my grandson . . ."

Jamil never heard again of his wife and daughter, nor of the fate of his grandchild.

Sariya Talibova — "They took us over to the Armenian cemetry. It's hard for me to describe what happened over there. Four young Meshketian Turks [deported from Georgia by Stalin to Uzbekistan who then had to flee bloody persecutions under Karimov] were shot dead on the graves of Armenian militiamen as a sort of blood sacrifice. They cut the heads off the bodies. Then the Armenians started torturing the children to death before their parents' eyes. Later a lorry came and dumped the bodies into a ravine. Again later, two Azeris in army uniforms were brought in whose eyes had been stabbed with screwdrivers . . ."

Shanan Orudniev — "We tried to escape to Agdam through the woods, but armed men near Nakhchivanik shot at us. A number of women and children were hit and died. My son was killed. They took away my twenty two-year-old daughter together with her twins, and my eighteen-year-old daughter who was pregnant."

Of their fate, nothing was ever discovered.

*

On the Armenian side such atrocities have been persistently dismissed as "Azeri propaganda", photographs of the events were said to be fakes, and even the Azeri army has been accused of having committed the murders in an attempt to pin the blame on the Armenians. A French reporter was even produced as a witness to maintain these allegations, his evidence received unquestioningly.

But a journey along the front in December 1992 provided images hard to erase from the memory. Agdam gave all the impression of a war-stricken spot. At the only hotel where any life survived, every windows without glass, officers slept there for shelter at night. Apart from the cold, shell salvoes kept us awake throughout the dark hours, most of them at a distance, but some fearfully close. However, not so close, as we were to see next morning, as the series of direct hits suffered by the central marketplace a few months earlier in broad daylight. Oleg Litvin, the press photographer who had documented the slain victims of the Khojaly massacres, happened to be around and produced a searing photo-report of the emergency operation during which over fifty dead and more than a hundred injured were dragged from the smouldering debris.

Even more dramatic were the traces of the conflict we were to see in Mardakert (Agdara), the capital of the north-eastern district of Upper Karabakh that bears the same name. The suburbs were an eerie copy of Beirut at the end of the 1980s: burnt-out apartment blocks, houses in ruins, shells of cars, smashed furniture and twisted lamp-posts. More than once Armenian troops had occupied the city only to be driven back; by the end of 1992 this was the only piece of Upper Karabakh which was still in the hands of the Azeri government army.

The following day we visited a number of army positions. The journey dragged on: each next army post again meant arguments, misunderstandings, waiting. The 'positions' offered a pathetic sight. No cover at the back. Commanders in their early thirties at most, soldiers most of whom were still teenagers. For shelter they had tents without any form of groundsheets — stuck literally in the mud. There was no transport available, not for the men and certainly not for the massive artillery guns fit to defend a fortress. It was evident the cannon were a burden rather than a means of deterrence to a field unit whose usefulness — and indeed survival — depended on its mobility.

More than once, the commander told me, this place became a scene of pandemonium and chaos: "If the shooting starts and we do nothing, we're likely to be slaughtered. If we shoot back we give our position away and get slaughtered as well."

With only a handful of walkie-talkies for communication, the unit sometimes had to wait days for supplies. Each time soldiers were killed or wounded nothing could be done except wait until help arrived, if it ever did. Young boys of fifteen or sixteen were forced to watch their mortally wounded pals scream in agony as they died a slow death. Later, an officer in Agdam described how lorries arrived from Baku filled with lads who had never even held a gun in their hands before. There they were shown how to load and reload a Kalashnikov — and then off they went . . .

However, not all fighters appeared to come straight out of mummy's lap. At another army post, we met Barad, a Red army veteran who had the character of the true seasoned resistance fighter: "As soon as I heard that the Armenians were harrassing this place, killing and routing its people, I got my old uniform out of the closet and reported to the nearest army command post. A few days later I was right on the front-line, with the dead and the wounded all around me — but no one's going to pull down this old guy, I assure you. Sure, I got hit in the leg, but I got myself treated and a week later I was back on my feet and ready for more. I'm not crazy about violence, you know, but you've got to understand that this is my country, and if I have to defend it against those who want to stamp all over it, I'll carry on doing so, even if I live to be a hundred. So there you have it."

As the 1992 drew to a close, there was only one road left, with a railroad running along it, that connected Zengilan with the rest of the country. The twin lines ran along the Iranian border and everything and anything venturing onto it was an open target for the Armenian snipers lurking on the northern side a few miles off. Here, the atmosphere differed sharply from the north. In more peaceful times the region had been friendly and prosperous, but now people walked sternly, their faces etched with their fears and worries. No one went hungry, but spare parts for machines, fuel, clothing and other things essential for a more or less sophisticated lifestyle could only be purchased on the black market at rip-off rates.

A few days before our visit, the town of Zengilan itself had narrowly escaped Armenian occupation. But the entire western part of the province had already fallen under the Armenian boot: village after village, settlement after settlement had been overrun, the houses set ablaze with tank grenades and mortars. Anyone found in the open was seized and brutally put to death by the sadistic Cobras — the elite units consisting mostly of soldiers of fortune and specialised in various forms of terror. Their particular skills were sniping and torture, and they were designed to be infiltrated into an enemy zone during the weeks previous to an attack with orders to spread panic among the population, only to return with the occupying troops in order to finish their butcher's job. As a job, it's a sadist's delight — but not without its risks.

On a walk in the area around Zengilan we found two dead bodies, already stiff, of an Armenian soldier and a Russian Cobra, lying in the mud at a crossroads. The stroll we were taking was not without danger still. Our military guide was a little nervous since he felt certain that Armenian snipers on the surounding hilltops had us in their sights. A dozen or so villages up in the hills had remained in the hands of the Armenians, while the others in the valley had been evacuated after being looted and burnt. Inhabitants took the opportunity of the lull in the fighting to go in to collect up the remainders of their belongings on tractors, lorries, cars and donkeys — then to leave for good without knowing where to go.

We walked along the railway track in the direction of Armenia and arrived at the station of the village of Sheyifly. On the street side, we spotted a fence reduced to splinters, an iron rod and a pair of boots. It was a modest monument for Adil Rustamov, a simple private who, in sharp contrast to most of his officers, took his job seriously as the Armenians approached the village. In an effort to give the civilian population the chance to escape he took up position in the middle of the street with his Kalashnikov. He fired round after round in the direction of the oncoming vehicles to keep the men pinned inside. After running out of bullets, he defended himself with an iron rod until his final breath. The way the paratroopers butchered him was gruesome to say the least.

In the town itself, chaos reigned. Thousands of people stood in the streets in front of the public buildings. Their anger was aimed less at the enemy — "War is war, sadly enough . . ." — than at the Azeri government.

"They could hardly be more right," the district's governor Telman Kazimov flatly agreed.

He described how, only a few days earlier, he had to take personal action. The Armenians were only seven miles from the city but from the nearby Azeri positions, not a single warning shot could be heard. The governor took his car to see the situation for himself and was amazed and appalled to find only a few soldiers there smoking cigarettes without an officer to be seen. He immediately drove back to town and rounded up a handful of policemen and personal friends, returning with his motley crew to the artillery position. There they fired on their own initiative and kept the enemy at bay.

The day after the event Kazimov filed back a detailed report to the ministries of interior affairs and defence in Baku. Later, he made a direct appeal to Parliament after weeks of silence. Months later again, a debate behind closed doors was held on the matter, with the only result that Kazimov and his senior staff were told they were fired.

After the invasion of Zengilan it looked for a while as if a political solution for the conflict was at hand. That hope, however, was to evaporate with what is perhaps the most inhuman of all the inhuman tragedies of the Karabakh war: the occupation of Khelbajar.

With Khelbajar the world woke up for a while: pictures and television images of a 60,000-strong flow of exhausted, hungry and traumatised refugees, tales of murders and abductions which made earlier tales look tame by comparison, all this contributed to the first formal condemnation of the Armenian side in the struggle by the Security Council of the United Nations.

The number of refugees who perished on the journey through the mountains that separate Khelbajar from the plains around Ganja is likely to have been closer to two thousand than to one thousand. The number of inhabitants of Khelbajar who were slaughtered on the spot by the invading Armenians is estimated at up to two thousand as well. The number of "missing" — most of whom were supposed dead months later — must be in the region of five thousand.

On her arrival in Dachkesan, one woman from Chestak described how, whene her village was occupied, she saw a pregnant woman drown herself in the river so she wouldn't fall into the hands of the soldiers. She told of another woman who ran away but lost her child to the paramilitary chasing her. From her hiding place the witness was forced to watch as children were tortured, raped, beheaded. The Armenians relaxed afterwards by playing a game of football with one of the heads.

Scenes like Chestak have been exhaustively reported from Lachin (not to be confused with the border town between Armenia and Karabakh further to the south), Zhomar, Baslibeyl, Jinsal, Selok, Kichiligaya, Kilsati, Zulfugardi, Joldar, Abdullavagi, Esrik, Jorman, Agchakend, Oruchlu, Alivalar and Merjimek. One of the most extensive massacres was carried out in the town of Ayrim, where less than half of its five thousand inhabitants managed to escape with their lives across the mountains to the north.

Yussuf, a sprightly old man in his sixties, is one of those heroes who, unlike many mass murderers, is rarely remembered in the official records. Singlehandedly he took eleven children whose parents had been killed or abducted to a remote store-hut and there hid them from the enemy. After a few days, he set off for the mountains together with his young wards and brought them safe and sound to Dachkesan. Along with a number of other survivors he spoke of the inferno that was Ayrim: scenes like those in Chestak and other localities, but also reportedly three (presumably, there were more such cases in Ayrim alone) separate cases of people driven to a square in their hundreds to be gunned down with mortar and machine-gun fire.

Another blood-soaked tragedy took place on the north-east road out of Khelbajar. Unlike the majority of the other occupied towns, the capital's population had been granted a few hours to leave. Those who stayed were cut down without mercy, and the numerous cars and buses crammed full of refugees drove stright out of the tunnel that links the Tutkuchay river valley to the northbound road straight into a welcome of mortars and bullets from the Armenian units that were waiting there. Anyone who tried to escape from the flaming inferno was gunned down indiscriminately. Few survived this massacre, but the stories of those that did are chillingly similar, and reconstructing the event puts the estimated number of killed between five and seven hundred.

Many of those inhabitants of Khelbajar reported 'missing' are supposed to have met their fate in one of the mass detention centres created by the Armenians in the area. The most notorious was in Istusu, a disused sanatorium 10,000 feet up by the glaciers of the Terter river, between the mountain ridges of Ketidag and Galingaya, south west of Khelbajar. Mamish Aliev was one of the few prisoners who managed to escape from Istusu. He later described how mass executions took place there on a daily basis, along with systematic rape and torture. From time to time, the centre would be evacuated in order to show, among others, an Australian television team and the French section of Médécins Sans Frontières, that nothing was going on there. Of course, this casts some doubt on the allegations that Istusu was used to hold over 7,000 prisoners, but nevertheless there were more than enough reports to justify the setting up of an investigation.

But this was not to be. Shortly after the invasion of Khelbajar, ICRC (International Committee of the Red Cross) delegate André Picot declared: "All of us have been able to see with our own eyes how in this place the Geneva Convention has been systematically violated en masse with respect to the population in the battle zones and occupied territories. I uphold this conclusion one hundred per cent. Unfortunately, political institutions are in only a position to act according to the consequences."

The taking of Agdam that summer, followed in the autumn by the occupation of all territories from Fizuli to Gubatly, meant only the continuation of the Armenian policy of ethnic cleansing. Still one remark should be made concerning the taking of Agdam as described earlier. On the eve of the final assault, a field hospital doctor nearby told us how a few weeks before he had received about thirty wounded from the villages of Gzulangardly and Boyagladuky. They had been hit by shrapnel and none of them showed injuries that were likely to endanger their lives. Yet, each one died mysteriously within a few days. Analyses made later of blood and tissue samples as well as pieces of shrapnel and the soil they fell on showed that the projectiles fired by the Armenians on the villages contained a form of organic phosphorus concentrate, a substance that passes into the blood and burns the organs from the inside. The effect can only be lethal.

Rotting on the plains

In contrast to those before them, the refugees from the last occupied territories in the far south west of Azerbaijan were not transferred to the hinterland in a more or less organised way. Thousands of families were settled arbitrarily in fields around Agdam after its fall, traumatised, desorientated and without anyone to take the trouble to bring some order into the chaos. Within the space of a few months, they were concentrated in camps that were hardly less depressingly primitive than their initial places of settlement. These people, over a hundred thousand of the quarter million victims of the last ethnic cleansing operation by the Armenians, had arrived through the inaccessible mountains of northern Iran where they had been driven by the invaders, forcing them to leave behind their belongings and thousands of missing and dead.

The scene of the camps around Sabirabad in the plains of Mughan is just as desolate as in the refugee centres near Agjabedy already described: noon temperatures in mid-summer rise to forty degrees, not a single breeze, intermittent energy supplies and the same kind of mud and heaps of faeces between which dirty and empty-eyed children wander crying. At a railway station nearby the situation was even more pitiful. Here, perhaps a hundred cargo wagons converted into shelters had become so hot during the daytime that people were camping under them instead of in them.

A surgeon camping there between the rails with his family pointed to a country house newly-built on the other side of the road: "Look — I used to have a house like that. Now look at how we live here, like beggars, like rats . . ."

Again, the material hardship of people's lives appeared to be perfectly in line with their spiritual deprivation. The imam of one of the villages near Horadiz on the Iranian border, a place occupied by Armenian troops on more than once occasion only to be retaken each time by the Azeri army, described how the place was surrounded and fired at with mortars. The enemy then entered the village with tanks, driving the population in the direction of a bridge across the River Arax, leading to Iran. But on the bridge, an armed unit was waiting for the villagers and opened fire on them as they approached. Survivors did their best to find a place to hide, leaving dozens of dead bodies on the site and a large number of those who had jumped into the river drowned. The imam took refuge, together with a hundred of followers, in a remote farm. A few days later, most of them managed to escape across the river in boats.

The irony of the situation in and around Sabirabad, as aid workers on the spot confirmed, was that as tens of thousands of refugees were begging for alms, at the same time the crops were rotting in the fields that started at the edges of the camps. Since most of the former kolkhozes and sovkhozes (collectively and state owned farms respectively) had long since been abandoned, there was no one to harvest on the land. A Red Cross official spoke of the "highly artificial poverty" suffered by the displaced as the government categorically refused at the time to grant them the facilities to build up a new life worthy of a human being. Meanwhile, the refugees were exploited by farmers in the area as cheap temporary labour, to be disposed of at any convenient time.

In this way, the number of souls rotting away in the plains of Azerbaijan increased to about half a million, from a total of 1.2 million people displaced by the war. Nobody cares about their future (and this includes the majority of their compatriots) aside from a few aid workers who admit they cannot help where they are needed most and the odd reporter who appears from time to time on a war-tourist trip.

"Of course we thank you — an awful lot," said so many depressed refugees commented. "But we'd appreciate it so much if someone came and told us we could go home again . . ."

In the late summer of 1997 as I finish the English edition of this book, the families in the plains were preparing for yet another winter of famine, disease and other ordeals. The structure of the Azeri army had collapsed as members of its chiefs of staff awaited trial, accused of conspiring against the government. Moreover, there was not the slightest sign that Armenia — or Russia for all it mattered — had any intention of preparing for peace. Earlier, in the spring, the Armenian media had launched an intensive campaign under the slogan "Azerbaijan prepares for war!"

This was how Azerbaijan woke in 1991 from a long nightmare only to discover, too late, that a situation far worse was waiting in the daylight. On the Armenian side, the war fever that had been carefully cultivated for so many generations is now proving useful only to power-brokers caring for their own pockets, and certainly not for their victims who, bereft of property, health and hope, still rot away in the mud, haunted by despair.

5

Karabakh: the fatal apple of discord

"The city's in danger of attack any moment now. Enemy troops are only a few miles away. You've got to leave within a couple of hours at most — it's going to turn out be extremely dangerous here." The army commander in Agdam seemed more sad than nervous. In spite of the continuous gun and artillery fire he took us to the road that led south out of the city.

There by the roadside a tattered pile of women's clothing was the only memorial to the twenty or so women and girls who three days earlier had gone out in the evening in search of bread and other food. An armoured car had approached — nothing unusual in a city under siege — but before they realised what happened, this one opened fire on them. Seven were killed instantly, five wounded and the rest escaped in a state of shock.

We drove around the countryside. The villages were abandoned — although not entirely. A fair number of inhabitants, most of them elderly people with no place to go, wandered around. There was a plan for a general evacuation of the area, but there were insufficient vehicles to take all the people and their belongings to safer territory. Those left behind could only await what lay in store for them.

Our driver took the wrong turning. The officer accompanying us was from Baku — a director of the stage by profession, he had never been in this part of the country before. As we tried to find our bearings, thoughts turned to how it is that wars come into existence — a question filled with promise but whose answers can often be astonishingly banal.

Throughout history, world politics have by and large consisted of an uninterrupted series of intimidation, extortion and blackmail. If one's demands cannot be satisfied by such means, then there is always the option of mass extermination. Demands invariably consist of land, money and power, while the instigator of any war is invariably a murderer, and anyone claiming to instigate a war under any other pretext is a liar on top of that. Anyone who says they believe such a liar is an accomplice.

In explaining the reality of war — expecially in respect to its victims — it may be useful to take a look at the background of this particular one, if only to make it clear how pointless it is to conjecture which side is right and which isn't.

Karabakh means 'Black Orchard' in Turkish. The region is divided into mountains to the south, gentler slopes to the north and plains to the east. Upper Karabakh embraces the first two divisions while the plains in the region of Agzhabedy are usually referred to as Lower Karabakh. Artsakh and Utik are the respective names for the areas in Armenian. It is Upper Karabakh that became the focus of what started out as a quarrel in 1988 that got out of hand and then disintegrated into all-out war in the years that followed.

According to hardline Armenian propaganda, Artsakh has been "Armenian territory" ever since the dawning of time and therea re even those that claim this was the spot where the avatar Hayk (see above) is supposed to have founded his mythical kingdom. As things stand, however, no written independent historical source exists to justify the claim. Both Upper and Lower Karabakh have followed the same destiny as the rest of Azerbaijan throughout ancient history, incorporated into Albania as after the collapseof the Seleucid empire (see above). The first recorded Armenian presence there was in the eighties of the first century BC when Tigran the Great incorporated the area into his Roman buffer state. From that moment on, Armenian clans of rich property owners, or *meliks*, were to maintain a potent role in local political events, but they never managed to turn their authority into sovereignty — although this wasn't for lack of trying.

In the days of the bitter struggle in Azerbaijan between the Seljuqs and the Atabeks, which was to lead to the latters' downfall, a (Muslim) Armenian landowner by the name of Hassan Jallal Dawla (his descendants were to call themselves the "dynasty" of the Jallalids) stood up in Zangezur and proclaimed himself lord of Khachen and Akhvank (Zangezur and Albania respectively in Armenian). His venture was to come to a swift end and neither he nor his successors were ever to set foot in Baku. However, they did act as governors of a large part of south-west Azerbaijan for their Seljuq and Mongol overlords over a number of generations.

No word has come down to us about social tensions between the Christian and Muslim inhabitants of Transcaucasia during the times of the restricted rule by the Armenian *meliks*. In fact, half the Armenian feudal class were themselves Muslims, as well as perhaps a substantial part of the rest of the Armenian population.

Ironically enough, and perhaps not quite by coincidence, the first ethno-religious conflict in Karabakh broke out at the same time as the Russians established their foothold in Azerbaijan. It seems that during the 15th century, the Karabakh *meliks* saw their political influence and wealth waning to the advantage of the Christian clergy. In 1722, Peter the Great's campaign in Eastern Azerbaijan coincided with an attempt by the Armenian Church leadership to conclude a pact with Georgia and Russia with the aim of turning the area into a "Christian stronghold" and an "outpost in the campaign to reconquer Constantinople." The attempt came to nothing, but the power vacuum it created was seized upon by Davit, claimed to be a descendant of Hassan Jallal. He proclaimed himself *bek* or lord of Upper Karabakh and Geranboy. His initiative was regarded with suspicion by his peers, whose discontent grew as David's troops began raiding their lands and Shusha became the scene of events of Byzantine proportions. In 1728, a number of *meliks* called in the Ottoman army which promptly occupied the area and restored the *melik* properties to their rightful owners.

In 1735, the future Persian shah Nadir occupied Upper and Lower Karabakh after defeating the Ottomans. A descendant of the old Mikhranid dynasty was appointed governor. In 1750, after Nadir's murder and the outbreak of civil war in Persia, Prince Panakh Ali-khan proclaimed himself sovereign and extended and fortified Shusha, which he renamed Panakhabad, on a grand scale.

The khanate of Karabakh, which stretched from Western Nakhchivan to the mouths of the Kura and Arax, including Zenguzur and Mughan, was an oasis of stability and prosperity in years when the rest of Azerbaijan was the setting of constant struggle and disruption. The most celebrated prince of Karabakh, Ibrahim-khan, was also the last. His days of glory he largely owed to his grand-vizier Mullah-Panakh Vagif, one of the most talented diplomats, philisophers and poets of his time. Among his admirers was the Russian Empress Catherine II who eventually consented to a military alliance with Karabakh in case of attack by the Persians. Unfortunately, this was not to prevent Shah Aga-Muhammad from taking Shusha in 1796, after a bloody series of battles, due in the main to the treason of one of the khan's relatives, who was rewarded with the governorate of the area and had Ibrahim and Vagif thrown from the rocks to their deaths.

After the Russian occupation under Alexander I, Karabakh was virtually erased from the records for a century or so. It was not here but in Baku, Yerevan and Nakhchivan that the ethnic havoc of 1905 first broke out — only at a later stage did Shusha became involved. By then, the Dashnaks (see later chapters) had become active, and according to tradition, the conflict was sparked by starving, vengeful incomers from the Armenia of the teetering Ottoman Empire rather than by local Armenians.

The first eruptions of violence were in February 1905 and the exact reason why they came about has remained the subject of speculation to this day. However, the evident unwillingness displayed by the Russians to intervene has led to the accusation (voiced by both sides) that the Tsarist authorities themselves provoked the violence as a psychological lightning-rod that would distract Armenians and Azeris equally from their rekindled aspirations to sovereignty and to ultimately justify the logical general crack-down that ensued.

It all started in Baku with the murder of an Azeri schoolboy by a Dashnak brigade and the gunning down of an Azeri shopkeeper by an Armenian soldier. A rich Azeri tradesman, Babayev, a relative of the shopkeeper, was then shot dead in the bloody clashes that followed. The general mood darkened when gangs of Azeri youngsters marched on the Armenian quarters of the city. Knives were drawn, blood flowed. Before anyone realised what was happening, the situation was already horribly out of hand. Four days later, 126 Azeris and 218 Armenians had lost their lives inthe slaughter. The rich and the influential of both sides in particular were targeted by the mobs and scores of them perished. Their religious leaders, the Armenian bishop and the Azeri *sheikh-ul-Islam*, called on the people to calm down, and it was only then that Russian troops started patrolling the streets again.

In the meantime, similar scenes were taking place in Nakhchivan and on February 20th Armenian armed units began massacring the Azeri minority in the city. Tension mounted throughout the country, especially after the governor of Baku, a Georgian nobleman by the name of Nakashidze, died in a bomb-blast on May 24, presumably the work of the Dashnaks who had accused him of taking sides with the Azeris during the riots.

Finally, on August 29th, mass violence erupted in Shusha after a series of incidents and a manifesto issued by the Dashnaks calling on all Armenians to "purge the holy place of Armenia from all Azeri, Persian and other heathen elements." Within the space of three days, hundreds of Azeris who used to live in the down-town area were killed and dozens of houses set on fire by Armenian gangs making incursions from their up-town stronghold. It was only by September 1st that the vice-governor of Elizabetpol was able to talk some sense into the leaders of the differenct sides and thereby return calm.

The bad news from Shusha had meanwhile reached Baku. Unfortunately, the good news of the truce failed to do so. Since in the capital things were more or less under control, the oil fields surrounding it became the centre of complete pandemonium. Crowds of furious Azeris attacked Armenian-owned oil installations and soon almost the entire oil-field areas of Bibi-Eibat, Balakhany and Ramany were ablaze, engulfing Baku in a thick mass of ink-black smoke. After the fires had died down an apocalyptic landscape of ruined derricks and pipes was all that remained amidst a layer of thick black oil slicks. Meanwhile, fighting between Azeri and Armenian workers had left over 600 killed.

By the end of the year, Baku, Ganja and Kazakh minor disturbances occurred, but on the whole Azerbaijan passed a relatively quiet winter. However, total uproar was to start in the early summer of 1906, this time in the countrysides of Upper Karabakh and Tauz where wholescale battles were waged between Armenian and Azeri village communities. By the end of June, Shusha had seen itself converted into the anachronist satte shared by latter-day Beirut: the upper part of the city, occupied by Armenians, was now separated by a no-go zone from the Azeri-dominated lower areas. Anarchy ruled and there was such fighting everywhere that people began to lose all track of who was fighting who. Panic spread in early July as Armenian forces commenced shelling the Azeri quarters from the city citadel. With great effort, fresh Russian troops brought in from Tblisi and Ganja restored order. This. however, was implemented with dubious efficiency since the authorities proved to be more corrupt than ever, arrests were made in a most arbitrary way and the Russians did not even remotely consider any attempt at reconciliation of the warring sides.

The final downfall of the Tsarist Empire downfall in 1917 resulted in the creation of the Transcaucasian Federation consisting of Azerbaijan, Georgia and Armenia. For a while, it looked as though Upper Karabakh became the Federation's fourth member as the Azeri and Armenian communities joined forces in an unexpectedly fraternal way and formed a coalition government whose first decision was to return the land to the farmers. At the same time as Armenia and Azerbaijan were fighting a frantic war over Nakhchivan and Zangezur, Upper Karabakh remained, odd as it may seem, an oasis of peaceful coexistence.

May 1918 saw the Federation split up, and with this the fate of Karabakh was sealed. At once, Armenia openly claimed the area as its territory and in the late summer a shady guerrilla by the name of Andranik entered Karabakh from the south after spreading chaos among the Azeri cattle-farmers, who once formed the majority of the population of Zangezur, killing about half and driving the remainder into Iran, Mughan and Lower Karabakh. To the north, however, Nuri Pasha's troops stormed

Shusha, swiftly taking it. After the Turks surrendered and left, the British took their place and Governor-General Thomson declared Upper Karabakh "provisionally" Azeri territory, giving a wealthy Azeri land-owner, by name Sultanov, control over the district. In the south Andranik and his fellow Armenians blithely left a river of blood behind them, leaving their kinsmen in the north of Karabakh to pay the terrible price for their actions, and many hundreds of them died at the hands of Azeris thirsty for vengeance.

Yet, not all hope for an eventual peaceful solution to the current dead-lock seemed to have vanished. At several stages, the parliament of the failed 'second republic' of Upper Karabakh had negotiated with Sultanov in an effort to restore harmony. Time and again, however, particularly because of pressure from the Ottoman Armenian newcomers from Anatolia, the peace plan fell apart. At a one stage, the non-republic of Upper Karabakh even had two assemblies: one in Shusha in awkward coexistence with the governorate, and the other in the near-by town of Shosh, in collusion with the government of Armenian government with a view to annexation of the district.

Although the Anatolian exiles continued to foment unrest in the self-same country that had granted them refuge after their ordeal, it should be borne in mind that they in turn were manipulated by Western politicians who made repeated high-profile proclamations of a presumed solidarity with *"notre petit allie vaillant"*, as Clemenceau himself put it. But of course these political giants nurtured quite different thoughts at the back of their minds. This is a game that is still very much alive — as the new millennium dawns, the sons of the Armenian Diaspora continued to unceremoniously flow in to the area. Some of their number were indeed respectable businessmen; others, however, ruthless soldiers-of-fortune with a somewhat less than respectable past in Lebanon . . .

The truth is that long before the First World War came to an end, France and Russia had already decided to split up Eastern Anatolia between them, leaving no space for an Armenian state in any shape whatsoever. In pretty much the same way, the British occupation of Transcaucasia was to end in a comparatively smooth Soviet take-over as the nations of the region involved were simply abandoned to their fate. Whitehall or the Kremlin: it made little difference.

After the pseudo-wisdom of the West had thus made way for the international proletarian brotherhood, the Federal Soviet Republic of Transcaucasia was solemnly proclaimed, on March 12th 1922. As commissar entrusted with carving of the newly acquired territories, Stalin signed a decree in 1923 whereby Nakhchivan and Upper Karabakh were given autonomous status within Azerbaijan while Zangezur was made an integral part of Armenia. Even though this 'judgement of Solomon' was not entirely without reality in itself, the soon-to-be dictator clearly failed to demonstrate that he needed to convince the communities involved that more than just a decree was required to build up a rosy future.

The times of 'glasnost' and 'perestroika' that shook Russia and other Soviet states, were times of grim apathy in Azerbaijan. Anyone uttering these words today in Baku is looked upon with cynical pity.

"Perestroika? But that meant social degradation, poverty and tanks in the streets! Gorbachev destroyed our society!"

It should be pointed out that most of those who speak like this once belonged to the old grey-suited elite, the privileged class who never did anything wrong because they never did anything in the first place.

The general lethargy which Heydar Aliev had tried so hard to eliminate during his first mandate, returned under his successors Karaman Bagirov and Abderrahman Vezirov, who were colourless conservatives. Corruption now returned in full flood albeit dressed up in grey, and had disappeared from public debate. The street rabble vanished from the city centres and were shut in behind their slum walls. Outside, the streets were clean and the parks were green. Elsewhere in the USSR life was jolted to its marrow by reformism, but in Azerbaijan the clock stood still under a useless leadership while Aliev had broken through to the highest echelons of power after Andropov had appointed him member of the Politbureau. In 1987, he returned to his homeland of Nakhchivan just as those in Baku who had taken his place were about to let things get completely out of hand during the following year.

"Suddenly, we saw people fighting on a variety of street corners. Nobody could explain what was going on. Some tried to call the police in, but the police stations appeared to be closed. The guards at the public buildings had all left their posts. Someone called a group of soldiers on the street for help. He got battered against the roadside for his pains — it was clear the troops were blind drunk. You could hear screaming blocks away. Some people came up and told us that the best thing we could do was to stay inside and not let anybody in. Our neighbours and best friends were Armenians and they were as confused as we were.

"Nothing unusual had ever happened before in Sumgayt — although hooliganism with the odd bout of street-brawls at the weekends was nothing strange because of the general mood of bored lethargy. But this time it was no ordinary hooliganism. We're still ashamed for ourselves, those of us and the few Armenians who didn't flee. Each and every one of us is only too aware of the fact that this was no spontaneous outburst of violence — nothing was ever spontaneous in the Soviet Union."

The young school-teacher in this concrete desert prefers not to have his name mentioned: "Besides, there'd be little point. Ask anyone in the street and he'll tell you exactly the same story, just the words will be different."

Sumgayt should never have been built in the first place. It is a dormitory-city of a grey uniformity that makes its average Western counterpart look like a pleasure ground. Here, certainly pleasure is hard to find: there are hardly any bars and the few cinemas that function show a sad prgramme of trashy movies. Streets and staircases stink from leaking sewage-pipes. Alcohol and drugs abuse get the highest score for how people spend their free time. The city is surrounded by derelict industrial sites sprawling over an immensely vast area which chemical contamination has turned into a virtual moonscape: Silent Spring turned into reality. In 1988 most of the factories were still functioning, but five years later most were deserted and anbandoned, rotting away like a giant scrap-heap from some science-fiction novel.

Many middle-of-the-road authors — Armenian ones to begin with — place that first spark that led the conflict over Karabakh in Sumgayt. In reality, what triggered the whole thing off was the murder of two Azeri youngsters on the road between Stepanakert and Askeran, in the very heart of Upper Karabakh, by a group of drunken Armenians, followed by the familiar see-saw of attacks and raids by one community against the other. Only after the arrival in Sumgayt of the first busloads of survivors, despatched by the local authorities, did the tension start to mount.

According to some witnesses, a reported rape within an Armenian family, by the name of Grigorian, may have triggered off the fighting. Conflicting rumours had spread, some claiming that Azeris had been the perpetrators and others that the victim was an Azeri girl — none of which proved correct in the end. Whatever the case, in the scenes that followed, 26 Armenians and six Azeris lost their lives as the authorities stood by and looked the other way.

But they were capable of doing hardly anything else. Officially, fighting between fraternised proletarian nations was incompatible which what they had always been trained to do. Only what was in line with Moscow's directive was conceivable; anything else simply could not, did not exist even if you saw it happening right under your nose. Identifying this syndrome does not come from opinions based on Western liberal snobbery; indeed, Communism has no patent on the phenomenon, this weird, Vatican-like inclination to push people en masse into believing the unbelievable, getting them even to slaughter one another in order to perpetuate this. In this respect, Stalin and his contemporaries were as Catholic as the most gruesome Pope in history, but then, so too were the meek followers of the Victorian demagogues, the fascists marching blindly behind Hitler,

Mussolini and Franco, the motley OAS-clique from the 1960s, the hysterical Peronists in Argentina, the Iranians and Afghans who allowed themselves to themselves be palmed off with beards and veils by mentally disturbed illiterates . . . All of them have run as fast as they could behind those unscrupulous and half-witted torch-carriers of the *idée-fixe* we call conviction: fate summons you and you can do little else but run after it in full self-surrender until you smash yourself upon it. It's not unlike the dog who jumps into a dirty pond over and over again just to bring a useless stick back to his master, although it should know after all these years that its master will only brainlessly throw the stick back into the water.

This political 'charnel-priests' are everywhere about us, and whether they are called Brezhnev, Woytila, Reagan, Thatcher or Smith or Jones makes little difference in respect to their psychology. One of the key figures in the history of this Wagnerian scenario was Karl Marx. He, for one, never suggested that the oppressed of the earth should unite on their own initiative to defend themselves and regain their self-respect. This was simply to happen, whether the oppressed liked it or not — the process Marx had in mind boiled down to a drama of suitably apocalyptic proportions. There was no way any poor devil of an individualist could withstand the fateful events Marx had prophesied, for all his sad 'bourgeois' thoughts.

If Marx had been a contemporary of Martin Luther or Catherine de Medici, he would have claimed that God wanted things to happen this way. Millions were to believe him, just as they did after Kant's revolution of thought and the nit-picking of Hegel and Feuerbach with mysticism, as the white-bearded prophet hewed new images of new gods, flaunted as much as previous ones and proving to be as effective if not more, as their use by the colourful company of acolytes Marx left behind would show. There are some, however, who are left behind in the mad rush towards any the world's tragicomic leaders — no matter if they used crucifixes, hammers and sickles, cryptic guru-speak or false election promises to get what they want. These are the generations who have learned what there is to learn, often the hard way, and what they know is that they should be wary of making judgements on others and, especially, of justifying their position based on those judgements.

The bickering prior to the spiral of violence leading to Karabakh seems almost too absurd to mention. Rows would break out over the question of whether the director of a bread factory in Stepanakert was to be officially allowed in Agdam. Whether the head of a state school or library was to be either an Azeri or an Armenian. Whether the location of a new, subsidised commercial venture was to be sited in an Azeri- or Armenian-populated village. Bureaucratic squabbling at peasant level.

According to some, the double murder near Askeran had been a common crime, while others claim it was all part of a deliberate master-plan by the Dashnaks to help things get out of hand. As for the Sumgayt events, the judicial inquiry began by the Azeri prosecutor-general Ilyas Ismailov resulted in 86 prosecutions most of which were against Azeri citizens and one of which resulted in a death sentence subject to appeal — which in those days in the Soviet Union was more or less automatically converted to a life term.

No official eye-witness reports on the events in Sumgayt exist; when the unrest broke out there were no journalists in the vicinity and shortly afterwards the city was sealed off from the outside world. Elsewhere, reactions to the first rumours of what was happening in Sumgayt came rapidly: raids and reprisals in Karabakh and, more systematically and on a larger scale, in Armenia, where on March 10th 1988, armed gangs surrounded and attacked the village of Mehmanlar, killing ten and injuring scores of its Azeri inhabitants. The survivors were told they had 24 hours to leave, and to never return. In this way, within the next two months, seven villages and a hundred or so settlements were emptied.

In order to prevent scenes from earlier generations from taking place once more, the authorities in Baku decided upon the mass 'temporary' evacuation of Armenians — which meant evacuated for a long, long time. By the summer of 1988, fighting in Karabakh had subsided. But the cracks in this peace grew ever wider as by mid-June the Armenian Supreme Soviet declared Upper Karabakh "Armenian territory," a move followed by the local Soviet of Karabakh which, boycotted by its Azeri minority, proclaimed "provisional secession from Azerbaijan in order to facilitate reunification with Armenia."

It was only then, and even then only to a limited extent, that those in high places within the Kremlin started worrying. At first, it was decided to form a special committee (they were good at that) in order to negotiate a way out of the deadlock. After this attempt failed, as expected, Moscow imposed direct rule by the government of the USSR on the rebellious enclave. Trusted by Gorbachev, Arkady Volsky was sent down as plenipotentiary governor. Volsky definitely knew his business — most of all his own business. Years before the USSR's collapse he had already become one of the richest men in the Socialist realm of peace.

Spring 1993. On the Caspian sea shore it was still chilly, but inland in the Qobustan desert, temperatures were already rising to way over thirty degrees. After wandering along deserted roads that seemed to lead nowhere, we arrived at a complex of shabby barrack huts.

The camp's commander stared at us in disbelief: "Who on earth sent you here? Don't you realise this place isn't even supposed to exist?"

I handed him a letter from the minister of public security, Namiq Abbassov. The commander tried to call Baku for verification, but got no connection and eventually gave in. "Oh well, I suppose you'd better come in now that you're here. After all, it's high time somebody blew the whistle on what's happening here. But all I ask is that when you write your story, say that as far as I'm personally concerned, these poor bastards should be sent home today, right now, rather than tomorrow."

The prisoners had committed no crime, except for being at the wrong spot at the wrong moment. The men were skinny and pale, but the women looked significantly better. The arrival of outsiders had given them some source of cheer. As we were leaving, one woman burst into tears — of joy. "Your coming gives us hope, that the world hasn't forgotten us. That we might be released soon. God bless you!"

These were the last 36 Armenian 'hostages' to remain in the hands of the Azeri government. During the final months of Mutalibov's sway (see below), hundreds of them had been picked at random from trains and public buildings to be held until they could be exchanged for the many hundreds of Azeri citizens held in the same way by the Armenians in Yerevan, Shusha and Stepanakert. Shortly afterwards, the whole group of Qobustan did get released. They were all understandably happy, except for a solitary Armenian who all the time had feared the very thing the others hoped for: to be sent back to Armenia.

Confused, stammering and trembling, he told his story.

He was an Armenian from Azerbaijan who, after an Armenian raid on a neighbouring Azeri village, was hounded from his home in a reprisal attack. Having fled to Armenia, he found that he was viewed with deep suspicion. "You see, I'm from Azerbaijan and I can't speak Armenian. As soon as they realised this, they took me away to Spitak where I was forced to work at the construction site of a giant underground arms factory under a mountain in the area."

He escaped, making his way northwards to Georgia on foot. How exactly he managed it, his confused and chronologically wandering narrative did not make clear, but at some point he found himself stranded in Azerbaijan once more, got picked up by the Azeri police and was finally brought to the desert. Six months later, after the detention centre had been closed down, I heard that he had been offered a haven in a 'special sanatorium', the nickname for the special hide-aways kept by the Soviet KGB to discreetly house individuals who had reason to keep out of the public eye for a while — in their own interest, in society's interest, or both — individuals they would rather not put behind bars.

Funnily enough, that factory in Spitak does exist. And its main investor would seem to be a certain Mr Arkady Volsky.

Soon after arriving in Karabakh, Volsky realised that there was little he could do to restore peace in the short term. He therefore proclaimed a state of emergency. The result: more raids, more street battles, more hatred than ever.

Meanwhile, in Baku, the situation was worsening by the week as slowly, gradually but ever so firmly Azeri temperaments became heated according to age-old tradition. From mid-November 1988 on, the daily rituals of picket-lines gradually expanded to mass demonstrations that attracted thousands and subsequently tens of thousands. This latest wave of protest was masterminded by the so-called Popular Front, an organisation more or less analogous to its Baltic and Georgian counterparts in regard to its rather simplistic ideology that from now on everything had to be different — although exactly how, they failed to explain.

For three weeks, the demonstrations in the centre of town continued. At first, the local police watched the scene with curiosity rather than animosity. They chatted casually with the demonstrators and were happy to drink a glass or two to the future, provided by cheery bartenders from the nearby Apsheron and Azerbaijan hotels. But when, during the first week of December, police reinforcements were brought in from the countryside, and even from the other Soviet republics, the mood changed for the worse. Skirmishes with the police took place. Neither First Secretary Abderrahman Vezirov nor any member of his cabinet showed their faces at the scene. Then, on December 4th, the demonstrators were delivered an ultimatum: by sundown the streets were to be empty, anyone still there would be immediately arrested. As it happened, only a few hundred hung around to be carted off by the forces of law and order. It was reported that a few dozen "hooligans and extremists," as it was put, were subsequently held — and mistreated — in jail for months without a single charge being brought against them.

But the demonstrators' demands had been unambiguous: independence and the restoration of the republic of 1918. The real reason behind it all, however, was undoubtedly the situation in Karabakh. The public did not consider their Soviet puppet regime capable of handling the crisis over there properly. They were hardly mistaken in this respect in thinking this. Where they were mistaken, however, was in thinking they could do any better.

Strikes broke out in Ganja and Baku the day after the break-up of the opposition. In Nakhchivan clashes broke out between armed citizens and Russian border troops, killing a number of both. During 1989, largescale violent confrontation was a rare occurrence, although skirmishes and occasional murders as a result of ambushes became increasingly frequent in and around Karabakh. The Kremlin, meanwhile, tried to smooth things down through legal — or rather somewhat less than legal — action. In January, accordingly, the members of the Armenian Karabakh committee were arrested and taken from Yerevan to Moscow — only to be legitimised in June under the title of the Hay Hamaskayin Sharzhum ('Pan-Armenian National Movemen). Back in Baku, by springtime, the Azeri exiles from Armenia and Karabakh whose numbers by now had already swelled to around a quarter of a million, organised themselves into a movement they called Grunk ('Godwit'), led by Arkady Manushehrov. He and his fellow-leaders were promptly arrested, and were released until the summer of 1990.

During the remainder of 1989, it looked as if the Armenian and Azeri sides of the conflict were basically trying to starve one another out. Road-blocks appeared throughout the area, lorries en route to Karabakh were stopped by Azeris, while those trying to get to Lachin and Nakhchivan were turned back by Armenian units. By October, raids carried out by both parties flared up again. In November, Volsky quit his job amidst a situation he described as "all-out civil war." Meanwhile, in Armenia and Azerbaijan alike, more and more committees were being formed and petitions proclaimed.

Transcaucasia is a place that seems sometimes as if it is filled with an overwhelming tranquillity. Nothing seems able to stir the rustic villages with their aluminium-roofed mansions, their lavish gardens and orchards. In the fields, boys tend the herds of cattle as their fathers, grandfathers and great-grandfathers did before them. Here, it looks as though everybody lives for themselves, out of touch with the great wide world out there.

And then, all of a sudden, things explode, seemingly without reason or sense, and rapidly spread throughout the area. That was how events in Azerbaijan suddenly fell into place with whirlwind speed after that fateful January 12.

It was mid-afternoon in Khanlar. In the town and its surrounding villages and farms the major event of the day was drawing to a close: lunch. Suddenly an army helicopter appeared in the sky. Nothing worth noting in itself, since there has always been a Soviet air force base in Ganja nearby. Even as the helicopter landed at the edge of a village, nobody paid any attention to it. By the time masked gunmen had sped into the village opening fire on everyone in sight, it was too late.

Half an hour later, the helicopter took off again, leaving about a dozen dead and scores more injured. A policeman who had watched the scene in sheer disbelief, later claimed he had heard the attackers speaking in Russian and even English. After the carnage was over, he immediately phoned the governor who, it appeared, had consumed more than his fair share of vodka at lunchtime and wasn't much use. The mayor of Khanlar managed to get through to the authorities in Ganja, but he was informed that the case had already been "reported" and that he would not have to wait long for the results of the inquiry, which was already proceeding at full speed.

The mayor is still waiting. Those, however, who had no intention of waiting were the opposition in Baku and elsewhere in Azerbaijan. In Lenkoran, as soon as the news was known, Popular Front activists occupied government buildings, decalring they were "provisionally taking control." In Nakhchivan, the local soviet proclaimed "provisional independence" until "state affairs in Azerbaijan are settled properly". In Baku, the first barricades appeared early next morning in both Azeri and Armenian areas. Soon, shouting and screaming could be heard in the slums north of the city centre. Shots were heard. In the course of the day, the sounds drew closer to the centre as fighting broke out in Fizuli Square. Twenty-four hours later, the death toll had mounted to over a hundred. Well over half the slain were Azeris, including several policemen. This failed to prevent Armenian propagandists from labelling the events a "carefully pre-planned progrom."

The greater majority of the city's inhabitants were baffled by the intensity of it all and professed to understand nothing, except that it was more hazardous than usual on the streets. The authorities for their part remained deaf and mute; the evening news on the state television that day made no reference to the violent events, even partially, and broadcast the usual good-news shows consisting entirely of non-events.

January 16th 1990. At the instigation of the Popular Front, a crowd gathered on Lenin Square, its ranks dwarfing the protests of 1988. A call for a general strike is heeded far and wide. Two days earlier, Yevgeny Primakov, chairman of the USSR Supreme Soviet and a specialist in putting Machiavellian principles into practice, had arrived in Baku to inform Vezirov in person that a convoy of 11,000 Soviet troops was on its way, "passing through Baku" to "restore legal authority" in Talysh and Nakhchivan. Primakov's performance was discreet — unfortunately, not discreet enough. The Popular Front was perfectly aware of what was about to happen — and, again unfortunately, Primakov was all too well aware of that as well. Early in the evening, AFP leader Etibar Mamedov appeared on television to tell the people the implications of the threat from the north. At six o'clock, straight after the broadcast, KGB terrorists blew up the national television transmitter.

Mamedov got the message and realised that the city would be sealed off from the outside world within a matter of hours. Without hesitation, he fled to the airport and hopped on the last flight out to Moscow.

Karabakh: the fatal apple of discord

"Not quite according to regulations," he was to admit later. "But I made it, and with the law at my heels I had just enough time in Moscow to get together a number of Western correspondents. I told them what was about to happen. You should have seen their faces — 'That nice Mister Gorby would never do such a thing!' I reminded them of what had happened in Tbilisi the previous year and of current events in the Baltics. If they had flooded the world's TV screens with images of Baku that evening, they would have saved a lot of human lives. But nothing happened. Most of the correspondents simply reacted by saying they'd believe it when they saw it."

They never would. When the news broke finally in the outside world, the hundreds of dead had already been buried.

At dawn, the first tanks had appeared on the roads leading to Baku. Shots were fired at random on residential blocks. Barricades were fired at first and rolled over next. A number of tanks set off in the direction of various office buildings occupied by the Popular Front. These were blasted until they burst into flames — mostly with the people still inside — except for the headquarters, which were spared until a number of trucks arrived: the occupants of the building were wanted alive. However, it appeared to be well-defended. A few tanks came under fire and a number of Russian soldiers died in the crossfire. But in the end the sheer numbers of the attackers proved too much and resistance crumpled.

The ensuing pandemonium was to last four days, while in Moscow the correspondents waited for news that never come. All the roads leading to Azerbaijan were blocked, telephone connections cut. Meanwhile, the Russian army spread mayhem throughout Baku, executing people on the pavements and in the courtyards, machine-gunning groups of citizens and carting thousands more off to an unknown fate.

Finally, on the fifth day, the Kremlin issued a statement stating that Baku had been "cleared of hooligans in a security operation" in the course of which, "regrettably," 69 lives had been lost. An inquiry held later at Mutalibov's orders confirmed a more realistic figure of at least 120 civilians and 12 soldiers killed. Allahsukur Pashazadeh, the mufti of Baku, claimed a total of 180 civilians killed, among which were a significant number of firemen, police officers and ambulance personnel whose vehicles constituted the Russian tanks' favourite targets. A dozen or so reporters who had tried to document the events as they unfolded had been killed as well.

And still that was not all. In December 1993, a mass grave was discovered in the Qobustan Desert containing over a hundred bodies of individuals who, according to autopsy results, all died together more or less at the same time. Evidence of bullet holes and strangulation was found. Here was the grisly answer to the terrible question asked by those families desperate to know where their relatives had gone after they had disappeared without trace during the weeks that followed 'Black January'.

Through four days of nightmare, 'order' was thus restored in Baku. But in the rest of the country the events soon became known in detail. Down in Nakhchivan, Heydar Aliev, putting aside for a while his usual contempt for the Popular Front — seized as he was by the thought of his arch-rival Vezirov in trouble — at once proclaimed the "Sovereign Republic of Nakhchivan," while sending an urgent request to the United Nations for protection. In Ganja, the local leadership followed his example. It is of interest to note that the Popular Front played no part in either act.

The answer was soon to come. Gorbachev had meantime received a call from his American counterpart George Bush who had expressed his "understanding" at the necessity to "maintain order" and so congratulated his colleague for the way he had done so. Thus secured, Gorbachev threatened to "reduce the west and the south of Azerbaijan to ashes" if there was no "complete surrender" within 24 hours. And so Azerbaijan surrendered — only too aware of the fact that no one was prepared risk a Third World War for its sake. For this was the 'New World Order', a licence to kill for political butchers who afterwards could celebrate by decorating each other for it and make a toast to a happy ending.

In Baku, the Azeri National Soviet, in a move to regain some of its moral authority over the population, adopted a resolution by which this "aggression against the Azeri nation" was condemned in the shrillest tone possible. As for Vezirov, his position had become untenable, resulting in Moscow replacing him with a man whose name was to become synonymous for disaster in Azerbaijan: Ayaz Mutalibov.

Meanwhile, in contrast to what they were to do in later times, Armenia and Karabakh refrained from using the situation in Baku to their advantage. The main reason was that a struggle for power had broken out in Yerevan between the Soviet government and the nationalist 'Hay' movement which had resulted in armed intervention by the Soviets in late spring, although with far less bloody results than had been the case in Baku. This paralysed the movement in Karabakh and the precarious stalemate managed to hold out there.

The fighting, however, shifted west in August, as the Armenian 'David of Sassun' and 'Tigran the Great' brigades crossed the border into Azerbaijan near Tauz and occupied a number of villages. Infuriated, Mutalibov telephoned Gorbachev and warned the Russian leader that if Moscow did not react, Azerbaijan would declare full independence without delay. For a while, the threat seemed to work. Gorbachev, for his part, called the new Armenian head of state Levon Ter-Petrossian and demanded withdrawal of his troops. The latter's answer, however, was evasive and no troops were withdrawn. However, Mutalibov too refrained from carrying out his threat. In November, things went from bad to worse as an entire Armenian army now marched on Khanlar. The force was only stopped by Soviet troops at Martushen, which was the place where the incident that led to the Baku massacres in January had taken place. However, Armenian troops managed to occupied most of the district of Geranboy (at the time still called Shaumian) without anyone intervening. Finally, in April 1991, the very thing Volsky had warned against and a blundering Gorbachev had tried to prevent was to happen. It became a war — a real one.

In mid-April, Soviet troops embarked on a campaign to clear the south west of Azerbaijan, including Karabakh, of armed Armenian elements. By and large, they were successful in their task whereupon the Azeri security service entered and started a search of the area for stocks of weapons, which they discovered in astonishing quantities and calibres. Large numbers of Armenians, who had squatted the properties of Azeri citizens they had driven out, were deported back to Armenia.

It was this group of displaced 'kolons' who were shortly to form the hardcore of the so-called Karabakh Self-Defence Forces, whose avowed mission was revenge at any cost. During the military operations Shusha had been under artillery fire from Armenia almost on a daily basis. It was not for the first time, and certainly not the last. The downfall of Gorbachev and that of the Soviet Union in his wake caused a lull in the fighting, but at the same time it only served to contribute to the general state of confusion. In September 1990, Boris Yeltsin and his Kazakh colleague Nazerbayev attempted to get the parties around the negotiation table but failed. In October, Armenian forces poured into Upper Karabakh through Lachin with the Azeri troops stationed there powerless to stop them. As it was, there hardly was anything like an Azeri army present.

On August 30th, Mutalibov, who had earlier publicly cheered at the military putsch in Moscow, proclaimed an independent Azerbaijan and thereupon appointed his old pal Rahim Ghaziev as defence minister. Activities from there on were strictly limited to decorating and toasting each other for some time to come.

In January 1992, an ill-sorted company of Azeri soldiers, on the loose and with neither proper command nor strategy, stormed Shusha like a pack of mad dogs — only to be pushed back by Armenian forces much to the despair of the city's Azeri inhabitants who were trapped like rats. In Ganja nearby, the commanders of the former Soviet army garrison there maintained a strategic distance and confined itself to lucrative arms trade with whatever customer turned up. In the meantime, Armenia took over command of the 366th regiment in Karabakh. On January 26th, the Azeris were routed in a full-out battle near Dashalty, a defeat more resounding than Napoleon's at Waterloo.

In Baku, Mutalibov put on a brave face and declared that Azerbaijan for the time being would refrain from membership of the Commonwealth of Independent States (CIS) and declared Karabakh's previous autonomous status to be "void." He had every intention of doing the same over Nakhchivan's status but held his tongue after threatening noises from Heydar Aliev who had since been chosen head of the local government in the southern enclave.

The political fall-out resulting from the Armenian offensive in spring 1992 has already been indicated. On February 26th, Khojaly fell and in the months that followed the Armenians were able to get their hands on Lachin and virtually all of Upper Karabakh without the Azeri forces having done as much as to try to protect the local Azeri populations. Details of this bloody and unequal struggle can be found in the next chapter.

Only Aliev, in his 'finest hour', managed to ward off an Armenian attack on Nakhchivan, by having Özal in Turkey threaten to bomb Yerevan if the Armenians made such an attempt, while Özal's Iranian counterpart Rafsanjani said he would close the Armenian border with Iran and have all Armenian border posts on the Arax river occupied. Ter-Petrossian could only mutter that Armenia had played "no military part" in the conflict. Of course, nobody believed him. Whatever the case, it would crop up time and time again in later days that this had been the precise moment when the Turkish and Iranian leaders had spoken the only language that could be understood in Yerevan.

Mutalibov's successor Abulfaz Elchibey had promised on his election that he would have all Armenian troops forced over the border within half a year. The only success he had, however, in the June offensive that was to follow was the temporary relief of Agdara (Mardakert) and the recapture of Geranboy. Fighting on the Tauz front ended in stalemate. The remaining Armenian villages and settlements in the area were evacuated in a way that resembled more a campaign of revenge for the earlier massacres of Lachin, Khojaly and Shusha than a military operation.

The deadliest move by the Azeri army was the deployment of aircraft after an Armenian counter-offensive in August. The raids lacked any form of coordination and pilots flattened many residential areas without managing to neutralise a single Armenian brigade. It had to be finally admitted that the summer offensive was a complete disaster and signalled the beginning of the end: within little more than a year, all the territory between Belagan and Geranboy would fall into Armenian hands for a long time to come.

By the autumn of 1992, however, things had not gone that far yet. It was the time when the so-called peace diplomats had started moving in fromoutside. These were of different breed and represented different organisations, but at least they have two things in common with their local counterparts: they are immensely well-paid and are no less fond of wining and dining. One of the most unlikely organisations behind these fancy paraders is the Organisation (initially called 'Conference') for Security and Cooperation in Europe (OSCE). For years, its minions shuttled blithely between Moscow, Yerevan, Baku and even Stepanakert as though on a school trip. In June 1993, after the umpteenth cease-fire was concluded far from the front — since at the front the fire continued as before — the leader of the OSCE delegation present proudly declared that this incredible achievement had finally proved to the world that his organisation was of use.

It should be observed that the gentleman concerned was an honest man insofar as he openly admitted that he cared about little more than securing his own job. This however, as it would appear, was where his frankness ended. A few months later, he had to face charges over his alleged involvement in a mega-corruption scandal back home in Europe, an implication which cost him his passport while awaiting trial and therefore his job. And so, the battleground continued to reap the benefit of the input of such dedicated helpers.

Early 1993 and spring was in the air for most of the northern hemisphere. But on the plateau of Yerevan winter lingers on. Although the snow had gradually stopped falling, the mixture of snow and mud would melt during the day only to freeze again at night, creating a sea of black ice upon which, each morning, the unwary pedestrian would invariably slip. Electricity was available but for a few hours a day if you were lucky, and only then at the most impossible times. All a journalist could do was make a few notes on paper and, if the electricity came on, rush madly to the computer before it goes off again.

My interlocutor is the effusive Mr Abrahamian, the friendly presidential spokesman who has swiftly become a media star in spite of himself thanks to the fact that his boss Ter-Petrossian hardly ever made public appearances and failed mostly to show up even on those rare cases he had consented to an interview.

It makes little difference: Abrahamian has the answers to every question to hand — he would have written them in any case for his master whether he'd shown up or not.

Negotiate with Azerbaijan?

"Of course. We have always said that we are ready to sit down at the negotiation table without so much as the slightest precondition."

And what would be, in such a case, the position of the self-proclaimed government of 'independent' Upper Karabakh?

"We have nothing to do with them. We provide political and humanitarian support, but there are no Armenian troops in Karabakh."

But the numerous eye-witness accounts plus the press and satellite photographs which have been published — all of which prove the opposite?

"But that's all Azeri propaganda!"

Then, what about all the Azeri civilians who perished in Lachin, Khojaly, Shusha . . . ?

"That was all carried out by the Azeri army itself in order to pin the blame on us for everything!"

Do you yourself *really* believe that?

". . ."

In Baku, where political debate remained no less remote from reality, people would merely shrug at the Armenian allegations. In Yerevan it seemed that Karabakh was the only thing that kept debate alive while the socio-political desolation that affected everyone was largely attributed to it. In the West, a blanket of apathy prevailed, cultivated by the shady echelons of 'international diplomacy' already mentioned, disrupted but momentarily by non-events from time to time. Meanwhile the pseudo-experts queued up to deliver their learned opinions on such buzz words as 'regional conflict' and 'conflict resolution' in diplomatic club fanzines, invariably omitting to mention their habit of spending tax-payers' money on futile trips such as those of the OSCE.

Except in late August 1997, Sergei Karaganov, an influential political adviser of Boris Yeltsin's, declared that the OSCE had no future and that "we should accept the fact that it is dying." There's irony in his remark, since Russia more than most has abused the organisation for its own political schemes since the moment it came into existence — not unlike the way it has played with Upper Karabakh for even longer, like a cat with a mouse, only to feed it to her kitten in the end. Whatever triggered off the fighting over Karabakh, the real finger of blame points north. There are even Armenians who readily admit that, although they have have held on tight to the "territorial rights" and "security guarantees" acquired on the warpath, there was always a certain "Russian interest" in the background with some hand in the way the conflict escalated. Added to which, the hatred and mistrust long held by Armenian communities around the world easily made them willing toys in the hands of the Kremlin. But then, war always looks different in reports and propaganda than it does in reality — as an acquaintance with its victims will show.

6

The long-lost world empire

The flight from Paris to Yerevan was at dead of night. Arrival was joyless and waiting for baggage seemed endless. Even more joyless, if it were possible, was the Armenia Intourist Hotel. It was February 1993 and there was no electricity, no water, no heating. Once a day a shockwave stirred the whole hotel: the lights would come on for an hour or so and simultaneously (cold) water would stream from the taps.

The only place you could find any refreshments or entertainment was the hotel restaurant where during the evening hours a noisy orchestra rendered any attempt at conversation futile. Still, this did not prevent a number of groups from feeding on limited amounts of solid food and impressive amounts of strong liquid. Sometimes they would get up and dance, throwing handfuls of banknotes into the air — members of staff were allowed to pick them up. They were Russian roubles but, even so, not without value for a population of which over two thirds lives below the poverty line.

High-ranking visitors experience hardship in the same honoured company. Such worthies include the friendly and informal chairman of the French Parliament Philippe Seguin and the unlikely doyenne of the British House of Lords, Baroness Cox. Her presence here, she insists, is "strictly private" and she surrounds herself with a strange band of British-Armenian Christian fundamentalists who spend most of their time praising the Lord and singing gospel hymns in and (mostly) out of season.

In Stepanakert, the baroness was to stage an extraordinary performance in which she assured the "brave freedom fighters" gathered there of the eternal and unconditional support of the British nation — perhaps unaware that among those she took in her arms in tears were individuals whose names sat on the wanted lists of half the world's police forces, sought for the most brutal acts of terrorism.

*

From Yerevan you can clearly see the twin peaks of the holy mountain Ararat. It's a source of continuous provocation since the symbol of the nation lies just over the other side of the Turkish border. The ruins of the ancient city of Ani, until the late Middle Ages the cultural heart of Armenia, are also outside present-day Armenian territory. The 15th century monastery of Echmiadzin, however, the heartbeat of the nation's religion, is still intact and has been renovated to create a palace for the Catholicos of the Armenian Orthodox Church. Many of the other old churches and cathedrals in the countryside have been reduced to ruins. The country is littered with them, and they stand in solitude like rotten teeth spread over an enormous muzzle. Those churches and convents, many of whose structures are still recognisible, slotted perfectly into the landscape's character: grim, gloomy and unapproachable.

According to their own mythology, the forefather of all Armenians was Hayk, the descendant of Japeth, one of Noah's sons. Hayk is said to have lived during the time of the Tower of Babel and rose against the Phrygian ruler Bel. After failing to overthrow his sovereign, Hayk and his followers fled to the north and founded their own principality, Hayk Dzor, on the upper reaches of the River Tigris.

Judging by the evidence of their language, the Armenians are of Indo-European stock. The oldest sources to make mention of the Armenians — Hekatos of Milete, Herodotus and the Old Testament prophet Jeremiah — place them on the upper Euphrates between the sixth and the second centuries BC, in the present-day Turkish district of Van. After forming part of the realm of Urartu, the area seems to have been independent for a while until the arrival of the Medean, Akhemenid, Macedonian, Sassanid and Roman empires (see chapter 1). In 189 BC, present eastern Turkey was incirporated into the Roman Empire, who created two Armenian vassal kingdoms in the dominion: Armenia under the last Persian satrap Artashak, and Sophena under the his rival Zareh. One of the former's descendants, Tigran II — better known as Tigran the Great — seized power in Armenia in 90 BC and proclaimed himself king of 'Greater Armenia'. Still under Roman dominion, Tigran managed, however, to obtain a high degree of autonomy within the empire thanks to his support for the Romans against the invading Parthians. His overlords even allowed him to extend his territory over most of Transcaucasia and north-west Syria.

It is the very thought of this Great Armenian Empire, although it was never independent of Roman control, which fills the hearts of today's Armenians with joy and sorrow at the same time. Books, brochures and maps explaining and showing the glory of old sell like hot cakes and from that first day at school onwards children are imbued with the ideal of Greater Armenia. All of Armenian history is bound to it and everything that happened after Tigran's downfall is explained as outrageous injustice inflicted upon the nation.

As for Tigran himself, he rose against the Romans in the seventies of the first century BC together with his son-in-law, the king of Pontus, today's Trabzon. Tigran had disinherited his own son in favour of his daughter who was married to the vassal prince of Pontus, and that was why, in 69 BC, he found himself facing his son at the head of Roman legions sent east by Pompey to subjugate the Armenian insurgents. Tigran's army was defeated and his kingdom reduced to a tiny independent buffer state in the present border area between Turkey and Iran. Over the subsequent centuries, both the Romans to the west and subsequently the Parthians and the Persians to the east were to choose hapless Armenia as the battleground for their armed conflicts, not unlike the way the French and the Germans were to do with Belgium in later ages.

During the eighties of the third century AD, yet another struggle for the throne broke out in Armenia, which would be decisive for the nation's future and the formation of its character. The struggle was between Prince Artavazd, who enjoyed Persian support, and Tiridates III, a protegé of the Roman Emperor Diocletian, who in the end was to help him subdue his rival. Enlightened in respect to the new wind that was about to blow in Rome, Tiridates had himself converted to Christianity by a missonary named Gregory the Enlighter, and it was thus that in 314 Armenia became the world history's first nation where Christianity was proclaimed as the sole official state religion. In the sixth century, the Armenian Church then split from Rome as the Armenian Patriarch created his own pontificate, awarding himself the supreme title of Catholicos.

In the meantime, nothing but memories remained of the sovereign Armenia of old: by the end of the fourth century, the territory of Tiridates had been divided west and east between Byzantium and Persia. In 451, the Mazdean east Armenian vassal prince of East Armenia was ousted by Vahan Mamikonian, a rich land owner. Mamikonian extended his rule over all over Armenia and his dynasty was subsequently to rule over it in the name of the Byzantine emperors, the Persian shahs and the Caliph of Damascus until 772 when, after a year of bloody internal conflict, the Bagratuni clan took over the helm. As in the course of the tenth century Arab control over the region declined, dozens of Armenian petty princedoms sprang up only to be incorporated one by one into Byzantium during the first half of the 11th century.

Byzantine hegemony was to be succeeded in the region by Seljuq and Mongol supremacy (see chapter I). By the time of Timur Leng, Armenia had been literally and figuratively wiped from the map, with the exception of a tiny principality in Cilicia, where the ruling families were continuously engaged in an Armenian style War of the Roses. But by the second half of the 15th century the country was overrun by the Egyptian Mamluks. Soon, the latter were to make way for the Ottomans, by which action the fate of present-day Western Armenia was sealed for a long time to come. As for Eastern Armenia, it too soon fell, this time under Persian domination, to be followed in turn by the Russians during the last years of the Napoleonic Wars.

From the first moment on, the fact of 'Russian Armenia' tended to be a bitter pill for its inhabitants who, driven as they were by fear of the Islamic Turk, had hailed what they deemed to be their their Christian brethren from the north. Although to this day the Russians are seen by most Armenians (in contrast to the Georgians who see them as their one sworn enemy) as the lesser of two evils, true love has never flourished between them — and for good reason.

The Russians reduced Armenia to an area between Yerevan and Lake Sevan, which in 1828 was proclaimed the 'Armyanskaya Oblast' until its break-up and incorporation into the Transcaucasian viceroyalty. In 1836, the Armenian Church was deprived of all canonical authority and placed under the supervision of the Holy Synod of the Russian Orthodox Church in Moscow. During the 1840s, the rights of the *meliks*, traditional Armenian landowners, an important number of whom had become Muslim, were restored, an action which made the hardships of the common people only more unbearable.

Little if anything was noticeable in Armenia of the fresh wind of change blowing from St Petersburg during the 1870s. Whoever could afford to do so moved to Tbilisi, Baku or St Petersburg. It was there and in Europe but certainly not in Armenia where Armenian political initiatives were taken, such as the foundation of the Dashnaktsutiun party (better known simply as the 'Dashnaks') which was created in Tbilisi in 1890, three years after the founding in Geneva of its Marxist counterpart, the Hinchak party.

The fact that the Dashnaks were admitted to the Second International in 1907 was interpreted as a significant tactical move. According to the party's manifesto, written by its founder Simon Vratsian — the same who was to later head the Armenian republic of 1918 — the movement's sole aim was the "liberation of all Armenia" by means of "revolution" by any means possible. What those means exactly were was made clear soon enough: robbery, kidnapping, assassination, raids on Turkish and Kurdish settlements in Eastern Turkey and other acts of bravado which led to little positive resonance in the better educated circles of Armenians within the Ottoman conglomerate. But they certainly struck a chord among the poor countryside population as well as the Armenian communities abroad — and in Transcaucasia in particular where the Russian authorities encouraged rather than restrained Armenian war fever against the traditional Turkish foe.

That proved to be a fatal error. Yet even to this day this policy is still pushed by the Russians. The Dashnaks' campaign was stepped up in terms of intensity and frequency after the bloody suppression of a mass uprising in Eastern Turkey in 1896-97. Over the following years, entire Turkish and Kurdish villages were massacred in revenge and attacks by suicide-bombers resounded as far as the cities of Constantinople and Sofia.

Meanwhile, a graveyard peace ruled in Transcaucasian Armenia. Whatever remained of Armenian culture had been annihilated by Alexander III: in 1885, the Armenian schools had been closed down and in 1903 the last remaining church property had been confiscated. It was thus that, especially after the failed revolution of 1905, followed by the shockwave of ethnic violence in Azerbaijan described above, most Armenians focused on Baku and Eastern Turkey. It was there that freedom was to be gained, not in Yerevan.

As for Turkey, as early as 1893 the Sultan had imposed a number of civic reforms, *tanzimat*, in favour of the Greek, Jewish, Serb and Armenian minorities. They were granted their own individual 'people's statute' which granted, among other things, the right to elect their own people's assembly, the chairman of each of which was given the position of supreme councillor at the court in Constantinople. In the case of the Armenians, it was the Patriarch of Cilicia who took on the post.

The winter of 1914-15, however, brought with it a dangerous turn of developments for the Turks in the course of the First World War. Enver Pasha's Caucasus offensive had failed and the British landing at Gallipoli, although a Turkish victory, had shown how vulnerable the vast but highly disintegrated Ottoman Empire already was.

In January 1915, a general uprising of the Armenian population broke out throughout the countryside between Kars and Van. Most of the insurgents' leaders were linked either to the Dashnaks or the Hinchaks. All had gambled on the intervention of Russian troops, which indeed were at the heels of the withdrawing Ottoman armed forces. This optimism, however, led to an ill-conceived reaction by a panic stricken Sublime Porte. On April 24th, all Armenian institutions in major cities were closed down and thousands of Armenian citizens presumed to be politically active were arrested. There were some instances of attempts at resisting arrest by arms. According to the official Armenian version, over two thousand Armenian leading politicians were summarily executed by police in the streets — a fact which has always been contradicted by subsequent Turkish governments. It is not that the fears of the Turkish authorities were entirely groundless to begin with. But whatever the true dimensions of what was to follow in fact were, it all shows at the very least that fear is the hardly the best counsel in times of extreme crisis.

Three weeks after this wave of arrests, general uprisings broke out once more in Van, Bitlis, Mush and Zeytun (Cilicia). The city of Van itself stood at that time in a strip of no-man's land created between the retreating Turkish army and the advancing Russian troops. Of the 70,000 souls who had remained there no more than 40 per cent were Armenians. Yet, 4,000 armed men were enough to enable Dashnak leader Vazgen Manukian to take control of the city's military stronghold and to proclaim himself "Governor of Van in the name of Nicholas II, Emperor of all Christianity."

On May 14th and 15th, it was time for the Armenian rebels in Van to take revenge for the 1896 pogroms that had resulted in the massacre, at the very least, of 9,000 Turkish and Kurdish citizens and farmers in the areas of Van and Bitlis. This 'victory' at Van triggered off uprisings that spread like wildfire westwards. Everywhere around Erzurum, besieged as it was by the Russian army, the Dashnak was lord and master and busy spreading his own brand of terror. Tens of thousands of Turkish and Kurdish refugees poured into the beleaguered city straight through the lines only to be net with disease and famine in their place of refuge, where life had seemingly overnight turned to hell.

Nobody wished to qualify it that way but in the end it was hard to deny: apart from being the scene of international battle, the east of Turkey had also become the desperate theatre of civil war. The realisation of this drove Enver and Talaat Pasha to an even more drastic decision: no less than the deportation of the entire Armenian population of Turkey from Asia Minor to the north of Mesopotamia. According to Armenian conspiracy theories, the whole plan had been conceived months before and included a 'secret paragraph' according to which the entire Armenian 'exodus', once underway, was to be liquidated to the last man, woman and child. What is beyond doubt is the fact that tens of thousands of Armenians at least were slaughtered in the raids that were to follow. Many more died on the way towards the south-east at the hands of Kurds and other bandits — more often than not in collusion with the Turkish soldiers who accompanied the condemned columns.

Many have objected to the estimated figure of half a million, or even one and a half million, who perished. Indeed, hundreds of thousands of Armenian exiles managed to reach north-west Syria and northern Iraq where they joined the Armenian communities already in existence there. Another 400,000 Armenians managed to take refuge in Transcaucasia where they also joined their distant brethren. In all, as the figures suggest, perhaps there were never more than a million Armenians in Asia Minor to begin with, half of whom had already fled to safer areas after the catastrophic events of 1896-97. But then, the more realistic estimate of between fifty and eighty thousand victims as a result of Enver Pasha's shameful action is bad enough. Of course, the whole of eastern Turkey was then the scene of wholescale civil war, where everybody was fighting everyone else and the vestiges of authority had long since disappeared, where the population had to take the law into its own hands and did not hesitate to do so at the slightest provocation, leaving at least four million dead by the end of the ordeal — but still, that is no excuse.

The joy over the occupation of Van was to be short-lived. In the course of July 1915, the Turkish army engaged in a counter-offensive which drove the Russians back into the Georgian hinterland. In their wake — as they had done at the time of the Russian offensive, over a hundred thousand Armenians are said to have followed this retreat of their 'protectors', fearful as they were of reprisals for the havoc they had helped spread — and not without reason as it would appear.

But the hour had not yet come. Most Armenians managed to escape — only to return, once more in the wake of the Russian army, in February 1916. This time, Erzurum was briefly occupied but the subsequent withdrawal of the Russians was conducted with such haste that it left the Armenians in the jaws of their foes thirsting for revenge, leaving, according to US academic Bernard Shaw, some 40,000 Armenians slaughtered. And Shaw can hardly be considered an advocate for the Armenian 'cause'; in 1982, Armenian students broke into his classroom at the University of San Diego, California, accusing him of "Turkish propaganda." Shortly afterwards, a bomb exploded in front of his house and after repeated threats against his life he was forced to go into hiding.

In fact, there have been very few serious researchers in the West who have tried to evaluate the debate — which has continued for nearly a century now — over the Armenian Holocaust according to the factual record instead of supposition. Much of what has appeared in word and writing ever since the tragic events themselves happened — and very much it is indeed — is conflictive as regards fact to say the least. Historians such as Walter Laqueur and William Lange have come to the conclusion that seen within the general framework of the 19th and early 20th century Ottoman state system, the uprisings of 1915-16 in Van and elsewhere could hardly be expected to provoke anything less than the harshest possible repression. The French author Georges Melville pushes the controversy to its limit by expressing doubt as to whether the massacres of Armenians really took place at all.

On the other side of the argument, there are straightforward propagandists for the Armenians such as Lord Pryce, 'observer' from several thousands of miles distance in spring 1915, who in his publications entirely disregards the terror previously spread by the Dashnaks. His interest extended further than his writings alone: in early 1915, even before the mass deportations had started, he had started collecting money for his 'Armenian Friendship Society' without making much secret of the fact that it was in fact intended to furnish the Dashnaks and other Armenian brigades in eastern Turkey with arms.

Another armchair advocate of the Armenian cause found himself operating on grounds far less secure. This was a German Protestant by the name of Dr Johannes Lepsius, who as early as 1896 was targeting German country clergymen with newsletters couched in such a passionate language that the good pastors were all too ready to read them before their flocks without the slightest thought for any critical approach. Shortly after the First World War broke out, Dr Lepsius was forced to dismantle his foundation, the Deutsche Orient Mission, but this did not prevent him from completing his masterpiece *Der Todesgang des armenischen Volkes*, which was published in 1919. It hardly represents more than an abundant and very demagogic flow of words in which facts and figures are dealt with in somewhat less than German way of *Gründlichkeit* . . .

Aside from Shaw, there is another, earlier author who at least tried to look at things from both sides although sometimes giving in to the temptation to blow up figures no less. This is the Swiss historian Jacob Künzler, who first of all warns against jumping to conclusions over matters difficult to verify after all this time, and then points to the fact that in those days other populations under Turkish occupation in the region, such as the Druzes, the Syrian Orthodox Christians and even the same Kurds depicted by the Armenians as the henchmen of the Turkish butchers, in fact suffered no less severe losses among their civil populations. In all, whether or not such qualifications as 'genocide' or 'holocaust' to the same proportions as the anti-Jewish programmes of mass destruction employed by the Nazis could be used in this respect has been subject to a variety of views so far and will no doubt continue to remain so in the future.

What remains is that beyond any doubt the Via Dolorosa suffered by the eastern Turkish Armenian community in those days triggered off a second wave of the 'Hay Tahd' — as the Armenian nationalist cause was baptised — emerging by the end of the 19th century to demand a return to the kingdom of old as Tigran once established, including the Kingdom of Pontus (which he never possessed in the first place) . . .

Thus the Hay Tahd, to which any Armenian not wanting to risk a feud with his brethren had to be devoted, comes down to eternal revenge and full recompensation for the 1915 Holocaust in the form of restoration of 'historic' Greater Armenia and anyone settling for less was considered a traitor to the cause.

Whatever sentiments the Armenian lobby had managed to stir up in Europe, concrete political support by foreign governments was for the most part non-existent. As early as 1916, the governments of Britain, France and Russia had agreed in St Petersburg that in case they won the war (which at that stage was far from certain), the area was to be split up between the 'French Protectorate of Anatolia' and Russia. Before the year was over, the Russians had occupied most of Turkish Armenia, but instead of Armenian colonies they preferred to install Cossack ones up the Euphrates. Right after the February Revolution in Russia some hope still glimmered on the horizon for the Armenians as the Kerensky provisional government appointed an Armenian general by the name of Averian (or the Russified 'Averianov' which he preferred) as commissoner general over the the southern Caucasus and the 'new provinces' in eastern Turkey. As it was, the situation was too complex to impose any real Russian authority; in Transcaucasia the Seim was virtually acting as an independent government while in Anatolia Averian had allowed Armenian colonists to build settlements in the districts of Vaspurakan and Turberan which resulted in less building than the destruction and ransacking of existing Turkish and Kurdish settlements in the area, and the deaths of thousands of their inhabitants.

At first, little had changed after the Bolshevik take-over in October 1917; only on December 31st of the same year was a glimpse of relief felt by the 300,000 plus refugees stacked up in Yerevan when Lenin issued a decree whereby they would be able to return to Turkish Armenia, which was to exist as a buffer state where they could spend the rest of their lives in freedom and security.

However the Treaty of Brest Litovsk in March 1918 was to propose a 180-degree turn-around instead as the Moscow government promised to return all the Eastern Anatolian lands to Constantinople as soon as the promised withdrawal of Russian troops from the region was complete. Initially this provoked a fresh offensive by the Turkish army to recapture all the territory, including Transcaucasia. However, an ill-prepared attack was repulsed by Armenian armed forces against all the odds on May 28th near Sardarabad, an event which resulted in the official recognition by the Sublime Porte of the Republic of Armenia on June 4th. It was agreed on that occasion that for the moment the status quo would be maintained until a proposed international peace conference sealing the end of the Great War had ratified future international borders in the region.

At least, this was what the parties promised each other, but naturally each had quite different plans in the back of their minds. The ink was hardly dry on the agreement when Armenian armed forces followed by settlers broke through westwards. On May 28th 1919, the first anniversary of the new republic, the Armenian government proclaimed the "reunification of Turkish Armenia with the Armenian republic." All the terms of the June 1918 agreement had been broken; this was to be silently confirmed by the treaty of Sèvres of August 10th 1920. The Armenian occupation of Kars, Ardahan and other areas was not even mentioned and the Turks were told to comply with "mediation" over Van, Bitlis, Erzurum and Trabzon by the United States of America!

At first, nothing happened since there appeared to be not a single American diplomat available who possessed a map of the area let alone the situation on the spot. Moreover, the new government in Turkey, led by Mustafa Kemal, which had recaptured most of the occupied territories in the western half of Anatolia — and exiled or jailed most of the country's previous leadership — refused to comply with the Americans and on September 23rd the Turkish army moved eastwards, taking all the lands west of Yerevan. Finally, with Turkish troops within shooting distance, on December 2nd the Armenian Dashnak ruler, General Dro, handed over all power to the Soviets. On the same day, an armistice was concluded with the Turkish government in Alexandropol.

On February 18th 1921, Soviet rule over Armenia was disrupted by a putsch perpetrated by the Committee for the Liberation of the Fatherland, a Dashnak-dominated movement. After having concluded, on March 16th, a "pact of friendship and brotherhood for the struggle against imperialism" with Turkey in which the Sèvres treaty was declared "void" and all the lands west of Yerevan returned to the Turkish government, Soviet troops stormed Yerevan on April 2nd for the second time and this time they had come to stay.

Only in Zangezur to the south did the Dashnaks manage to hold on to a small stronghold from where they were eventually ousted during the summer. The Dashnaks may have been defeated in a military sense, but throughout the Soviet era they continued to keep their underground structure and maintained tight control over the area — which in fact they do to this day. On September 26th, the borders between Armenia and Turkey were once more confirmed in the Treaty of Kars. The betrayal was complete, and as in early 1923 the Treaty of Lausanne officially put an end to the First World War, the word 'Armenia' was nowhere to be found in any clause.

Later that year, Stalin ordered the Republic of Armenia to be liquidated and integrated into the Transcaucasian Federal Soviet Republic, which in December 1923 signed up to the new Soviet Union together with Russia, Byelorussia and the Ukraine. In 1936 the Transcaucasian Federation was split again but the borders between the three republics were modified. Thus, Zangezur was handed over to Armenia, where the majority of the population had originally consisted of Azeris who had, however, been wiped out by Andranik in 1918-19 (see previous chapters), Georgia gained the area of Javakheti — a region even today still heavily populated with

Armenians — while Azerbaijan acquired both Nakhchivan and the time-bomb that was Upper Karabakh.

In the meantime, the first Armenian Bolshevik leaders — two rustic thugs by the names of Sarkis Kassian and Avis Nurijanian — whose sadism and cruelty had paralysed the entire region, had been replaced by Armenians from Moscow who toed the Party line. From there on, farmers were paid for their harvests according to Lenin's 'New Economic Policy' instead of being robbed of them, and security returned at least in the countryside. In the cities, however, food prices were sent soaring by the agricultural policy and the steady disintegration of society continued. Soon another struggle for power started up, involving most of the main figures in the government, paralysing the state. Murders, disappearances and threats were to last until 1927.

Between 1921 and 1924, the number of party activists had dwindled from 7,850 to 4,230. Both Lenin's NEP and the government's general state of disorder had brought the country down to a beggar's level. The 'agricultural mechanisation programme', noisily trumpeted by the government at its launch, appeared to consist of thin air: by 1926, the country possessed the grand total of 187 tractors while the 'industrialisation programmes' had created little more than 7,000 jobs in all. More than half of the 65,000 residents of Yerevan lived in shanty towns around and in the city. Pollution, disease and crime ruled daily life.

In 1925 the mysterious murder of First Secretary Alexander Miasnikian (nobody believed that he had died in an air crash since nobody had witnessed it and no planes had been reported missing) provided a new impulse to the proletarian War of the Roses, leaving once more dozens of prominent leaders dead. Most of the killings were officially attributed to the Dashnaks, the Hinchaks (originally pro-Bolshevik but marginalised soon after the Soviet take-over), the Socialist Revolutionaries or Trotskyist opposition, but in reality they were the handiwork of warring factions within the party, the government and the local branch of the 'TseKa', or secret police — though this was probably not true for all killings since the still active Dashnaks were not averse to carrying out a murder or two themselves.

It was not until 1927 that this internal strife appeared to grind to a halt. Who had fought against who was never to get any clearer; moreover, fresh trouble was already brewing. In 1929 and 1930, half of the country's livestock was slaughtered and 25,000 farmers and their families were dispossessed. This new proletariat among proletarians moved en masse to the cities where unemployment and poverty awaited them, while the new collective farms in the countryside remained unattended by lack of labour force. One of the compelling reasons that nobody dared stay outside the main population centres was the nightly raids by the Dashnaks from their hide-out across the border in Iran in Daralaguyaz and Zangezur. Only major intervention in the south by the Red Army in 1934 put an end to what had got so out of hand it amounted to a counter revolution.

The main executor of the Armenian 'de-kulakisation' on Stalin's orders was the controversial First Secretary Aghassi Khandzian. Disregarding the gneral state of catastrophe into which he led the country, this theologian, born in 1900, educated at Echmiadzin and one of the founders of the Communist youth organisation Spartak, was not altogether evil. After having come to his post in 1930 at the recommendation of Kirov, who was his brother-in-law, he soon started acting as a 'wartime mayor' on behalf of Armenia and argued against the Kremlin's 'Russocentrism' wherever he safely could. He seems to have been particularly infuriated at the rehabilitation of the dynasty of the tsars, since he saw in it — and not without some truth — a continuation of the colonial policy of old. But the rise of Khandzian's arch-enemy Lavrenti Beria in 1936 looked set to seal the former's fate, which it did. One day, the Armenian leader entered Beria's office in Tbilisi for 'counsel'. He never emerged alive.

According to the official version, he committed suicide, but it was simply the prelude to a new series of purges which was to last until the Second World War and to continue well after it. It is estimated that the total number of victims of Stalin's purges in Armenia between 1926 and 1953 was as much as 300,000 — not including 174,000 killed in the Second World War, over a third of the number mobilised. In 1937 and 1938 alone, more than 20,000 officials and intellectuals, including the entire party leadership consisting of the 'second generation' of Bolsheviks who had taken over after Lenin's death, disappeared. After the coming of the Bolsheviks the clergy had taken over the torch of national conscience, and for this they too had to pay dearly. Thus, in 1938, the Catholikos Khoren I was strangled in his palace in Echmiadzin after, it is said, he had refused a gang of TseKa agents access to the treasury they intended to loot.

Most of the 22,000 Armenian prisoners-of-war returning from the war never saw Armenia again but were rewarded with a one-way trip to Siberia on their journey back from Germany. During the early 1940s, Armenia's population had dwindled to some 1.2 million. But despite all this misery, some hope glimmered on the horizon for those who still hankered after an Armenian reconquest of north-eastern Anatolia. After the occupation of Moldovia and the Baltic states on the eve of the Second World War, Molotov was now keen on occupying much of the territory west of Mount Ararat and even considered taking Trabzon. This scheme, however, was blocked by General Rommel who convinced Hitler of the convenience of an alliance with Turkey — or at least to keep it neutral in case of armed conflict with the Western powers. Soon afterwards, however, this flirtation between

Hitler and Stalin came to an end. In 1945, there was a last-ditch attempt by the Soviets to take Kars and Ardahan back from Turkey, but according to many Armenians the intention was to attach these areas not to Armenia but to Georgia, as they had been in the cradle of the ancient kingdom. But at the Moscow Conference of 1946 it appeared that the Allies were little charmed with the idea of any border shift between Turkey and the USSR.

It was then that the Armenian First Secretary Grigor Harutiunian came up with the idea of a 'mass repatriation' of half a million of ethnic Armenians to their 'birthplace' after the example of the Jewish exodus back to Israel. Indeed, thanks to Mikoyan's support, some 100,000 Armenians from all over the world migrated to Armenia. The plan was intended to convince Moscow of the 'necessity' of reclaiming Kars and Ardahan. It was in vain: in 1953 Molotov and Malenkov, who was then prime minister of the USSR, let the Turkish government know once more that there was no serious Soviet claim to any Turkish territory.

Many Armenians had come a long way in the Soviet hierarchy. On the eve of the Second World War, aside from Mikoyan, who by now was president of the USSR (although this was essentially only a ceremonial office since all real power remained in the hands of the Secretary General, i.e. Stalin), the Red Army in particular had quite a number of generals and at least one admiral among its top ranks.

But as for Armenia itself, it had become the (Adriatic) Albania of the USSR. To their shock, the immigrants of the late 1940s discovered that in the land of proletarian social discipline they could not go out on the street after dark without running the risk of being raped, robbed, killed — or all three. Alcohol abuse, opium and morphine were visible on every city corner and the negative effect they had on society as a whole was far heavier than evidenced in any Western metropolis.

In 1966, the French travel writer Albert Mahuzier described how he had met Suzanne, an Armenian from France in Yerevan who had been lured by Mikoyan's propaganda and come with her family to Armenia in 1947. On arriving, it was immediately clear to her that nothing was available: no home, no jobs, no food. For a preposterous amount of money she was finally able to rent a small, shabby, leaking apartment, and it was only after much trouble that she was able to find a job with a salary that brought in enough to stave off starvation. On more than one occasion, she and her relatives were robbed and beaten up without any authorities around to report to. During the first weeks, having run out of food, Suzanne had fallen ill from sheer exhaustion on more than one occasion, and she would burst into tears at the thought of her comfortable family apartment in Paris by the Gare de Lyon. Her elderly father went to the government house to complain about their situation — and never came back.

The policy of migration was stopped in 1956, but from 1949 onwards Armenia was forbidden territory to all non-Soviet citizens. Only during the 1960s, after a steady flow of publicity, did the French government start issuing the necessary documents to facilitate the repatriation of Armenian immigrants who had been lured to Soviet Armenia fifteen years earlier.

As for Armenia itself, by the end of the 1960s the general state of degradation into which it had sunk met with a response all too typical of the system. The 50th anniversary of the founding of Soviet Armenia was fast approaching and it was therefore decided that everything should be polished up in the spirit of Potemkin, who would put up hardboard facades in front of the impoverished village huts as the train of Empress Catherine II puffed by. The monarch now was Leonid Brezhnev, not as brain-dead as in later days but already well programmed on waning glory. And so it was that the countless congresses, speeches and proclamations all glorified the gigantic achievements of the Revolution, heralding a future shining brilliantly for the next generations . . .

'Brilyantovich', in fact, was the nickname of Anton Kochinian, the man who at that time was Armenia's First Secretary. However, he had not earned the nickname on account of his brilliant mind. The reason was that he was extremely fond of precious stones, and paid for them at the expense of the tax-payers of Armenia. In 1974, he was forced to step down for having committed 'ideological errors'. In this atmosphere of frustration, bitterness and backwardness, Armenia waded towards perestroika and eventually independence. And a new war.

Beyond doubt, the Armenian nation throughout its long and turbulent existence has fallen victim to many fateful events — including mass deportation and mass destruction. But the most serious thing they have mainly fallen victim to in our times is mass confusion. First of all, the location of the 'historic Armenian birthground' has remained subject to dispute up to this day and its relevance remains no less doubtful.

Whatever the case, the present-day nation of Armenia is small and ill-situated, and to claim a territory more than twice the size of Britain in order to harbour a few million people at the expense of those others whose roots have been there for eons, is ludicrous. All the more so since the intended 'reconquista' is driven by revenge rather than justice.

The Armenians won their war with it, but they lost their peace, as well as their senses, in the process. In previous chapters the turmoil wrought on a local scale by such a philosophy has already been well illustrated. However, it has also been exported to greater dimensions in the shape of international terrorism.

7

Hushed-up terror

The area around Baku's Central Station is one of the city's busiest spots. Travellers have to force their way through a lobster-pot of people trying to sell vegetables, fruits, other foodstuff, stationery, cigarettes and currency. It is one big swarming mass and an ideal playground for pickpockets, racketeers and cut-throats. The carousel starts before dawn and ends well after dusk.

At sunrise that fateful February 1st 1993, the whole racket had already been going on for several hours when a shockwave ripped through the crowd as a huge explosion resounded from the railway station. Panic-stricken people, blood streaming from many of them, came running out of the station's main hall and after some minutes the air was filled with the sirens of ambulances and police cars.

The bomb had exploded in a wagon of the train which had just arrived from Kislovosk in the North Caucas, resulting in three killed and some twenty injured. Another bomb at the border station of Khudat, between Daghestan and Azerbaijan, was to result in material damage only. Both terrorist attacks, however, were to seem almost minor against the calculated carnage of the bomb placed on the Baku metro. As a train entered the tube station near the central railway station, in the middle of evening rush hour. Fourteen died and over fifty were seriously injured. The first half of 1993 will always be marked by such a senseless loss of life.

Nevertheless these events only represented the rare moments when Baku was confronted directly with the reality of the political conflict which was usually confined to the country's remote south west. On January 3rd, the latest (and last, as it turned out to be) Azeri offensive on the Karabakh front had been initiated. But since no reports from the front were seen either on television or on the front pages of the press, no ordinary citizen in the nation was motivated to care about the onslaught in the slightest way. At first, there were indications that the Turkish Grey Wolves — the attempt to kill Aliev was still fresh in people's memories — or even the Russian intelligence services may have been behind the bomb attacks. But it was soon clear that Armenians were to blame. Within a few weeks the perpetrators were identified, with the aid of Interpol, as members of an Armenian terrorist organisation operating under the name of Vrezh ('Revenge'), believed to have ties with the Dashnaks. According to some reports, the Armenian Hrayr Marukhian had founded it while outside the Soviet Union. Towards the end of the 1980s, Marukhian was expelled from the USSR only to pop up once more in Rostov after the collapse of his ertswhile host.

Armenian terrorism certainly has a colourful history. As early as the end of the 19th century, a whole stream of terrorist attacks were carried out within the Ottoman Empire, responsibility for which was claimed by the Dashnaks. Not that they were the only ones, there were many such groups within the crumbling empire that did not shrink from bringing their agendas to fruition though kidnappings and shootings.

During the second decade of the 20th century, the Dashnaks embarked on a programme of hunting down leaders of Enver Pasha's Ittihad party, who were judged responsible — and indeed were partly so — for the Massacres of 1915 and previous. Accordingly, on March 15th 1921, Talaat Pasha, interior minister under Enver, was gunned down and killed in Berlin, followed on December 6th in Rome by Turkey's ex-president Ghina Sais Salim, and then, again in Berlin on April 17th 1922, by another of Enver's ministers, Baetdon Shakir, who was accused of having ordered the drowning of thousands of Armenian children in the Black Sea during the 1915 'razzias'.

Among the members of the hit squad responsible for these assassinations were two Armenians of obscure origin by the names of Arshavir Shirakian and Aram Erkanian — the latter was also the assassin of former prime-minister Fathali Khan-Khoiski in Tbilisi in 1920. This particular killing, along with that in the same year of Khan-Khoiski's interior minister Peyut Khan Zhoanshirov, carried out on July 19th in Istanbul by an Armenian named Misak Tarlakian, cast an intriguing light upon this new wave of terror. Had there, at some stage or other, been some form of gentleman's agreement made between the Soviets and at least a section of the Dashnaks? The hypothesis becomes even more plausible if one considers the 'volunteer batallions' who played a key role in the 'dirty war' waged by the Soviets against Enver Pasha after he had proclaimed himself emir of rebellious Bukhara in Central Asia. The would-be emperor met his end in an ambush in 1922, which was the handiwork of an armed group commanded by a certain Hagop Melkonian, who was under the direct orders of the Soviet defence ministry.

In 1923, the Dashnaks were officially disbanded and their leader General Dro fled to the United States where, in collusion with his former comrade-in-arms Karkin Nezhdeh, he created an openly racist movement he dubbed Tzeghagrons ('Devoted to the Race'). During the 1930s their organization found protection under Rockefeller's political umbrella. Units recruited from the ranks of Tzeghagrons were sent to Germany immediately following the outbreak of the Second World War. There they formed Batallion 812, which was to wreak havoc with no less zeal than their German mentors among the 'enemy' communities of the Crimea, the Ukraine, the Caucasus as well as other areas on the Eastern Front. By the end of the 1930s, Dro himself had settled down in Berlin with his cohorts for good.

The development of post-war Armenian terrorism found its origins in the work of a loner by the name of George Yanikian, who, on January 27th 1973 at the Biltmore Hotel in Santa Barbara, California, shot and killed the Turkish consul-general Mehmet Baydar and his first secretary Bahadir Demir.

Yanikian had migrated to the USA shortly after the Second World War, and meanwhile attained the blessed age of seventy-eight. With his conviction for the killing and subsequent imprisonment, he started writing and distributing pamphlets offering convoluted explanations for the motives that had led him to commit the deed. These leaflets were rapidly disseminated among the Armenian community in the West where they struck a surprisingly major chord.

On April 4th of the same year there followed two bomb attacks on the offices of the national Turkish airlines and the Turkish tourist office in Paris, followed by another explosion on October 26th at the Turkish tourist office in New York. In all three cases, the bombs were of similar construction. An organisation calling itself the Yanikian Commando admitted responsibility for the bombings, a terrorist group that has long been assumed to form the initial hardcore of what was later to become the ASALA — until it eventually looked as if there was more to the ASALA, a subject discussed below.

At a fairly early stage, the Dashnaks had jumped onto the bandwagon of these rapidly unfolding events, in the form of the so-called Justice Commandos for the Armenian Genocide, later rebaptised as the Armenian Revolutionary Army. One of their first acts was the murder of the Turkish ambassador to Austria, Tanis Tunagilil, on October 22nd 1975. On May

28th 1976, their bombs destroyed the Zurich offices of both the Turkish Garanti Bank and the Turkish embassy's second secretary, followed, in Rome on June 9th 1976 and April 17th respectively, by the killings of the Turkish ambassador to the Vatican Taha Karim and the his successor Vecdi Turel.

The JCAG equally bears responsibility for, among others, four bomb attacks on one and the same day in Paris, July 8th 1979, on Turkish institutions, a similar series of attacks in Madrid on January 20th 1980, the bomb attack on the 'Turkish House' in New York on October 12th the same year, and the murder in Sydney, on December 17th, of the Turkish consul general Sarik Ariyak. The JCAG's final acts took place during the first half of 1982, and included the murder in Boston on January 4th of the Turkish honorary consul Orhan Gunduz, and the killing of the Turkish embassy's military attache, Colonel Atilla Altikat, on August 27th in Ottawa.

The JCAG's successor, the equally Dashnak-affiliated ARA, was responsible for the lives of around twenty victims among Turkish diplomats, their wives and their children in 1984 alone. At an earlier stage, the organisation's entry on the scene had been rather spectacular with the hostage-taking at the Turkish embassy in Lisbon — the incident included a bomb attack that left the mission's deputy head's wife Cahide Mihcioglu dead of her wounds and her husband and son seriously injured. Four of the terrorists themselves died in the explosion, while another was killed later on in a gun battle during which a Portuguese policeman was fatally wounded as well.

The list of the more notable attacks carried out by the ARA in 1984 includes the car bomb in Vienna on June 20th in which the Turkish embassy official Erdogan Ozen was killed, the murder of his Brussels-based fellow Dursun Aksoy on July 14th, and the killing of a UN official of Turkish nationality named Enver Ergun in Vienna on November 19th, who was killed by a sniper while driving his car. The final and probably most dramatic terrorist attack carried out by the ARA was the hostage-taking indicent in Ottawa on March 12th 1985, when three heavily armed men stormed the Turkish embassy and shot three guards — one of them fatally. After blowing up the front gate, the three attackers forced their way into the building and made their way upstairs. The ambassador Coskun Kirtca managed to escape by jumping from the window, but his wife, daughter and staff were taken hostage. After four hours, the terrorists gave themselves up.

The strange thing is that if the existing links between the ARA and the Dashnak lobby in North America and Western Europe were common knowledge at the various levels of offical circles, then the terrorists were evidently given free rein to continue the various ranges of their activities without so much as being hindered by Western security services. Not once was there an official investigation co-ordinated and launched by Western security services into the ARA networks and their activities. The same may be said about the competing organisations of a more left-wing inclination such as Yanikian's 'heirs', who have become better known under their sinister acronym ASALA — the 'Armenian Secret Army for the Liberation of Armenia'.

Summer 1988 in Bourj Hammoud, a suburb east of Beirut. Civil war had already raged in Lebanon for thirteen years now. But that hardly seemed to bother the suburb's mainly Armenian denizens — nor did they appear to notice the piles of domestic garbage, the unworkable sewers, the failing electricity supply and other parts of the crumbling infrastructure. Here, Lebanon ended for a while.

Banners across the streets, signs over shop windows (for a desolate neighbourhood like this, the number of jewellery shops was remarkably large), newspapers, magazines, nearly all of them were in Armenian. A narrow shopping street runs from one end of the centre to the other. At either end of this particular street stands a church. Underneath each church there is a basement. But those 'souterrains' did not harbour, as one would expect, a fine collection of bishop's robes, chalices, monstrances and other objects of beauty. Here instead you would discover that the walls could not be seen for the rows of Kalashnikov and M16 rifles that hung from them, while the floors were piled with boxes of hand-grenades, all kinds of ammunition, leaving barely enough space for a narrow shooting gallery down the middle.

One church basement was the Dashnak hide-out, the other functioned as headquarters for the ASALA. The latter's leader was a short, sturdy, balding man with a Charlie Chaplin (or Hitler) moustache. On the corner, there was a roadblock where his men checked passing cars. Each time they spotted something suspicious, he would arrive and arrange things in a most gentlemanly fashion with the driver, who'd meantime be nervously wringing his hands.

While Yanikian is considered to be the ASALA's 'spiritual father' (the organisation's first three attacks, in early 1975, bore the hallmark signature of the so-called 'Prisoner George Yanikian Group'), a certain Hagop Hagopian is considered to be the movement's founder. Yet, at least as far as we know, he never played an active part in any of the terrorist attacks. At the earliest stage of activities, two Lebanese Armenians, Khachig Havarian and Viken Ayvazian, both of whom maintained strong ties with the

Armenian community in California, had a reputation as leading field commanders. As for 'Field Commander' Monte Melkonian — the short man with the moustache — his career as commando leader and subsequent leader of the entire organisation was yet to start. But still, anyone seeing him coming down the streets of Beirut in the late 1980s would have been better advised to take a sidestreet instead.

This fact had been discovered — a little too late, it would seem — by Havarian and Ayvazian when in July 1983 they were ambushed while travelling in the Bekaa Valley and butchered in cold blood by Melkonian and his cohort David Davidian. From that point on, Melkonian was the undisputed leader of the ASALA. The very mention of his name provoked the same shudder in the forces of law and order from Los Angeles to Hong Kong as those of Hussein Mussawi, Carlos or Abu Nidal.

Understandably, little love was lost between the men of ASALA and their fellow Lebanese Maronite Christians, although the latter themselves were not exactly innocent little lambs — and, indeed, precisely the same could be said about Yasser Arafat's Palestinians to the south. Quite a different matter, however, was the relationship of the ASALA with the many enemies of Arafat within the fractious Palestinian community and with Islamic Jihad. ASALA availed itself of such dubious alliances to make extensive use of the facilities offered by the training camps of Abu Nidal and Ahmed Jibril in the Bekaa Valley in order to prepare for terrorist operations, while with the Mussawi brothers they ensured that a lucrative drugs and arms trade flourished.

In terms of attacks, the ASALA had already made its reputation in 1975, in a Lebanon as yet untouched by the outbreak of war but filled already conspiracies and bellicose rumblings. A bomb planted by the group exploded at the Beirut office of the World Council of Churches. The pretext was that the Council had suspended the Armenian Church's membership after the shameless apologies for terrorism which the Armenian Catholicos had recently made. On February 7th, the attack was followed in the Lebanese capital by two bombs at the Turkish tourist office and the offices of Turkish Airways.

In a place where Israeli agents used to take potshots at and blow up Palestinian leaders on a weekly basis and where Arab underworld figures too chose to settle their scores, the Armenian attacks attracted no more public attention than a minor note on the inside pages of the press. It was only after the murder on October 24th 1975 of the Turkish ambassador in Paris, Ismail Erez, followed four days later by a rocket attack on the Turkish embassy in Beirut and the fatal shooting of Oktar Cirit, the embassy's First Secretary, in a barber shop on Hamra Street in broad daylight, that the realisation began to sink in that Armenian terrorism represented a far more substantial threat interantionally than it had been so far supposed.

Such suspicions were confirmed beyond doubt on May 27th 1977, when in Istanbul two powerful bombs exploded: one at the airport, killing five and injuring 42 people, and another one at the central railway station killing one and injuring around ten. Initially, the attacks were attributed to those who had claimed responsibility for them: an organisation operating from Greece by the name of the Armenian May 28th Movement. However, later analysis concluded from the style of the operation that its origin would be better sought in the circles of the ASALA.

From then on, the ASALA acted as if there was nothing that could stop them. They were on a roller-coaster ride of destruction. No single ASALA activist had been caught so far, and in war-torn Lebanon at least they considered they were free to do whatever they felt. Amongst the most spectacular acts of this period were the attack on June 2nd 1978 in Madrid when the Turkish ambassador's car was hit by a hail of automatic gunfire, in which his wife, his predecessor and their Spanish driver were all fatally hit (both ASALA and the GCAG were to claim rsponsibility), and October 12th 1979 in the Netherlands, when the Turkish ambassador's son, Ahmet Benler, a student at the Technical University of Delft, was shot dead in his car. Over the rest of the year, the scenes for other attacks which failed to kill their intended victims included Milan, Rome, Madrid, Paris and Amsterdam.

The most striking reaction from Western authorities to the terrorist acts, which were openly cheered by the Armenian community, was one of sheer indifference. When, for example, on June 11th 1981, police in Paris got word that a group of ASALA terrorists led by a certain Ara Toranian, who was sought by the police in connection with previous acts of terrorism, had forced its way into the Turkish Airways offices, the authorities flatly refused to intervene until the Turkish ambassador had furiously called the interior minister from his bed. If the French government had thought its lenient attitudes would spare the country from fresh terrorist acts, they were to be proved fatally wrong when, on September 24th 1982, Paris became the scene of a dramatic hostage situation at the Turkish consulate, where a guard was murdered and 56 people held at gunpoint. After 16 hours the terrorists gave up, but only after they had been guaranteed political refugee status by the French government.

Yet again the treacherous attitude of the French government failed to pay off. On February 28th 1983, a French employee was killed after a bomb exploded at the office of the Marmara travel agency, and on June 8th another bomb exploded at the British Council. The bloodiest incident, however, was on July 15th when a bomb went off at the Turkish Airways desk at Orly Airport killing eight and injuring some 60 bystanders.

Meanwhile, Belgrade had become yet another target on the ASALA's list. On March 9th 1983, two Armenian terrorists by the names of Hartunium Levonian and Raffi Elkbekian shot dead the Turkish ambassador Galip Balkar in an ambush, murdering a Yugoslavian student in the course of their getaway. Back on familiar territory — historically at least — on June16th, an ASALA armed unit threw two hand-grenades into the packed central bazaar of Istanbul and opened up with automatic gunfire at random on bypassers, killing two and injuring 21 others.

These two last attacks in particular, aimed as they were at innocent victims most of whom had probably never even heard of Armenia, showed the true mindset of the future commanders of the Upper Karabakh Self Defence Forces, no matter how heartily embraced they came to be by the hypocrites of the West. The ASALA's last major wave of terror came on March 28th 1984, when five separate terrorist attacks were carried out on the same day, three of which were unsuccessful. The husband of one of the targets, a female employee of the embassy, was killed exactly a month later as their car was raked with bullets.

The very final act of terror known to be the handiwork of the ASALA was at Lyons railway station on August 13th, where an explosive device went off too early, causing only minor damage. That summer, however, the ASALA had launched a massive hate-mail campaign, the language of which suggested that the movement, which at the time was labelling itself 'Maoist-Trotskyite', had lost its final touch with reality — if it ever had one.

The most important reason that both the ARA and ASALA went under for the time being was their mutual enmity and their internal animosity. The JCAG leader Apo Ashzhyan had been shot dead in Lebanon in December 1982 as a result of an internal feud within the Dashnaks. His successor, ARA chief Sarkis Aznavourian, was murdered in Bourj Hammoud by the ASALA a few years later. Meanwhile, the murder of Havarian and Ayvazian had sealed the struggle for the leadership within the ASALA. As for Melkonian, he was arrested in 1985 in Paris as a suspect in connection with a series of bombings carried out to put pressure on the authorities for the release of Varuzhan Garabedian, one of the terrorists who had carried out the Orly bloodbath.

Under which precise conditions and through what kind of 'arrangement' Melkonian was eventualy released has never become known in any great detail. Whatever the deal, it didn't stop him from cropping up again in 1992 in front of the television cameras in the uniform of field commander of the Armenian Karabakh armed forces. At the occupation of Agdam, in October the following year, he was fatally hit by a stray piece of shrapnel. In fact, his death is assumed to be one of the reasons why almost no prisoners were taken at Agdam — almost without exception, the Azeri soldiers and officers who surrendered were butchered by the attackers.

One explanation that clears much of the obscurity around the ASALA but at the same time throws strange but clear light on the remarkable course justice has taken in various countries in respect to the organisation, consists of some facts revealed by two Russian journalists, Gyorgy Podlyessky and Andrei Chereshonok, in their booklet *Vory v Zakony* (literally 'Thieves Within the Law' — an expression used to describe mafiosi who get away with everything). Published in 1995, the report contains data which even during the heydays of Gorbachev's glasnost would have been considered utterly taboo. Based on the information provided by the authors, taken directly from KGB sources, one can reach only one conclusion, that the ASALA, if not actually set up by the KGB, served in its employ for a fair long time.

Possibly this was not the last time this sort of arrangement was, and it most certainly was not the first. In 1976, the prosecutor general of Armenia, a certain Mr Serobian, received a remarkable file of an investigation that has gone into history as 'File No. 100' and which, although it grew thicker and thicker throughout its long existence, never once came to trial in a court of law.

The investigation originated from a bomb scare at a trade exhibition in Moscow. One of the clues from the scene of the crime led to a certain Dmirtabian, who, it was discovered, was not only a component of a subversive group, Paylak, but also worked for the Yerevan branch of the TseKa secret police. He was able to moonlight in this way thanks to the protection of the local KGB chief Yuzbashchian, whose presence was frequently noted in Beirut and the Bekaa Valley in those days. Paylak, a rival of the ever-active Dashnaks, had been set up to neutralise the latter. In 1981, the organisation was dismantled under pressure from officials high up in Moscow who feared a major scandal, after (many) failed and (few) successful acts of terrorism.

That, however, did not mean the end of File No. 100. The ASALA had also shed a little light on its own workings. What had been kept secret for a long time was the fact that one of its co-founders, Zhor Martirossian, had been trained at a KGB camp in Laos under the command of the high-ranking Armenian KGB officer Khachur Artakovich Avakian. Remarkably enough, one of Martirossian's comrades-in-arms during the training programme, a certain Unjian, was also working for the CIA — as were several of his relatives.

Melkonian was far from being the only Armenian terrorist leader to find a safe berth in Armenia and/or Karabakh aided by being able to pass unhindered through the same countries in which they were wanted. According to persistent rumour, Hagop Hagopian, long viewed as ASALA's principal architect, is supposed to move freely in Armenia, despite his presumed murder in Athens in 1988 — a hoax according to many. As late as 1993, Yuzbashchian was spotted in Yerevan. At the same time, Martirossian, featuring on an impressive number of arrest warrant lists issued by the world's police forces in connection with a no less impressive list of bloody acts of terror, had quietly lived for years in London alongside another terrorist named Hovanissian, only to escape to Armenia with Scotland Yard snapping at his heels.

Yerevan, March 1993. Half of the university's student hostel had been crammed with 'volunteers' who keep a hotline open with Karabakh. I was waiting for a car in the company of two Swiss journalists. A fat, puffy young man was hanging around near the entrance. He was unwilling to reveal his name. But he did want to tell us something.

"Do you remember that attack on the Turkish ambassador in Berne . . . ?"

We certainly did.

"That was me."

The name of the victim who survived the shoot-out was Dogan Turkmen. The gunman's name was Max Klinjian. He sat out his term in jail after his arrest in Marseilles and extradition to Switzerland.

It was not coincidence that he had fled to Marseilles. There lived the Armenian Protestant clergyman Harutiun Helvajian, founder and chairman of the Comité pour la Défence des Prisonniers Politiques Arméniens (CDPPA) who took care that arrested Armenian terrorists were looked after and provided with legal assistance. However, this shepherd of pious souls did more than that with the many millions of francs he collected annually from the Armenian community there. In fact, everyone in those days, including the local criminal investigation department, was in no doubt that a substantial part of the money the pastor collected went towards arms purchases. But if this was true, no one ever got in his way.

In Yerevan, the question of terrorism is an awkward subject to discuss. But no one will allow themselves to show any unease if the subject is brought up, and they will invariably qualify any remark they make with the statement "self defence." Presumed factors that play a key role in respect to the mass psychosis which induces entire communities to applaud the bloodiest forms of aggression have already been subject to much speculation. Reality, however, dictates that a world that intends to progress can never do so without individual and collective self-control.

Hushed-up terror

It is for this reason that the mainsprings of terror and the mass inclination towards terror must be sought in the tendency to revolt against this reality. As a rule, intelligence — i.e. the ability to weigh one thing against another and thereby draw a conclusion — will constrain such tendencies or at least make them subject to control. However, there are individuals who lack the mental capacity to bridge the concept of impression and interpretation, a situation which leaves them unable to argue their unargued discontent, inept at distinguishing facts as they actually are from facts as they observe them.

Some individuals are born with this handicap, whereas others develop it, for whatever reason, at a later age. Usually, it expresses itself through short-temperedness, distrust, hostility and aggression. Such people are better known as complainers or troublemakers. They are not dissimilar to a plague and — in the event verbal aggression degrades to physical violence — a direct threat to their environment. In some cases, but by no means all, early treatment by experts can save the day.

Things get substantially more complicated, however, if the victim of the syndrome is not a single individual but a group of individuals — or even an entire community. One does not necessarily have to be a psychologist or soiologist to imagine the result: at such moments, the chain reaction of frustration–irritation–aggression is no longer a deflective phenomenon in an otherwise controlled society, but the deflective syndrome takes over the place of the normative and the norm becomes deflection.

At such moments, the socio-mental disease tends to adopt the guise of what we loosely term 'politics'. Why in some societies such things happen while in others they do not is a question which can be debated endlessly. Many communities that have been subjected to terrible ordeals in the past have escaped the syndrome while just as many whose ordeals have been far less fall victim to it.

Whatever the case, what actually happens is no less clear for it: once the process kicks in, neurotic obsession under the delusion that some fatal force is supposed to drive people to deeds (often resulting in misdeeds) will drive whole communities straight towards the abyss. Acknowledging the symptoms — such as delusions of superiority, hunger for revenge and tendency to self-destruction — is often to little avail. As long as people prefer to pamper themselves at the conference table instead of searching for effective remedies against the disease of (collective) hysteria, a great many Palestines, Rwandas, Yugoslavias and Karabakhs will continue to develop without so much as a look-in from a world where understanding prevails over unreasoned jealousy.

As if determined to prove this theory, the driving forces behind the ASALA and the ARA went back to work with a vengeance after the demise of their respective organisations. Only this time, after the implosion of the clandestine networks of the old guard throughout the world's capitals, the arena for their operations now consisted mostly of those areas directly neighbouring Armenia. By the end of the 1980s, raids and attacks on trains and buses between Baku and Nakhchivan and elsewhere in and around Karabakh by local gangs from nearby Armenian villages was soon to attract the attention of hardcore survivors within the former shells of both the ASALA and the Dashnaks. It is probable that it was Melkonian himself who laid the basis for the so-called Armenian Secret Army (ASA) in order to revive the fortunes of the ASALA of old.

The existence of the ASA was brought to the authorities's attention after the confessions of a well-known Armenian railway prostitute nicknamed 'La Vartouche' who worked the train between Yerevan and Baku and who was arrested on May 27th 1989 in possession of enough explosives to blow up a whole carriage — which was exactly what she had intended to do. Once in court, La Vartouche claimed that she had been ordered to carry out her mission by leaders of the ASA leaders, whom she named as Teroyan and Sos Eloyan, and that both had told her that the scheme had been set up "with the full consent of the authorities."

Not much more was heard of the ASA in later days. Much more dangerous, however, was the rise shortly afterwards of Vrezh, a new, Dashnak-sponsored organisation already mentioned here. Vrezh's composition and structure only came to light in 1993. Apart from its involvement in the various attacks described earlier, the group was also held responsible for the attack on the bus from Tbilisi to Baku on September 16th 1989 in which five passengers were killed and seventeen injured. A similar attack on the Tbilisi to Agdam bus, on August 10th 1990, killed seventeen and injured another twenty, followed by others on the Moscow to Baku train on April 13th and July 31st 1991.

There were those who assumed Vrezh was the alter-ego of Dro, another Dashnak military wing which had been set up to operate in Armenia proper with the purpose of undermining President Ter-Petrossian's government. Others, however, pointed the finger of suspicion in the direction of the Armenian government itself — a supposition that was closer to how things were than was thought, although as late as summer of 1996 the Armenian head of state still spoke of "Azeri provocation" and an "anti-Armenian witchhunt" intended to disrupt the peace negotiations over Karabakh.

Azeri provocation? In March the same year, a Russian court had sentenced three Armenians, Boris Simonian, Ashot Galoyan and Jahan Hovanissian, to one-and-a-half, two and six years apiece for their parts in the 'train bomb campaign' of early 1994. The mild sentences provoked a storm of anger throughout Azerbaijan. At the time, the first two bombings had targeted top officials in the Armenian state security service while the third had gone for one of the leading commanders of the Russian Federal Intelligence Service's anti-terrorist department.

The Armenian community, both in and outside Armenia, can basically be divided into two camps: those who dismiss the existence of Armenian terrorism as "Turkish and pro-Turkish propaganda," and those who claim that "you have to do something to defend yourself against the enemy." We have already seen how the present-day Azeri nation emerged from a lengthy, geographically ambiguous history. But, in contrast to the citizens of Azerbaijan who tend to consider one other Azeri, no matter one's ethnic background, for the simple reason that they have all grown up together within the same borders, Armenians tend to attach land to people and not the other way round. Thus is justified, at least according to an influential section of their leadership, the practice of ethnic cleansing and geopolitical isolation in their most extreme forms.

I have heard it time and again from defensive interlocutors in Armenia and from Armenians elsewhere: "But look at us here surrounded by our enemies! Can't you understand that their fathers and fathers' fathers from the earliest generations onwards have always been our deadliest enemies. If we don't strike first, they'll come and exterminate us all. It's simple: we're only defending ourselves."

Naturally, "the enemy" are Muslims in general and the Turks in particular.

This bitterness of the Armenian nation over their 'hereditary enemies' could be sensed everywhere by anyone visiting Armenia during the early 1990s. Blind, naked paranoia and a lust for revenge could be encountered at every level of society — with the notable exception of a few young people who bravely struggled to give pacifism some semblance of a hearing. In this respect, the contrast with the Georgians — even though they have been fellow Christians of the Armenians since the early Middle Ages — was striking.

But do I deliberately wrong the Armenians in this respect?

On the one hand, it could be argued 'yes, of course'.

On the other hand, however, it would be utterly nonsensical to deny the facts as they are, facts that have even been confirmed and condemned by independent institutions whose reputations are not exactly based on their objectivity. One also has to take into account the process whereby nations rightly depicted as the very symbols of terror at earlier stages of the world's history have demonstrated an ability to adapt to more civilised standards with the passage of time, whereas others which once were paragons of respectability turn themselves into mass murderers without a single clear indication as to why. All of which leads to the obvious conclusion that although the future may sometimes appear bleak, it will be never entirely bereft of hope.

8
Playing poker on Vagramian Boulevard

Vagramian Boulevard starts near the Yerevan opera house, a pompous, fortress-like building. The garden that surrounds it also serves as the local Speaker's Corner in London's Hyde Park: a sanctuary where everybody and anybody can stand up and address the crowd as they want, something that happens frequently and wholeheartedly all the time. The boulevard itself features the almost threatening House of Parliament, the somewhat less imposing presidential palace and a number of smaller villas where ministries and foreign embassies such as those of China and the USA have settled.

But anyone thinking that Armenia is a perfect example of solidarity as far as the nation's geopolitical renaissance is concerned, would appear to be mistaken. This was the last week of May, 1993. Midnight of May 26th was the deadline for Armenia to respond to the latest in a long stream of proposals drawn up by the Organisation for Security and Co-operation in Europe, which this time boils down to withdrawal from all occupied zones except Upper Karabakh and Lachin, and the establishment of a demilitarised zone around the disputed area under international supervision.

Twenty four hours before the deadline still no official reaction was reported. But since no one in this part of the world is any good at keeping his or her mouth shut, it had been a public secret for some time already that the government had a declaration already drawn up to the effect that they were prepared to co-operate fully . . .

". . . Only so far as Armenia's involvement in the conflict is concerned," added presidential spokesman Abrahamian. "And there is no such involvement!" There was a slight twinkle in his eye as though asking 'are we clever or are we clever . . . ?!'

The opposition evidently did not think so — and it took up its role in the colourful way all oppositions are supposed to.

"We think the president should step down," Dashnak leader Ruben Hagopian fulminated in joint chorus with, among others, Vigen Khacharian, party leader of the Liberal Democratic Armenian Organisation, who in turn declaimed:

"The people do not accept the peace plan brought in by the international diplomacy. For the people know what the government has so far apparently failed to realise: war has its own reality and its own rules. Anyone failing to realise this reality and these rules cannot possibly claim our co-operation . . ."

Involvement or not, Karabakh was far from absent on the political scene. A nervous young man wearing a shining blue blazer and a multi-coloured necktie was stealing the show in Parliament's lobby speaking in no less colourful terms of a "conspiracy against the Armenian nation" and "the beginning of a national campaign which shall lead us to final triumph." This was Robert Kocharian, 'chairman of the national self defence forces' in Upper Karabakh.

Triumph?

The history of empires that rule the globe or substantial parts of it, their campaigns, triumphs and their conquests is a fascinating topic for serious study or, indeed, leisurely reading. Standing eye to eye with somebody who intends to put these things into practice once more, however, gives one a deeply unpleasant feeling in one's gut, to say the least.

"Karabakh fighters?" exclaimed youngsters in one of Yerevan's bars with rare frankness. "'Desperados' — that's what they are! Don't be sorry for yourself if you don't get the chance to go there. A German journalist was robbed of his cash and his equipment by his own escort out there. They would have shot him just like that if an officer hadn't happened to come by . . ."

The landscape along the way to Goris, which lies within shooting distance of the Lachin 'Corridor', was gruesome and dreary. Once these hills and mountains must have been a natural paradise, but erosion and deforestation had scalped it in more than one way of speaking. Nonetheless, arrival in Goris meant an unexpected view: factories were working, residential complexes were being erected and the lights were all burning thanks to a hydraulic power plant nearby that was up and running.

The general mood, however, was deflated by the sandbags stacked up in front of the doors and windows and the ruins of buildings caused by the (frequent) stray artillery projectiles. The nearest Armenian positions were miles away from the city, "but those guys on the other side haven't got much clue about how to take aim."

Gormidzor, a village at some twelve miles from Goris, was a far more grimly visible witness to the war, since it was sited right in the crossfire. Hardly a house had stayed without damage. Still, there was something unnerving about this place: positioned as it was on the front-line you would have expected intensive military activity and yet there was not a tank nor soldier in sight — much to the population's frustration.

"The Armenian army?!" a hale and hearty old lady rages. "Don't talk to me about them! Those good-for-nothings never show their faces around here. We've got some weapons for ourselves from paramilitary units in Zangezur and set up our own civil guard. If we hadn't, you wouldn't see a single soul around here."

What is particularly intriguing is that these "paramilitary units" appear to be none less than the military wing of the Dashnaks, the self-same terrorist organisation whose units only days before presidential spokesman Abrahamian had sworn were all "dismantled and disarmed."

On the horizon, near Vardenis, the non-stop crunch of artillery fire continued relentlessly.

"That's the Azeris bombarding us," insisted the people in Goris, under the strong but mistaken impression that this correspondent was unable to tell the difference between an artillery projectile being fired from one impacting. On the way back, we saw dozens of military lorries carrying men and arms moving in the opposite direction. One day earlier, the invasion of Khelbajar had started — the same move which Armenia would ever keep claiming as having "nothing to do with." And Armenia never officially recognised the 'Republic of Upper Karabakh'. Just before he had to send the OSCE his answer to its latest proposals, President Levon Ter-Petrossian declared in Parliament that he had no intention whatsoever of doing so.

Ter-Petrossian is the model exponent of the wave of immigration from eastern Turkey inhabitants whose parents or grandparents moved across in the aftermath of the First World War and whose younger generation embraced the Soviet regime with an ardour characteristic of the true 'desperado'. After all, civil democracy is unlikely to thrive on an empty stomach. But he is also the exponent of the political heritage left by the 'war generation': the Armenian 'reconquista'. During the mass demonstrations of 1986 and 1987, he fervently led the chants with choruses of simple but direct slogans such as "Our Lands!"

Armenia can be no less disconnected from the Karabakh issue than Azerbaijan. However, whereas in Azerbaijan most of the visible and audible symptoms are indifference and collective self-complaint, collective obsession is its main feature in Armenia. This is what pushed Ter-Petrossian quickly into the Artsakh Committee that lobbied for the Azeri province's 'liberation' — and armed its clandestine militias to the teeth.

But the president symbolised more to Armenia than nationalist rhetoric alone. To the Armenian citizen he stood first of all for Andropov's 'conducted reformism', i.e. 'adaption' of the totalitarian system in order to guarantee the system's survival without submitting its basis to discussion. Power for power's own sake, and democracy in order to maintain power instead of the contrary.

In order to materialise this principle, Ter-Petrossian had surrounded himself by the eve of independence with a company of people of unquestioning loyalty that resembled more a version of Valhalla. Among his foremost acolytes were Varo Siradeghian who was to become interior minister, future defence ministers Vazgen Sarkissian and Vazgen Manukian and most of all his 'special personal adviser' Ashot Manucharian — nicknamed 'Rasputin'. Moreover, once in power the head of state did not forget to endear the old Soviet clique to him by granting ministerial positions to people such as former Communist officials Gagik and Khosrow Arutunian. Unsurprisingly, he attempted to lure representatives of the Armenian Diaspora from the West into Armenia in much the same way. However, the response of the Diaspora was less than impessive; one of the few of its number who did get a seat in the cabinet was the American Sebu Tashjyan, who in 1992 became minister of fuel and energy.

The hapless American, however, was to bash his head against a brick wall. Fuel was only available on the black market at prices which were less than a quarter of what consumers could afford, whereas energy supplies were available a few hours a day at most, if at all. Tashjyan was of the opinion that the solution for the deadlock had to be sought in a commercially run distribution sector. Which meant that he would have to neutralise a corrupt network of civil servants. Who were far from ready to be neutralised.

When Tashjyan called on finance minister Zanik Zhanoyan to obtain state credit for imports of fuel and electricity from Iran, what he in fact got was a categorical *"nyet"* — 'former' Communist Zhanoyan was the uncrowned king of the 'grey-suit mafia' to whose own fingers the profit margin — which the commercial sector Tashjyan dreamt of had to bring in — was meant to stick. Moreover, the deposits needed to cover state credits for fuel and power supplies had been transferred to Moscow at a much earlier stage as a 'guarantee' for the import of 'crucial provisions' — such as vodka.

The unemployment rate in Armenia in 1993 stood at a shattering

75 per cent and, in some areas such as Spitak, which had been hit by a devastating earthquake in 1989, it was way over 90 per cent. Out of 3,000 factories only some two hundred were working, most of them small manufacturing plants with minor energy requirements. Levels of production for grain, dairy and other agricultural products were less than a quarter of what they had been in 1991 and less than ten per cent of levels for 1987. However, whether these figures for the previous years actually represented any form of reality is doubtful.

In summer 1991, Ter-Petrossian fulfilled one of his earlier promises and had 80 per cent of all the agricultural land in the republic converted into private property. What he omitted to do, however, was privatise the distribution sector for agricultural products — the only means by which agriculture could have become financially sound — as a result of which farmers were forced into a position where they could only sell their products to state distribution companies at below market prices, the reality of which meant that they sold their products instead on the streets and elsewhere on the 'parallel market', and the state shops stayed empty.

Thus delivered on a platter to the cut-throat free market, the ordinary citizen in Armenia was delivered a deadly blow by the government — to his wallet. Officially, inflation was at 830 per cent annually, but in reality 90 per cent of the population's loss of purchasing power was three times as high. Business life, which had been booming by the end of the 1980s, lay moribund as only a hundred or so trade firms were still functioning, and no one was harbouring any illusions as to what sort of trade firms these really were.

"I have been praised here for three weeks with great ceremony," a Lebanese businessman told me on the eve of his departure in the forever lifeless Intourist restaurant, "and I've got an long list of orders from cherry bonbons to concrete steel. But if you ask for a bank guarantee, they look at you as if they don't know what you're talking about. But then they straightaway start asking what your profit margin is likely to be and if they can't have a thirty, forty or even higher percentage of it slide into their own pockets. I have the severest doubts that any of these would-be clients I've got here even remotely thinks of ever paying the bill. And I've also got the strong impression that there's a lot of people here who think everything in life is free."

Just like Baku, Yerevan has its war refugee colony which lives on the seamy side of life. And no less than in the Azeri capital these uninvited guests appear to be welcome here. Most refugees in Yerevan have come here from poorer rural areas in Azerbaijan and only speak Azeri. In the capital, they are beaten up in the street and called "filthy Turks." In the refugee centres, most of which are derelict schools, offices and factory buildings, people noisily speak out their embittered hearts.

One tiny woman, barely five foot tall, spoke her mind: "The Armenian government? Crooks — that's what they are! Every bit of the foreign aid that comes in for us they just swindle away from us. Kerosine for our stoves we've been promised, as well as two thousand roubles [then worth $1.5] per person per month. But nothing — not a thing — has ever managed to reach us!"

Standing by me was Geldolph Everts, at the time head of the UNHCR delegation in Yerevan, who warned me in Dutch: "I've been through this before — this can take hours."

Then, with his interpreter's help: "Lady, we're doing what we can but we've been committed to work together with the local authorities. If you have any proof of what you are accusing people of doing then I advise you to go to the police or to the courts."

It is hard. Courts in this part of the world function but only for those who can pay. And as for the police, they are no less eager to fill their pockets in a somewhat less than legal way. When I was there my wallet was stolen and, as I went to report its theft, the head of the railway police visibily squirmed.

"Yes, I know that your property has been stolen," he told me. "But wouldn't it be more convenient to simply say that you've lost it? For you, that is. If not, then I've got to report the case to the examining magistrate, and you have no idea what a terrible pile of paperwork that means . . ."

Ter-Petrossian came to power thanks mainly to the support that was granted him by a majority in the old Soviet Assembly which had united in the so-called Pan Armenian National Movement (popularly dubbed the 'Ter-Petrossian Fanclub') with a view to having himself voted in as head of state at a later stage to formalise matters.

Nothing unusual here in a country that was passing through its post-colonial period. And, no more unsurprisingly, Ter-Petrossian reduced his own government to the level of a second-rate power-wielding body through the establishment of a form of intimate 'super cabinet': the National Security Council, featuring himself, Manucharian, the vice-president, the prime minister, the defence minister and the head of the security service. This was the precise apparatus that was to enable defence minister Sarkissian between 1991 and 1993 to allow tens if not hundreds of millions of dollars worth of weaponry and cash slip into Karabakh without so much as even informing the ministry of finance — and likewise, behind the backs of the ministers of justice and interior affairs, have international terrorists such as Monte Melkonian and David Davidian openly installed in the battleground.

The political motives behind these moves were clear for all to see: to cast the Dashnaks, who were in tight control of the rebellious enclave, from their throne. The remedy Sarkissian eventually employed with the president's approval was no less alarming, as he slipped in the ranks of the ASALA to bring the president's figurehead Robert Kocharian to power. It was only in Zangezur, that isolated and impenetrable fortress of old, that the Dashnaks managed to keep their crown, thanks to the local garrison commander, who was one of their own and obeyed or disobeyed orders from Sarkissian according to his whim.

Sarkissian was finally sacked in October 1992 in favour of former prime minister Vazgen Manukian. The official reason offered was that Sarkissian had signed an agreement with his Azeri peer Rahim Ghaziev. Designed by the Russian defence minister Paul Grachov, the deal included total withdrawal from Azerbaijan of precisely those Armenian troops the Armenian government had always insisted had never been in Azerbaijan. Eighteen months later Sarkissian was to be found sitting behind his old desk again as if nothing had happened. His reinstatement had come after a row between Manukian and the president, the exact cause of which has largely remained guesswork.

In spring 1995, with parliamentary elections in sight, the Dashnak leadership was suddenly placed under lock and key and the party outlawed for the remainder of the year. At once the Dashnaks proclaimed themselves the innocent victims of "grave violations of human rights." Ter-Petrossian promptly aimed a barrage of accusations at them, making constant references to "terrorism" (a linked underground terrorist organisation operating under the name of 'Dro' was claimed to have been been "dismantled") and to "drugs and arms smuggling." It is highly unlikely that the president's accusations were groundless. It is no less unlikely that the accused were the only ones involved in such practices.

Meanwhile, the occupation of Khelbajar (see previous chapters) saw all hopes for a workable solution to the deadlock dashed. Armenia's sole border post with Turkey, which had just been reopened for passenger, fuel and provision transport, was hermetically sealed again — as were the three border posts with Azerbaijan which had started functioning again only weeks earlier. Manukian had managed to draw Armenia into a such quagmire of warfare that it was difficult now to imagine how it could ever get out of it without losing a fatal amount of face.

Four UN resolutions were to be "duly noted" by Yerevan which doomed them to remain dead letters. Return to the *status quo ante* in accordance with the Azeri demand including the highest possible degree of home rule for Karabakh but only with the 1937 borders had become remote and beyond any ordinary human reckoning. Mediators were forced to admit that they were firmly back at square one — not that it was the first time nor the last. The stalemate which various diplomats, with their typical sense of understatement, would describe as a "first step on the road to peace" was in reality the de facto recognition by the international community of a phantom territory, a sanctuary based on the still smouldering remnants of an international terrorist movement which entitled itself to ignore whatever rules and supervision the outside imposed.

They had proposed recognition of a 'liberated area' in the most cynical sense, an area only half the size of the Netherlands where a few hundred thousand half-savage colonists were ruled by a self-imposed paramilitary group which answered to no one in the whole wide world.

Conclude peace with the Muslims?

"Never! Not at any price!" they raged at the Yerevan premises of what was cryptically called the 'Department for Special Programmes' — in other words the Artsakh Committee. "To survive means to fight. It's all very well for you over there in Europe, but you just wait until the Islamic hordes get their hands on where *you* live. They're already at it as it is!"

That's a tough conclusion.

But the word we have in Europe to describe this sort of language is a rather less flattering. The discreet, quiet intellectual people's deputy and supporter of the government Professor Karen Yuzbashian, who has the air of having seen it all before, merely shrugged at the suggestion

"I agree that this is no language any civilised human being should accept," she admitted. "But you must understand that at the moment Karabakh is suffering a flush of victory. But the very idea of a republic of Karabakh is naive — and the idea of a Greater Armenia which includes the territories of neighbouring countries is dangerous for our country's and our nation's survival."

Outside, little old women carried bundles of firewood on their bowed backs, and people queued for hours at the distribution centres for bread and dairy products. Elsewhere in the city, travel agencies were besieged by people who had scraped together their last savings for a one-way ticket out — where to hardly mattered.

Having dealt with the historical backgrounds of both Azerbaijan and Armenia in their present state of affairs and having taken a closer look at such phenomena as expansionism, ethnic cleansing, post-colonial political intrigue, counter-productive diplomatic interference, (oil-)business schemes, terrorism and general geopolitical abuse, it may help to review the principal causes underlying the present Azero-Armenian struggle:

Firstly, an age-old hatred inspired by mythomaniacs and cultivated by shrewd political leaders has led to a general mood among the Armenian population by which aggression towards neighbouring nations appears justified to them;

Secondly, Russia has used this state of mind to encourage the Armenian 'trouble-makers' to seize power on a local level in order to facilitate the spreading of conflict in the region, while to offer at the same time their 'protection' to Azerbaijan — in the violent conclusion of which the former colonial master can return in order to put things straight once more and thus regain control over the Southern Caucasus;

Thirdly, the whole scheme is designed — in full co-operation with the self-mythologising representatives of foreign nations and (most of all) of international organisations — to allow the issue to become as out of focus as possible so that Russia can dictate the terms for Central-West Asian oil and gas exports to Europe.

The only ones who are unwilling participants are the victims of the stalemate. And they have no one to turn to, since the political web around them is all but sealed.

As we shall see in the following chapters of this book, there are similarities between the political break-up in the south west of Azerbaijan and the cases of both breakaway areas in Georgia. But while Georgia has adapted and forged ahead regardless, Armenia still languishes in a state of somewhat less than splendid isolation — although one cannot help but admire the gritty resolution the community has shown in terms of its survival.

There has, however, appeared some glimmer of hope in this gloomy place. In the summer of 1996, inflation was halted and was later even reduced to less than one per cent a month. Ter-Petrossian had just had himself re-elected as president with an overwhelming majority of votes, leaving both the Karabakh hawks and Vazgen Manukian's Communist fossils far behind.

That was the good news.

The bad news for the Armenian political establishment came not from Azerbaijan this time, but from Georgia where, in the autumn of the same year, the Karabakh syndrome was rearing its ugly head in the southern districts of Ninotsminda, Akhalkalaki and Akhaltsikhe, areas populated by a narrow majority of ethnic Armenians. Unofficial roadblocks appeared, manned by just as unofficial Armenian militiamen. Pamphlets were distributed urging the Armenian population to "restore historic Armenian territorial rights." Georgians were subject to harassment, leading to thousands of them fled the area.

"We have seen this all before . . . ," it was muttered despondently in Tbilisi — echoed no less despondently in Baku.

Eyes full of expectation turned now to the most celebrated personality in the Southern Caucasus, Eduard Shevardnadze.

9

The cross, the sword
& the ram's horn

"The traditional Georgian is a voluptuous eater and drinker, a talented poet and artist and a tireless fighter." These words come straight from the mouths of people who are supposed to know what they are talking about: social scientists from Tbilisi, themselves born and raised Georgians. As if by way of proof, the Georgian version of the Arabic *salaam aleikum* 'peace be with you' is *gamarjobat* 'may victory be yours!' Returning victoriously and loaded down with booty from the battlefield is the best one can wish someone else. After the phlegmatic Azeri and the gloomy Armenian, portraying the Georgian character proves substantially more complicated.

Nothing is more hazardous than trying to put a 'nation's character' into words. In the case of the Armenians and the Azeris I have already wronged a significant minority among them; in the case of the Georgians I am more likely to wrong a significant majority. But then, what can one conclude in observing a nation that not only produced a Stalin and a Beria but also a Gamsakhurdia?

There are many nationalities and peoples living within the borders of present-day Georgia, most numerous of which by far are the Georgians themselves. The most important indigenous Georgian 'sub-ethnic entities' are the Kartlians, the Kakhetians, the Pshavs, the Khevsurs (who may or may not be the descendants of Crusaders driven out of Palestine by the Muslims), the Rachans, the Imeretians, the Gurians (whose offspring includes Shevardnadze), the Mingrelians (Gamsakhurdia's tribe), the Lechkhumians, the Ajarians and the Svans. All these ethnic subdivisions are considered 'pure Georgians', or 'Kartvelians', in addition to which are a significant number of non-Georgian minorities, including the Tsova-Tush (who speak a language akin to Chechen) and others to whom attention shall be given at a later stage.

Odette Keun, an ardent French Socialist who travelled through Georgia at the time of the Russian Revolution shortly after the foundation of the Transcaucasian Federation — a trip ending up in a romantic relationship with her guide, Prince Giorgi Tsereteli, after her first guide, another prince named Davit Chavchavadze, relative of both the illustrious poet Ilia and the last Georgian king Irakli II, had attempted suicide after squandering his employer's financial resources at the gambling table — tried to put into words her impressions of the various segments of the Georgian nation with the faultless intuition which is the privilege of a thoroughly spoilt Parisienne.

To the reader today the results must seem rather shocking. In the dedication to her book, the author renders tribute to "this loveable and virile race" as it had been revealed to her by her (second) prince — the details of which are not hard to guess. The Khevsurs and the Svans, for example, are singled out as victims of Odette Keun's wrath as far as the treatment of (their own) women is concerned, who are said to have little more status than domestic animals. In respect to the spiritual development of the male population, the Pshavs, however, had "made considerable progress" and therefore had become the "meilleurs éléments de la population géorgienne."

In reality, the mountain peoples north of Tbilisi had already gathered up a considerable number of poets, scientists and other men of the world well before the end of the 19th century. Rapiel Erestavi and Vazha Pshavela immersed themselves in the ancient mountain cultures and found significantly more than the rather anecdotic findings of Western accounts. The Khevsur tradition used to be — and these days is becoming once more so — a unique kaleidoscope of early Christian, Islamic and pre-Christian elements. In Shatili, the impressive rock fortress high up in the mountains of Khevsureti near the Chechen border, one can find shaman, polytheistic and other customs still very much alive up to this day. It is striking that in contrast to the warlike gamarjobat! the greeting formula here should be salaam! . . .

Still, insisted Mlle Keun, the Svans should be viewed as "greedy, aggressive" — and on top of that as sex maniacs in such proportions that Russian middle-aged women in the belle epoque are reported to have travelled there with no aim other than the resolution of the sexual problems suffered at home. Though she seems to have touched on a nerve (since even today in Georgia the Svans are the butt of many of the country's regionalist jokes), Keun throttles down at the end of her book, conceding the Svans a more noble "haute allure de chevalier."

The Svans themselves claim to be direct descendants of the Colchians — a claim by no means questioned by such historians from across the centuries as the Frenchmen Dubois de Montpereux, Chantre and De Bernoville, the Britons Telefer and Freshfield, the German Radde and even numerous Russian ethnologists. According to Svan legend, in Old Testament times their forefathers moved towards the north from Chaldea to finally settle in the lands between Ararat and the Black Sea, present-day Guria and Ajaria. Although most of the neighbouring tribes came to be driven eastwards by Greek colonists in later times, the Svans took to the snow-locked mountains of the Western Caucasus. Ever since then, they have stayed there among the peaks of their Svanetia, secure in their reputation of a proven allergy to imposed rule.

It is well beyond the limits of this book to give each facet of the Georgian its full ethno-cultural background, whatever gap in available documentation it would fill. Moreover, progress has turned most of these fierce knights and warriors into uniform tax-paying citizens who, instead of galloping on horseback over the mountain ridges and through the wild valleys, are content to drive their Ladas (and the odd Mercedes-Benz) along the motorways — it being only their style of driving which reminds one of the impetuous riders their ancestors used to be in days of yore.

The Georgians are one of the few nations which were already in existence before the waves of Indo-European invasions which started in the 12th century BC. This honour they share with the Lapps and the Basques, and there are those who claim the existence of some trace of an ethnic and linguistic kinship between the latter and the Georgians, even if numerous scholars are now beginning exclude this possibility.

The history here certainly has roots that are deep. In the company of countries like Lebanon, Iraq and Yemen, Georgia is one of those to claim the Garden of Eden was situated on its territory. And, as suggested earlier, the 'Land of the Giants' referred to in the Book of Genesis where Cain took flight was in all probability the Caucasus — the 'Giants' being the Titans, the cosmic warriors that come have down to us through Hellenic mythology.

Where the name Georgia itself originates from no one exactly knows. It is doubtful the country was simply called after its patron saint St George (although the country is dotted with his features in innumerable religious icons and other images) but such devotion to killers of dragons and other demonic creatures is hardly exceptional among traditionally warlike nations. According to less folklorical explanations, the root of the word may perhaps be found in *Horzh*, a word of Sumerian origin, which gave rise in later times to the Persian term 'Gurjistan', and still later to the Russian 'Gruzhia'.

The Georgians are descendants of the Ibero-Hittites, a people who during the gap between the Babylonians and the Assyrians, briefly controlled a vast empire that stretched from the Caucasus to Lower Mesopotamia. 'East' and 'West' Georgia developed separately over long sections of history. The origin of the western kingdom roughly coincides with the history of Colchis.

The first united kingdom in what was to be East Georgia dates from 322 BC when the *erestavi*, or lord, of Kartli, by the name of Azon, proclaimed the lands described by Greek and Roman historians as Iberia to be a sovereign kingdom with Mtskheta as its capital. The kingdom was to hold out within admittedly fluctuating borders until 69 AD, when the Romans crushed it under their boot.

As for the people themselves, the Iberians, in the annals of Urartu which have survived, they are referred to as the 'Diakhoni', whereas Assyrian records refer to them as 'Diaokhi'. In the oldest written records found in the area itself, the Georgians are referred to as 'Kartveli', a term they still use to this day. This has led to the name, both classical and modern, of Georgia, 'Sakartvelo' — as well as to the claim of the Kartvelians that they are the progenitors of all Georgians.

Throughout ancient history East Georgia, along with most of the other territories in Transcaucasia, found itself constantly trampled on by the boots of one global empire after another, while the West was meantime busy developing into an advanced organised state that somehow managed to preserve its independence until well after the beginning of our era. During the first century AD, the land was occupied by the Romans who renamed it Lazica after the Laz who lived there, ancestors of the Caucasian people who live in present-day Ajaria and north-east Turkey on the Black Sea coast. In time, one by one they conquered neighbouring tribes such as the Gurians and the Mingrelians. The Imeretians also fell to the Romans, although they gave their name to the kingdom which later cut itself free from Rome during the third century AD.

During the Middle Ages, both East and West Georgia were forced to defend themselves against the continuous stream of invaders pushing in from all sides: the Huns from the north, the Central Asians from the east, the Persians from the south and the Byzantines from the west. The relative strategic positions of both kingdoms as well as their internal divisions and struggles made them easy prey for any expansionist-minded power, including the most recent, the Russians, who to this day still have little ability to control their greed.

As a result of all this, the Georgians share with the Armenians and the Azeris the ability to blame others with astonishing skills of rhetoric and distortion through whatever stage in history the country was passing. Similarly to Armenia, Christian martyrdom and the Crusader syndrome still play a key role in any Georgian's interpretation of world history: "You should know in fact that Georgia is the oldest Christian country in the world . . ."

But isn't that precisely the same as what the Armenians claim for themselves?

"That's their problem. Whereas Armenia only became Christian as late as the fourth century, we were building cathedrals here as early as one hundred and fifty years before!"

So then, to the Faithful! — *Gaumarjos! Bolomde!* 'Drink up'! These are the Georgian passwords that signal that you have to empty your glass in a single gulp. It's a reminder of the tradition of when Georgians drank not from glasses but from ram's horns, which cannot be steadied on a table if there is wine still left in them. No more argument!

Dipsomania is the perfect way to save one's face in this type of awkward discussion and still keep spirits high, be it at festive or less festive occasions. And there are more festive occasions than others in Georgia — at least two per day, it sometimes appears.

As it is, during the reign of King Rev (187-213) Christianity was allowed to be freely practised in Georgia, while in Rome the Pope and his followers were still forced to operate in secret. At the Council of Nicea in 325 AD there was already a special envoy who represented the Georgian congregation. The following year, a Byzantine nun, Nino of Cappadocia, convinced the Georgian King Mirian he should proclaim Christianity as his state religion. In the fifth century, the Georgian archbishop, who so far had operated under the authority of the Antiochian Church, was granted the rank of catholicos and eventually came to claim the title of patriarch in the tenth century, head of the newly autocepahlous Church.

Georgia has even more worldly heroes than spiritual ones. The image of the Iberian King Vakhtang Gorgasali, 'Wolf-Head', has come to hold the same significance for the Georgians as that of Babek and Joanshir for the Azeris. In Ancient Colchis the Byzantines had usurped the Romans' role after almost two centuries of independence, and Iberia had come under Persian hegemony. According to Georgian tradition, it was Vakhtang who was stirred into taking up his sword and shield, mounted his warrior's steed and after years of battle managed to reunite Georgia.

In the process he managed to defy not only his foreign overlords but most of the local *erestavis* and *aznauris* — 'warlords' — many of whom put up resistance, unwilling to countenance such changes since most of them owed their own positions of power to those foreign superpowers that ruled from afar. The new king celebrated his victory by building a new city which he named Tbilisi and proclaimed it capital of the newly integrated Georgia.

Unfortunately, it was not to hold. Within less than a decade, the neighbouring superpowers had divided Georgia among themselves and Vakhtang came to a sad end. The Persians in particular wrought terrible havoc, ransacking churches and convents and giving the common people and the nobility the choice between conversion to Mazdeism or death. The oldest preserved manuscript in Georgian, which describes the life and death of the first martyr in Georgian Church history, St Shushanik, dates from this stage of the fifth century.

But the Persians were to suffer their own setback in the seventh century with the decline of the Sassanids (see above), upon which the Arabs and the Seljuqs subsequently filled the void and attempted to impose Islam upon Georgia. The fact that they failed to do so, in strong contrast to Azerbaijan, fills the common Georgian — believer and unbeliever alike — with glowing pride still to this day.

An end to all this religious, political and economic oppression arrived with the 11th century. This was Georgia's Golden Age, comparable with England under the Tudors, Spain under the kings of Aragon, the Netherlands under the early stadtholders, Germany under the Hohenzollern and France under Louis XIV. The names of the kings of the Bagrationi dynasty — such as Davit IV (the 'Reconstructor' or 'Builder') and, most of all, Queen Tamar — are to be found easily on any Georgian's lips. Any *tamada* today — the toastmaster who during endless banquets pronounces the most important toast speeches himself and designates other orators one by one — is not considered a good *tamada* if a toast is not especially made to Davit and Tamar and, ideally, to each of the other monarchs too.

Davit succeeded where Vakhtang had failed and, having consolidated his authority, managed to dispense gradually with all feudal privileges in favour of the growing merchant class — not unlike the way the later Tudors were to do in England. He also expanded the territory under Georgian supremacy, reconquering Tbilisi and for a time the Georgian banner waved from Erzurum to Baku — even if most of the more remote territories were Georgian in name only, their local princes ruling the same way they had always done in the guise of tributary lords.

Davit's most renowned feat of arms was the Battle of Didgori, the 'Georgian Trafalgar' which took place on August 14th 1121. With an army of only 80,000 men-in-arms he delivered a shattering defeat on a 600,000-strong coalition consisting of Persians, Arabs and Seljuqs — who for once in their history had united, having momentarily ceased their attempts to finish each other off. The only outsiders who came to the Georgians' aid in this their most glorious hour were a thousand or so Frankish Crusaders. As it was, Davit's army was considerably less 'Christian' than the cause it was pushed forward for, since its military core consisted of Turkish Kipchak warriors. The Kipchaks, inhabitants of the steppes to the north east, were part Muslim, part Buddhist and part animist, but had a general aversion for Persians and Arabs alike, while with the Seljuqs they also had old scores to settle. In similar fashion to the Swiss in Europe, they were widely in demand as mercenary warriors who looked favorably upon the Georgians as patrons.

The Bagrationi dynasty — to which Davit and his granddaughter Tamar belong — stretches back to the tenth century AD, when, on the initiative of the *erestavi* of Kartli, Ioane Marushidze, the torn-up feudal conglomerate of Georgia was reunited through the joining of the petty-principalities of North and South Tao, Kartli and Tegris Abkhazeti. The first king of the new entity was Bagrat III from whom the dynasty took its name.

Today, little more remains of the once glorious dynasty apart from three disparate royalist parties, each acting in favour of a different pretender, each of whom lives in voluntary exile: one in Italy, one in Greece and one in Spain. The last, Prince Mikhail, speaks no Georgian, is a former racing motorist and, at present, a Spanish branch director of a leading car manufacturer.

It is doubtful whether Georgia could ever become the first and, for the time being, only former Soviet republic to be transformed into a constitutional monarchy — even if reference to Spain where the royal house has proved to be such an effective buffer against Francoism has been the subject of national debate on more than one occasion. The fact is that ever since the Russian occupation under Alexander I, the Georgian royal house has seen its influence dwindle steadily from the scene. Even enlightened spirits such as Queen Tamar (the first monarch in world history to abolish the death penalty) to the late 18th century King Irakli II have always acted in an exclusively authoritarian manner that bears not even the remotest resemblance to the transfer of power to the people as effected in such kingdoms as Great Britain or the Netherlands.

Whatever the case, the fairy tale was definitively shattered with the advent of the Mongol invasions. The awesome extent of destruction the *Didi Turkoba* or 'Great Turkdom' brought along with it is the reason why so many works of art, documents and architecture from the times of Davit and Tamar have been lost to future generations. The Mongol leader Timur, who never permanently occupied Tbilisi but had it ransacked and burnt down several times — since he suffered from an insatiable tendency to turn everything that had an air of Christianity into smoke and ashes — more than decimated the entire Georgian cultural heritage.

One of the few works of literature that has been preserved, be it in a version written centuries later and which in all probability includes substantial modifications, is Shota Rustaveli's epic poem the *Vepkhistqaosani* or *Knight in the Panther Skin*. Rustaveli is for Georgia what Nizami is for Azerbaijan. The epic — which, curiously enough, is not set in Georgia at all but in India and the Islamic world — tells the tale of bosom-friends Tariel and Avtandil, noblemen who are both in love with the daughters of their respective sovereigns — one beloved being the Indian princess Nestani Darajan and the other the Arabian successor to the throne, Tinatin. Bizarre adventures by the politically inspired lovers (although the author, according to the extant edition, excludes any political or other non-spiritual interests and ensures that it is only noble passion that inspires both knights) featuring heroic deed after heroic deed end finally in sumptuous wedding feasts — and they all live happily ever after.

Rustaveli Avenue in Tbilisi is the Boulevard St Germain of Transcaucasia. It features the peculiar opera building built in fake Persian style on the orders of Tsar Nicholas I's viceroy to Georgia, Prince Mikhail Vorontsov. Sugar cake-like palaces and pavilions are here by the dozen, and appear rather well preserved with the exception of the belle epoque Hotel Tbilisi (the erstwhile Orient Hotel where the Republic of Azerbaijan was once proclaimed) which has been turned into a piece of holed Swiss cheese by Gamsakhurdia's weapons once he spotted his adversaries taking up position in its windows.

But today people lounge along the avenue like they once used to — only these days they stroll in jeans and T-shirts and drive like madmen in Ladas, Volgas and here and there a Mercedes or two. A century and a half ago, people strolled as well, but then they were dressed in stiff costumes and waving capes, and rode in carriages and coaches instead of four-wheel drives and trolleybuses.

Tolstoy provides an insightful description of the Russian upper class in the conquered Georgian capital in his novel *Hajji Murat* as a world of glittering chandliers, waving evening dresses and fountains of champagne. But there were also night-long orgies, widespread gambling, suicides and deadly duels over nothing. Along with civilisation, much-criticised Oblomovism was imported into Georgia as well. This was the period too when the writer Lermontov so tragically ended his life shortly after completing his first and only novel *A Hero of Our Time* — a book which, for all it mattered, sketches a far from friendly image of the Caucasian nations.

It certainly all mattered little to the Tbilisi elite: the party was to go on no matter what. And as they partied, half the country was ablaze, troops ransacked poverty stricken villages and ran women and children through with their bayonets.

"La Russie envahit pour detruire" — "Russia invades to destroy," Alexandre Dumas wrote bluntly in *Le Caucase*, his account of his travels there, and this he concluded despite the generosity and friendliness with which his Russian hosts in Georgia received him. He described how villages and estates were ruthlessly razed to the ground, how the country's 'reconstruction' remained a dead letter because of corruption and lack of organisation. Instead, the land and its nation were squeezed and plundered. Countless Armenian, Tatar and Georgian traditional feudal lords were reduced to beggars, forced to sell their properties to Russian peers at give-away prices only to lose that money through ill-judged speculation and nightly gambling sprees.

As described earlier, in a similar manner to Azerbaijan, Georgia was a chaotic conglomerate of feudal principalities on the eve of Russian domination, who were too busy fighting out their internecine feuds to the utter detriment of their communities. This placed them badly for resistance to the Persian threat from the south and the Ottoman from the west and so laid them open to Russian offers of 'protection'. The 'alliance' concluded between Tsar Paul I and King Giorgi XIII became a model for the scenario that was to repeat itself time and again in decades to come. After the treaty was signed in early 1801, the commander-in-chief of the Caucasian Army, General Knorring, who was in charge of the whole operation, already had the arrest warrants signed by the Tsar for the Crown Prince Davit and other influential figures at the Georgian court. Against all their warnings the Georgian sovereign bowed to the agreement, and so in effect sold out his nation.

It was not the last time something like this had happened — nor was it the first. Two decades before, in July 1783, King Irakli II had concluded a similar treaty of 'friendship and co-operation' with Empress Catherine II, after the Khan of Karabakh's example. Shortly afterwards, the Georgian monarch, ever loyal to his word, refused to comply with a plan devised by his neighbour Agha Mohammed to form a buffer state between Russia and Iran in the form of a federation with Azerbaijan under Georgian sovereignty. A large number of Azeri feudal lords, among whom were those of Shirvan, Sheki and the Sultan of Ilusu, showed their willingness to comply, but they swiftly saw their plan doomed to failure as it became clear that Khan Ibrahim and King Irakli refused to co-operate. Yet both leaders would later discover that the Russians were hardly appreciative of their integrity.

In 1795-96 the Iranians invaded Georgia and Karabakh and the Russians promised to send troops and arms, but after a month they informed their allies that, regrettable as it was, it was too late for action. Come 1801, the Russians did intervene, but not in the way the Georgians had expected. In 1802, the Russians occupied Kakheti and the local ruling family ordered to pack their bags. General Lazarev, who gallantly came to the Princess Miriam himself to offer her his personal escort to her place of exile, had a dagger run through his heart by his would-be protegée. Among the princes only one, Alexander, escaped to Persia where he immediately started gathering a guerrilla army.

With Alexander's backing, a popular revolt broke out in Kartli-Kakheti, in 1810, only to end in the mass destruction of villages and estates throughout the countryside. Over 20,000 farmers and townsmen were slaughtered by Russian troops and many more that number carted off to Siberia into exile. According to tradition, Tsar Nicholas I had toyed later with the idea of deporting the whole Georgian population to the Far East, and he would have done so had it not been for Vorontsov who persuaded him against it.

However, the suppression of the Kakheti revolt by no means meant the end of Georgian resistance. After two years of struggle and vain attempts by the ruling family to come to a compromise with the Russian governor Tomasov, who had taken over command in Tbilisi, the region of Imereti was occupied. In Guria, which had been occupied on paper but where there was little Russian military presence, revolt broke out in 1819 after an attempt by the Russians to dispossess all owners of private property. The results were massacres and ransackings. In Samstskhe, the region managed to entrench itself against the Russians until the Russian offensive against Turkey in 1828. In Mingrelia, the local leaders concluded a treaty with the Russians which permitted the ruling family to keep their throne as vassal princes. Only in 1857, after the Crimean War, did Tsar Nicholas I tear up the agreement and send the last remaining Mingrelian vassal princess into "honorable exile."

In that same year, the Russian army invaded the mountainous area of Svanetia. General Gagarin, who supervised the operation, personally went to the Svan Prince Dadeshkeliani with the intention of personally handing him the order for his surrender and the warrant for his arrest. The prince proved to be just as fierce as the lowland Princess Miriam had been and promptly delivered the impetuous general a bullet through the head. Sadly, the prince met an ignominious end before a firing squad, his family exiled to Siberia.

From that point on, the only corners of Georgia that remained unconquered were Upper or 'Free' Svanetia, where a unique communal system was preserved until 1869, and Abkhazia, which is a story in itself and a subject that will be attended to in later chapters.

Meanwhile, a Georgian intelligentsia *avant la lettre* had organised itself, shaped by a bizarre sequence of events. In 1825, the so-called December revolt of liberal tendency had been nipped in the bud. General Yermolov, under whose supervision the major part of Georgian occupations had taken place, had been behind the liberal revolutionary Decembrist movement but, in contrast to numerous intellectuals such as Pushkin and Marlinsky, no one had ever dared touch him. He had, after all, played a hero's role at the Battle of Borodino and enjoyed great popularity. As a result, he took a complete batallion of free thinkers such as Pushkin into the Caucasus, who took refuge in Tbilisi where they enjoyed the freedom to write as they pleased and to communicate with the local elite. The arrival of these Russian free thinkers naturally made a deep impression on the Georgian nationalists.

Invigorated by the fresh blood and in the wake of the recent failed revolts, these nationalists tried to deal with their new rulers through more advanced means: coup d'etat. In December 1832, however, their 'Conspiracy of the Patriots' was detected and its leaders arrested. It was not until 1870 that the intellectuals, united under the banner of the Meore Dasi or 'Second Circle', found the courage once more to write political studies, manifestos and hold demonstrations.

By now, the European upheavals of 1848 were already history and although those events passed unnoticed by the Russian 'Prison of Nations', the democratic ideas which in Europe were becoming reality gradually managed to find fertile ground in upper circles. At the same time, however, another ideological mainstream started flowing in from Europe — Socialism, which was to disrupt the flow of the resistance movement against their foreign masters. Thus, Georgia's poet philosophers, such as Akaki Tsereteli and Ilia Chavchavadze, whose statues still stand near the House of Parliament in Tbilisi (miraculously saved from the shoot-out during the coup against Gamsakhurdia when the rest of the area was merely blackened rubble), called themselves Georgian nationalists when, in reality, they were under the strong influence of Russian populism as expressed by Herzen and Belyinsky.

Alexander III soon put an end in the most radical way to all the free-thinking tendencies and reforms existing in his empire after his predecessor's fateful death — in all probability, not realising that in doing so he was already putting his own hapless successor's head on the block. As it was, if he had been able to have it his own way, he would have happily reintroduced serfdom.

*

As in other remote parts of the empire, there was scarcely any need for this in Transcaucasia. The abolition of serfdom in 1869 (eight years after its abolition in Russia proper) brought the vast majority of peasants in the Transcaucasus more misery than relief. Although they had the right to buy the land they worked on from its owners, the authorities set prices which were so high that those who did buy ended up in such debt they would never be able to repay it. As a result, the deal's security — the land — was returned to the large land-owners while the former serfs themselves were doomed to 'labour long-lease', which in practice meant the same conditions as the previous serfdom they had endured or worse.

Industry in Georgia was hardly developed in those days, the only exception being Batumi, which served as Baku's main oil output terminal. As late as 1886, the labour force of Kutaisi and Tbilisi working in the industrial sector only acounted for 12,000 and revenue for the sector as a whole was no more than ten million roubles. The rest of the country consisted of rural land managed along medieval agricultural lines, producing a similar revenue. As the end of the century drew near, social conditions in terms of inequality and lawlessness in Georgia were, to put it bluntly, appalling.

The appearance on the scene in 1892 of the Mesame Dasi ('Third Circle'), the Georgian equivalent to the Azeri Mollah Nasreddin group which was also active in Tbilisi, coincided therefore with a environment that was far grimmer than it had been for its 1870 predecessor. The leader of this latest movement was the Social Democrat Noa Zhordania — the same Zhordania who was later to become president of the first independent republic of Georgia in 1918. But tensions between radical Socialists belonging to the First International and their rival 'revisionists' soon showed within the Third Circle — although strenuous efforts were made to exclude the more radical elements. In 1898, for example, a young man answering to the name of Iosep Jughashvili, a.k.a. Stalin, was expelled from the 'Dasi' on account of his "aggressive behaviour and tendency to conspiracy." Other members, however, were allowed to proclaim the ideas of Marx and Plekhanov, provided they did it in a more discreet fashion; among their number was the future leader of Soviet Georgia Philip Makharadze.

By one of the gates through which one enters the old city of Tbilisi, a three foot high or so statue may be seen of an old fellow wearing a proletarian cap and leaning on a walking stick. All that remains of the stick is the handle in his hand. I have baptised him *'Muzhchinoshka'* — an expression in Russian similar to 'Pop' or the French *'Pépère'*. Who or what he represents I have never quite discovered, but he seems to me a shrivelled image of Stalin, stripped of all his glamour.

At the theological seminar where Iosep Jugashvili studied during his teenage years, the mood was less devoted than grimly nationalistic. The future Social Democrat leader Silvester Jibladze as well as the future Communist leader and president of Soviet Georgia Mikhail Tskhakaya studied there until 1886, when they were expelled because of their suspected involvement in the murder of the Russian head of their institute. Another suspect, Lado Ketkhoveli, wandered off to Europe where he fell in with the Socialist International, to which in later days he was to introduce Jugashvili. Another personality in the future dictator's younger years was a young Russian intellectual who had been exiled to Transcaucasia like Pushkin, but for different reasons: Mikhail Kalinin. Pushkin, after all, was hardly the left-winger and mass-murderer Kalinin would become, the clandestine co-ordinator of strikes, robbery and sabotage.

1901 was a most exciting year for Georgia and for the young Jughashvili — in a number of respects it resembled 1989. For the first time a May the First celebration was held in Tbilisi. But on March 21st most of the organisers were thrown behind bars after a crackdown by the authorities; it was only by sheer luck that Jugashvili managed to escape their net. From then on he was forced to work underground.

In fact the May celebration took place on April 22nd because of the difference between the Russian and European calendars. That Sunday, a crowd of some 2,000 'workers' gathered in the Soldatsky Bazaar, off Rustaveli Avenue The bazaar still exists, albeit now in grey concrete. Police and Cossacks waited, bayonets at the ready, around the corner. It was a miracle that only a dozen or so injured were reported and no one was killed. The number of arrests came to a mere fifteen.

But things were not set to remain so restrained. In August 1905, protest rallies in Tbilisi were repeatedly dispersed by Cossacks, resulting in over a hundred people killed within a fortnight. Mass detentions were to follow in which the main target was the Georgian clergy who had taken the lead in the national democratic movement that strived for the re-establishment of the old kingdom.

After the infamous 'manifesto' issued by Nicholas II, seen by liberal tendencies as a political breakthrough but as a provocation by the left, revolt spread from Tbilisi to the rest of the country. In Kutaisi in particular months of utter anarchy followed as Socialist cells paralysed public life.

The outbreak of the First World War created more rifts within the Georgian national movement than the existing controversy between 'nationalist' and 'internationalist' tendencies. Pitched against each other on both sides were supporters and opponents of fighting on the Russian side;

as it was, large factions made no secret of their sympathy for the Austro-German alliance. However, Turkish participation in the Axis was to tip the balance in favour of the pro-Russian party. Even the so-called Transcaucasian Commissariat, which was established in 1917 and acquired legitimate status after the first democratic elections in Georgian history and which was de facto a sovereign government, remained loyal to the old Russian Empire until April 9th 1918.

It was only the Treaty of Brest-Litovsk on March 3rd 1918 — in which, without consulting Tbilisi, the Russians handed over Batumi, Artvin, Olti, Ardahan, Alexandropol and Kars over to the Turks — that made the Seim (the federate government of Georgia, Armenia and Azerbaijan) decide to break with the Russians once and for all . . . or so they thought.

The Seim itself had been an ineffective body from the start. Its deputies had exhausted themselves through ceremony and symbolism as one cultural centre after another, one theatre after another was given a grand opening, and more money was spent on monuments than on provisions. Before spring 1918 drew to an end, all-out war between Georgia and Armenia over Akhalkalaki and Alaverdi had ended in a fragile truce without the central government being able to disarm the opposed parties. Azerbaijan and Armenia kept fighting it out over Karabakh as if no Seim existed. In reality, the authority of the commissioner of defence ended at his office's doorstep while his command over the federal army existed only on paper, as its regiments busied themselves fighting each other, every commander his own supreme commander.

Other departments were scarcely in a better position: salaries were no longer paid, and each sector had look out for itself. The Seim continued to take contradictory decisions, as both Parliament and the council of ministers ruled according to whoever of the various Dashnaks, Mensheviks, Socialist Revolutionaries, Mussavat and any number of splinter parties happened to be present.

Thus, property of the feudal land owners was nationalised in the summer of 1917. The decision, however, failed to be put into legislation, upon which two months later the whole matter had been reversed. In the meantime, farmers, encouraged by Bolsheviks and 'Narodniki' (countryside Socialists) operating from Russia, had taken the law into their own hands and continued to do so after the Seim had proclaimed that everyone would be free to buy and sell property but that disowning it would be out of the question.

So, on Febrary 24th 1918, in Stalin's home town of Gori, people stormed the local landowner's estate, murdered the inhabitants and established a farmers' council which divided the land among the peasants. Later, on March 15th, a train was seized by government troops which appeared to be loaded with Red Guards on the way from Rostov to Chiaturi, on the border between Racha and Imereti, where they planned to murder the local landowner Prince Tseretseli and proclaim a 'commune' there.

The Bolsheviks' actions were becoming more and more ruthless: on March 10th 1918, they captured two Russian cruisers and used them to bombard Sukhumi. On the same day, a terrorist group infiltrated from Russia blew up an ammunition depot in Trabzon killing hundreds. Sukhumi was occupied by Communists on April 14th and had the privilege of getting the first taste of what was to happen to the rest of Transcaucasia: ransacking, bombardments, destruction.

August Muls, a mining engineer from Belgium who owned a manganese mine near Chiaturi and whose diaries from those days (*In de Kaukasus*) have been preserved, wrote about the Communist intruders: "In my view they are simply bandits who seek to enrich themselves, only to disappear afterwards . . . miserable cowards!"

The first part of his description was undoubtedly true. As for the second part, the world would have to wait almost three quarters of a century to learn the truth.

On March 31st, things had got so out of hand in Georgia that the Seim finally decided to give in and nationalise the land. Two months later, the Seim was no more. In almost every corner, from Derbent and Poti, the lives of ordinary people had been turned to hell by famine, cholera and typhus epidemics. Food and other basic needs had become the monopoly of mafias who had used the general state of lawlessness to get their hands on stocks and the distribution systems. And as though this was still not enough, Bolshevik marauders made everywhere doubly unsafe.

In the third week of March, the Germans entered the Caucasian battle zone — ostensibly in a bid to tip the balance in favour of the Turks, but in reality to lay their hands on the oil wells of Baku and the lifeline connecting them between Baku and Batumi before the Turks had the chance to do so. The fact was that the Austro-German Axis had a formidable war machine primed to go, but no fuel to use it effectively since their access to Mesopotamia had been blocked by the British. In order to keep up appearances and to prevent the showdown from getting out of hand, the Germans opted for an offensive in the Northern Caucasus. On March 21st Nikolayev fell and six weeks later all the territory between Poti and Vladikavkaz was in German hands.

Meanwhile, on April 9th to be precise, the Seim formally abolished the Transcaucasian Commissariat and granted itself the status of government — this despite Denikin's threat to 'shatter' Transcaucasia (a fate shortly to be reserved for himself). Six weeks later the Republic of Georgia was proclaimed under Zhordania's leadership, soon to be confirmed through presidential elections. But this government had its say in Tbilisi and Kutaisi only. In the south west, the Turks were lords and masters, and on April 14th Sarikamish fell and a week later all of Guria and Ajaria was in Turkish hands. In the north west, the Germans set the rules, whereas in the Central Caucasus the Bolsheviks controlled all strategic spots. On top of that, local gang leaders fought out their own bloody feuds against each other as well as against anyone else who dared interfere.

Muls, himself a Belgian and fervently anti-German, vented his rage at one point — after the failed raid on Chiaturi — against the local brigands: "Germany will teach them what is most appropriate in this place: freedom . . . or the whip!"

On taking office, Zhordania signed the Treaty of Batumi, ceding all Turkish occupied territories and immediately afterwards sending a request to Berlin to become a German protectorate. Within two months, between 25,000 and 30,000 German troops had landed on Georgian shores.

The Germans were hailed by the Georgian population as heroes. Rather than the butchers of Verdun, they were viewed as bringers of order and civilisation — were not the Germans after all the proponents of Schopenhauer, Kant and Nietzsche?

But it was not to last. On losing the Great War, both Turkey and Germany evacuated the Transcaucasus with the British ready to take their places. Along with the Azeris and the Armenians, the Georgians were promised at the peace negotiations that "full consideration will be given in respect to either's national aspirations." How it all really ended is a matter of record.

Stalin had a number of fatal habits — fatal, that is, for those who came into contact with him. One habit was the ability to seamlessly convert difference of opinion and rivalry into rage and grudge-bearing. Zhordania, who knew him well, must have known at the back of his mind that Stalin installed in Moscow meant his own fate sealed from the very first day.

On May 7th 1920, the Moscow-based regime officially recognised Georgia as a sovereign state, making also the promise to refrain from all interference within its borders and to prohibit any similar activity aimed against Georgia from Russian territory. In his turn, Zhordania promised to have the Georgian Communist party legalised and to release all political prisoners.

Jean Marin, correspondent of the *Journal de Genève* who visited Georgia at the same time Odette Keun was roaming its mountain slopes, was forced to remark: "Russia is playing with Georgia like a cat plays with a mouse."

Before the end of the year, both Armenia and Azerbaijan were occupied. Meanwhile, Georgia had been formally recognised by 22 countries as a sovereign state. An army of 160,000 troops had been mobilised and arms and ammunition had been ordered — and paid for in advance — from France after the British had refused, "in order not to give the Russians a pretext for aggression."

In reality, Lloyd George and Krassin had already concluded their gentlemen's agreement in London according to which the British committed themselves to non-intervention and compliance with Russian domination over Transcaucasia in exchange for an attractive trade deal. This was how British troops remained in Iran. And the arms owed by France never came. On February 21st, Sergo Orjonikidze led the 11th Red Army into Georgia. On February 25th, Tbilisi fell. On March 17th, after several attempts to salvage what they could of Georgia's sovereignty, Zhordania and his ministers fled the country.

Merab Mamardashvili — a modern philosopher who out of principle never drinks vodka but sticks to Georgian wine — in 1990 on the eve of the great storm over the Caucasus wrote: "Each Georgian is his own king. This is exactly what has always preserved Georgia from total slavery."

He should have added that one cannot eat domination.

This cowardly attitude of the West did not prevent the Svans, who had revolted against the Bolsheviks in 1922, from calling on the governments of France, Great Britain and Italy for help at the precise time when these three governments were negotiating with the Kremlin on normalising relations. Earlier, in mid October 1921, a workers' revolt in Tbilisi had already been crushed mercilessly by the Soviets. The Svans' own rebellion soon spread to Kakheti where workers occupied the Muls manganese mines near Chiaturi. The results were devastating: mass executions, deportations, purges and the 'abolition' of Georgia, which Stalin merged into a new Transcaucasian Federation that heralded a treaty of 'Eternal Friendship and Co-operation' with the Russian Federation.

The bloody scenes of 1921-22 were to repeat themselves in 1929-30 on the occasion of the forced collectivisation of agriculture. There were uprisings, particularly in the western part of the country, and in many areas Soviet officials were forced to create 'patriotic committees' which then seized power. One event still remembered from this period is the tale of the 'Sun Virgin', a young woman from Tusheti who set off on a protest 'March on Tbilisi' followed by an ever-swelling crowd of women and children. But they never reached their destination — a Red Army brigade was waiting to ambush them on the road to the capital. Thousands died in the hail of machine-gun fire, and for the survivors a one-way trip to Siberia lay in store.

*

"What has happened here since 1921 is too horrifying for words. Never, not once, has the truth has been told, nor will it ever be written down. We have been educated with lies and even those few who imagined they'd caught a glimpse of reality kept their mouths shut and put it out of their minds," came the chilling words of my host.

I was in a rustic quarter, built in the 1950s, on the edge of Tbilisi. It could easily be the well-heeled outer ring of a French provincial town; it certainly looks plusher than the average suburb in any part of Britain, not to mention Spain or Italy. The trolleybus line ends here and the driver politely asked me if I was sure that this was the place I was supposed to go, and if I knew where to walk from here.

As it happened, I didn't, and so I requested, and got the help of a friendly woman who spoke fluent English, at a travel agency on the corner. She made a phone-call for me to the man I was to meet, a man you could say is a personification of the nation's history.

Nikolaz Cherkedishvili came to pick me up personally, as is the Georgian habit, casually dressed (shell-suits were so popular in Georgia that MPs who saw them as a trademark of their image even turned up to their Parliamentary sessions wearing them). After an uncomplicated walk (provided one knew where to go) through the apartment blocks, we arrived at the entrance of a staircase as dirty and neglected as any to be found between East Berlin and Vladivostok. But once inside his flat, everything was shiny and clean, with objets d'art on display as if there never had been a culture of the proletariat. In fact, if one disregards the staircases, there never was.

Nikolaz seemed not to be anti-Russian — in principle, at least. Instead of the fashionable English, he preferred to speak French.

"Before the Revolution, everybody spoke French," he mused. "Except Vorontsov, who spoke better English. But then, he was educated in Britain where his father had been ambassador."

He pulled out a few worn photo-albums — little more remained of the proud family whose descendant he is.

"All that we possessed in terms of trophies, paintings and other memories has been destroyed," he explained. "And all our property we lost too. In 1964, I went for the first time to the place where my father's estate once was. Hundreds of families used to earn a decent living there. But when I arrived there, nothing was left of it — the mansion was in ruins. All the farms and surrounding estates were collectivised in 1937, but no single farm in the whole area still functioned. Everything was dead, ruined, run wild."

Nikolaz's family, on his father's side, until the Revolution were the proud *erestavis* of Sakarejo, in Kakheti. Their line went back to the 19th century. The line of his mother, Princess Vadskhuadze, heir to the lords of Kardanakhi, traced its origins as far back as the seventh century.

"My grandfather on my father's side, Nikolai, was a high-ranking officer in the Russian army. He was wounded trying to save Lermontov's life. He was a personal friend of Alexander III as well as Nicholas II. He died, too young, on a campaign in Central Asia."

But it was not all stately nobility in the family. Even today, you could feel there was a slight awkwardness felt in respect to 'Aunt Sophie' Vadskhuadze, a notorious Bolshevik who married Serge Kaftaradze, one of the leaders of Communist underground, on the eve of the October Revolution.

"My father was no hero," Nikolaz declared with resignation. "As it was, there was no way you could resist the Soviets, and Stalin in particular. My father was a lawyer and remained the same anonymous office-clerk until the day of his retirement. Aside from my grandfather on my mother's side, who was a general in the Russian army, but who been long retired by the time the Revolution broke out and died in peace in 1941 at the blessed age of over a hundred, and another aunt who ended up as a dancer in Paris in Isadora Duncan's company, only my parents survived the onslaughts of the twenties and thirties. All the others, dozens of relatives of mine, were systematically exterminated."

Like Nikolaz, there are thousands with similar tales to tell in Georgia. What is certain is that unimaginable atrocities were committed by people who to this day have never had to face the consequences of their actions. But shoulders are merely shrugged at the question of whether something should be done about it.

What would be the use?

The use, of course, would send a strong signal to those who wield power today that they should think twice before flexing the slightest muscle of tyranny again.

Power wielders?

"The only ones who have any power in this place are the Russians," was the almost unanimous opinion of everyone I spoke to. And the suggestion that it was high time such a situation changed provoked the responce: "There's nothing anyone can do to stop the Russians. Not then, not now and not in the time to come."

Gamarjobat . . .

Such was the general mood in 1994. "They're back — they'll always be back whatever we try . . ." And so it had remained so for almost two centuries.

But all was not lost. Let us not forget there had always been those instances when their innate nationalism had burst forth, a phenomenon of such a proud and radical nature that it seemed almost impossible that those possessed of it were the very same traditional winers and diners who had a taste for leisure not work.

The most recent time this transformation took place was under the brief but turbulent rule of the man who became a phenomenon in himself: Zviad Gamsakhurdia, Georgia's very own 'phoenix on broken wings'.

10

Soviet frustrations & the Gamsakhurdia roadshow

O ld Gogi is 87. Every day, he takes his time as he trudges to a shabby office on Gamsakhurdia Avenue in the centre of Tbilisi. There, endlessly chatting and gossiping, the elderly men who make up the Stalyinsky Party come together on a daily basis.

Most of their number are Second World War veterans. "You want to know what the Nazis did to us? Twenty million Soviet citizens they massacred! Oh yes, then, after the victory, there could have been peace. But those treacherous social-democrat bastards in the West ruined everything. And there was no difference with their pals over here — I mean Khruschev and his cronies. Those idiots thought people could do without leaders. And they claimed that Stalin killed off intellect! But then tell me why they left us with a complete generation of engineers, artists, lawyers, men of letters, doctors and other talented intellectuals? Where did they all come from? One single generation earlier, 99 per cent of the inhabitants of this part of the world consisted of illiterate peasants, half savages. There you are, sir!"

Old Gogi could fulminate like this for hours without getting tired of it. He was the representative of an almost extinct species: the *rabochik* who, during the day, worked with the sweat of his hands, while at night he studied, by candlelight if he had to, from any book he could lay his hands on. Whole chapters he copied out by hand, thousands of references he could still quote by heart.

Being a Georgian true to his kind, Gogi had of course an opinion on everything — such as that fateful day, on March 9th 1956, when all of Tbilisi was turned upside down. According to Gogi, it was a "patriotic revolt against Khruschev and his gang of parasites, who smeared Stalin's name so they could drive the country into the abyss — which is precisely where they got it in the end!"

Others have different memories of the uprising. "It *was* a gang — of course. Thousands of former yes-men who had licked Stalin's boots for years and who all of a sudden played the valiant hero by heading off to the city centre to tear down the monuments. War veteran invalids were beaten up. I heard the slogan *'heil Hitler!'* being shouted out again and again! Patriots . . . don't make me laugh!"

What happened the next day had no one laughing, as Soviet troops entered the city centre of Tbilisi on a killing spree that left at least 500 dead — followed by over a thousand 'disappearances' as a result of KGB raids. The West simply watched silently, opting to ignore Khruschev's style of operating. Only when the blood started flowing a little closer to home in the shape of the Hungarian Uprising did a few Western eyes start to open.

The next time blood flowed on the streets of Tbilisi was not until April 1989. What happened in the 1960s and '70s is quickly told: pretty much nothing. If it was true that occasionally a person was picked up under mysterious circumstances by equally mysterious individuals in plainclothes, it was mostly someone who had studied in Moscow or Leningrad, moved into the upper circles of society and fallen foul of one of its more powerful members — or something of the kind. Better to stay here in Georgia, where things went much more smoothly. You paid a little — or a lot if you had some hotshots up against you — if you had a 'problem', but there was virtually no real danger.

Corruption both morally and economically was to reach its most shameful level during the rule of Vasili Mzhavanadze, the First Party Secretary under Khruschev, and one of the small number of the latter's protegés to survive unscathed under Brezhnev. By 1970, the agricultural sector had an official turnover of some four billion roubles as against $400 million generated in revenues from clandestine cultivation and sales. According to the official rate, that would have been 200 million roubles, but on the black market $400 million was worth anything up to 1.6 billion roubles. Industry, property and other sectors were subject to similar double-dealing. But in spite of this, not every Georgian was a wheeler and dealer on the sly. In fact, it was only an estimated five per cent of the population who earned a more than voluptuous income in the 'parallel circuit' — beyond any doubt at the expense of the remaining 95 per cent.

In 1972, things threatened to get completely out of hand as public buildings became the targets of a series of bomb attacks, blamed on people who had scores to settle with officials who were working in the buildings. By now, Mzhavanadze, the Georgian party leader, had provoked so much ill-feeling as a result of his personality that the Kremlin considered it wise to replace him with someone from the younger generation — although it was said that Brezhnev felt some mistrust towards the replacement since he suspected him of too much sympathy for Georgian nationalism. The object of Brezhnev's uncertainty was Eduard Shevardnadze, who was charged with purging Georgia of all less honorable practices "in the name of the People's Honour," and doing away with the "mafias" by the most thorough means possible.

How thorough had to be thorough, Shevardnadze came all too soon to realise. Scapegoats were easy enough to apprehend but the real masterminds behind the smuggling and extortion rings evidently had friends in high places within the KGB and elsewhere in Moscow. After being initially hailed by the population as their champion, he was soon met with cynicism and lethargy, upon which his euphoric patriotic words changed swiftly into threats. But this simply sparked the only reaction a Georgian will give in response to empty threats: he shrugs and orders another drink.

In intellectual circles Georgian nationalism had started to emerged once more in the late 1970s, although in the form of starting one committee after another, to the accompaniment of a never-ending flow of petitions and minor demonstrations on minor issues. Here Georgians bear a remarkable similarity to Dutchmen: get three of them together and you have four political parties and five committees. It was in this way that the Georgian Union of Writers in 1976 cried out in protest against the increasing use of Russian in educational institutes and the lowly level of the teaching of Georgian literature and history. On April 14th 1978, 20,000 people demonstrated in Tbilisi against a revision of the constitution which ruled that Georgian was to be supplanted by Russian as their official national language. The amendment was not implemented — according to the demonstrators, thanks to their persistance; according to Shevardnadze, thanks to his 'quiet diplomacy' in respect to Moscow.

Although its more extreme features were cunningly disguised ("Shevardnadze's an absolute master in that," one of his opponents would comment in later times), cultural repression still maintained an irritating presence. Arbitrary arrests of hot-shot activists were refrained from, but lesser gods within the intelligentsia were regularly put behind bars for shorter or longer periods.

"It was no gulag," one of their number recalled. "People were rarely ill-treated and it almost never happened that anyone got carted off to Moscow. In fact, people stood up for each other to a far wider extent than the authorities wanted to admit."

In this way, through almost weekly demonstrations in spring 1981, the students got their way and their leaders were released by the police without charge.

*

During all this, the opposition under Shevardnadze had gradually become radicalised, a fact which which was to lead to the rise of four men who were to play a role in the future political developments in the country no one was yet able to predict. Their names were Irakli Tseretseli, Giorgi ('Gia') Chanturia, Merab Kostava and last, but by no means least, Zviad Gamsakhurdia. As I put the finishing touches to this book, out of those four only the first is still alive, while the the last undoubtedly earned the most controversial personality in Georgia in the second half of the 20th century — unless Shevardnadze beats him to it, of course.

Gamsakhurdia was born in Tbilisi in 1939 — the son of a highly respected novelist and man of letters, Konstantin Gamsakhurdia. He developed a reputation as a troublemaker as early as his primary school years — indeed, more with with his fellow pupils than his teachers.

In 1974, Kostava and Gamsakhurdia founded the Initiative Group for the Defence of Human Rights, transformed in 1979 into the Georgian cell of the Helsinki Watch Group. After a series of public outbursts, both men were arrested and condemned to ten years in prison each. Kostava endured his full term in jail, and shortly after his release he perished in a car crash on October 13th 1989. But Gamsakhurdia walked a free man on the streets of Tbilisi as early as 1979, after he had 'repented' his earlier deeds in a melodramatic television performance.

Meanwhile, others had stepped in to fill the places of the barred Kostava and the neutered Gamsakhurdia. In 1983, neo-nationalists led by Chanturia and Tseretseli organised a protest rally against the celebration of the 200th anniversary of the treaty between King Irakli II and the Russian Empress Catherine II, which marked the beginning of the end of Georgia's sovereignty. Both men behind the initiative were swiftly arrested. But this time neither expressed any intention of 'repenting.'

There then took place a crucial event which was to leave its mark for a long time: the foundation in late October 1987 of the Ilia Chavchavadze Society (of moderately nationalist tendencies), the most important protagonists of which were Chanturia, Tseretseli and Kostava — the latter just having been released from jail. In March 1988, Kostava proposed Gamsakhurdia as a member, which was rejected by an overwhelming majority. Aside from Kostava, only Tseretseli and Chanturia were at the time prepared to admit Gamsakhurdia to their ranks; the others considered him, in the words of one of those who used to be on the board, to be "a quarrelsome idler and a disgrace to his father's memory!"

At this, Chanturia, Tseretseli and Kostava resigned from the Society and founded, under Gamsakhurdia's leadership, the Meotkhe Dasi — the 'Fourth Circle — intended as a successor to the Third Circle which once had rejected Stalin in such a disgraceful manner, and professing motives similar to those by which Gamsakhurdia had been denied membership. In both cases, it was clear that the individuals in question were hardly lacking in desire for retaliation.

The fledgling Circle refused to sit idle and was soon speaking out loud to anyone within earshot, denouncing the Ilia Chavchavadze Society as "a gang of KGB agents and enemies of the people," while the ranks of the authorities were abused ineven cruder form.

For the moment, it seemed that Gamsakhurdia's demagogy of exhortations and abuse started to cause a stir among the masses. Mass demonstrations in October and November swelled to tens of thousands of participants — be it with rather diffuse demands, which included stopping a planned trans-Caucasus railway for "ecological reasons" (there was indeed a natural reserve situated on the track, while Gamsakhurdia spoke of the "desecration" of a site containing the ruins of a medieval monastery), rejecting Moscow's proposals for a new constitution that threatened, the demonstrators were told, the "destruction of the fatherland's culture," and a welter of other demands of lesser importance.

The results, however, were somewhat less than encouraging. It was indeed agreed by the Georgian Soviet that the draft for the new constitution should to be sent back to Moscow for revision, but as for all the other issues, the series of protests merely ended in chaos — and in various bars. In December 1988, a row broke out within the Circle's leadership followed by the inevitable split: Kostava was no more, Chanturia went off to found his National Democratic Party, Tseretseli his National Independence Party, and Gamsakhurdia entrenched himself along with a number of his die-hards in the Tsminda Ilia Matlis Sazogadouabe — the Society of St Ilia the Just. Throughout the publications of this latter organisation, many elements of the quasi-mystical political extremism Gamsakhurdia was later to develop can already be recognised.

Such a mega-split was hardly a unique event: almost on a daily basis, committees, political 'movements,' parties and people's fronts for the liberation of the fatherland were created in bewildering succession, one more democratic in name than the other and almost each one doomed to a speedy rift or ignominious demise. And so, against this backdrop, there loomed ever ominously the Great Catalyst that would finally pack all these pieces together while unwittingly flinging the door wide open for Gamsakhurdia and his irrational *Sturm und Drang*. What exactly went wrong that fateful day is something to which many of those present return in wonder.

"The atmosphere was anything but violent or threatening," recalled a demonstrator who managed to escape with slight wounds from what was to follow. "We chatted to the police and soldiers, and the ordinary people there were eager to know what we wanted in detail and how we saw the country's future."

What happened then is now common knowledge. On April 9th at half past four in the afternoon, tanks rammed straight into a crowd of some thousands, including over a hundred hunger strikers who had stationed themselves in front of the city hall. Demonstrators were attacked with iron bars and instead of the usual tear gas, poison gas was used. Six died of stab wounds, around 14 of poisoning, while hundreds of people fell wounded.

Officially, the blood-bath's instigator was the secretary general of the Georgian Communist Party at the time, Jumbar Patiashvili, who two days earlier had telegraphed Moscow with a request for "military assistance in case the authorities in Tbilisi fail to keep things under control." At the time, both Gorbachev and Shevardnadze were absent on a diplomatic mission. On the initiative of Ligachov, Gorbachev's sworn adversary who aimed at undermining the democratisation process in the USSR at any cost, defence minister General Yazov had given the order to the commander of the Transcaucasus, General Igor Rodionov (the same firebrand who took care of the Baku massacre nine months later) to take on the population of Tbilisi as soon as the signal was given (from Moscow, not Tbilisi). Patiashvili was reassured that "extreme violence" would not be used and — even more crucial — that he himself would be guaranteed against any political consequences of whatever occurred.

Later, Gorbachev claimed he had been led to believe that it would all be a simple matter of "surveillance" based on the presumption that a "political compromise" between the authorities and the demonstrators had already been achieved. Shevardnadze, in a state of utmost embarrassment, refrained from comment. Although he had denied all knowledge, at home no one believed him. As for Rodionov, the fact that years later he was appointed defence minister of the Russian Federation and publicly refused to express the slightest regret over his role in both massacres, must have come as a slap in the face to both Georgians and Azeris.

After the break-up of the demonstration, Georgia was once more awash with newly created political organisations: traditionalists, Greens, monarchists (four movements to be exact — each with their own candidate for the throne), democrats, national democrats, liberals, liberal nationalists, national liberals, Christian democrats, social democrats . . . As before, barely any of these organisms were to be long-lived and even fewer related in any way to the nation's needs and the people's aspirations.

As for needs, these were reaching desperate levels. On the official exchange market, the rouble had plummeted from two dollars down to two cents. On the black market the difference between its own exchange rates and those of the banks had shrunk from 1,000 to less than 100 per cent. As a result the circuit of major investors, linked closely to mafias who in turn were tightly linked to upper government levels, stood at the brink of mass panic. Violence and criminality got the upper hand, and those wanting to simply preserve their lives were advised to get home before dark and, even in daytime, avoid dark corners.

"Who's talking about civil war, about how crime's getting out of hand after the collapse of the Soviet Union?" Peter Mamradze, the president's young counsel, was to exclaim in later days. "It's never been as bad as it was in those days."

There are many who have wondered what got into Gamsakhurdia once power came into his hands. Many have pointed out that schizophrenics are able to keep themselves together, externally at least, so long as they are denied realising their goal — whatever that may be. The moment they do, it swiftly beomes clear that they have been living outside reality all along, convinced as they are that their life is steered by some destiny of universal order.

Gamsakhurdia's *Georgia's Spiritual Mission* was not conceived originally as a book, but consisted of compiled lectures and essays penned by the failed helmsman. The work's main issue revolves around a single text — one of the earliest Georgian manuscripts whose originals have been preserved — taken from the work *Appraisal and Glorification of the Georgian Language* written by Ioane Zosime, a monk who lived in the tenth century at the Georgian convent of St Saba on Mount Sinai. The text runs as follows:

"The Georgian language shall be preserved until the Day of Return ithat it may bear witness before Him that God reveals all languages through this language.

And this language has been slumbering up to this day, and in the Gospel this language has been named Lazarus.

And the Virgin Nino and Helen the Queen converted themselves, as did Mary and Martha.

And David the Prophet spoke "four days dead" for a thousand years which is equal to one day, and in the Georgian Gospel according to Matthew its beginning is marked with the letter TS (ჯ) which stands for the four thousand *maragis* — prophecies. And these are four days and the four days of death, and [one] buried Him through His death and baptism.

And this language, haloed and blessed in the name of the Lord, humiliated, waits for the day of the Return of the Lord.

And this language has a sign: four and ninety years since the announcement of the coming of Christ until this day, and in this it is ahead of all other languages.

And of all this, that has been written, this letter of the alphabet shall testify."

It is a typical allegoric medieval work of poetry, which has much in common with the French, Bohemian and Byzantine mystics of the period. But Gamsakhurdia loses himself in wild fantasies that are even more difficult to grasp — if at all — and depicts a confused and confusing whirl of images in which Greek gods and heroes, Old and New Testament characters, mythological creatures from India and East and West European medieval saints are swept together with a casualness reminiscent of one who is suffering delusory hallucinations. But even this fails to give a full flavour of his phantasmagoria in full flow. Instead, a single striking quote may suffice:

> "The *Appraisal's* Author explains to us in Christian terminology the self-same story contained by one myth from the ancient mysteries: the once rising and mighty Nation of Kartveli — the Georgians — and its Language, which have been humiliated and thrown down for four thousand years. But then this humiliation is the same for the Georgian Nation and its Language as Christ's Baptism, Death and Burial, inevitably followed by Resurrection and Ascension to Heaven. Likewise, the Georgian Nation shall re-emerge after this four day-long baptism, and take its place once more at the Return of the Universal Spiritual Leader and Judge of Mankind, as it used to do in times of old. All this shall be returned to the Georgian People by He who resurrected and glorified Lazarus. It is thus that the Georgian People is compared with Lazarus. At the same time, it is not foretold that the Georgian Nation is to remain humiliated, thrown down and lifeless until the Return but that after four days (four thousand years) of death and burial it will rise again as did Lazarus. Sooner by far than Christ's Return shall it testify before Christ, whereas at the Return it is to designate those who are sinners . . ."

At the first — and last — elections under Gorbachev's perestroika, held in May 1991, Gamsakhurdia was elected with 87 per cent of the votes as head of the Georgian state. Earlier, on April 9th, his Round Table had held a referendum according to which 98 per cent of the population had voted for total independence. One minor detail was that Azeris, Armenians, Abkhazians, Ossetes, Russians and other ethnic minorities in Georgia were not permitted to vote.

What Gamsakhurdia had at the back of his mind we can suppose to have been revealed at a far earlier stage. His interventions at the Round

Table — into which he had forced himself, after the blood-bath of April 1989, to impose his presence as an angel of wrath, much to the irritation of the older members — are easy to imagine. One of his 'presentations', a speech which he gave at a rally organised by a committee called Democracy and Independence in Akhalsopeli, and which was published a week later in the Ilia Chavchavadze Society magazine, went as follows:

"We are gathered here together because those corrupt and treacherous Communists have allowed the Leks to burrow deep into the very heart of our own Kakheti. This area used to be ethically pure because the Georgian element was superior in it. Today, however, the situation has deteriorated to such an extent that we are now wondering how it can possibly be saved . . . Kakheti is being threatened from all quarters: from one side the Tatars are on the move, elsewhere the Armenians and the Ossetes are busy taking over these lands. So what those Communist traitors have done to us? They have sold off our sacred Kakheti, the birthplace of so many Georgian heroes and saints. They have overflowed it with foreigners and delivered us straight into disaster. But now the Georgian people have woken up. They will drive out the interlopers — an action, in fact, they have already started to undertake . . . Do you all understand what is going on? Can you all not understand that at this precise moment a conspiracy against your people is being put into action . . . ? There is no exodus — the 'Tatars' and the 'Leks' all prefer to stay put here . . . So open your eyes! The enemy is right here, disguised in our midst. Give him the reply he justly deserves. Go for these traitors, pour the melted lead of the Georgian nations over them! We shall not permit ourselves to be abused . . . We have the power, the Georgian people are on our side. We shall put an end to all these traitors, we shall put the truth under their noses, we shall work for the speedy dispatch of all foreigners living on our land . . ."

'Lek' is an abusive word for Russian, while 'Tatars' is a reference to the Azeris. It is true that way into 1993, long after Gamsakhurdia's downfall and the rise of Shevardnadze, Azeri villages were still being cleared and thousands of their inhabitants chased across the border to Azerbaijan. But in 1990, all this was yet to happen.

A hunger strike, during the second week of May, by a group of students demanding unconditional independence, was broken up by Gamsakhurdia with his promise that that he would convince Secretary General Gumbaridze — who ruled the nation in the name of Gorbachev and perestroika — to make "decisive concessions." This action of the future president drew jeers from moderate opposition circles and threats of retaliation from the die-hards. One of the latters' number was an ex-convict just out of jail, Jaba Ioseliani.

Jaba took advantage of the occasion to vow that from there on the struggle for the liberation of the fatherland against oppressors and traitors would be fought only with arms. Backing up his words, he founded a 'people's army' which he dubbed the Mkhredrioni or 'Knights' — making each recruit swear his loyalty to the Fatherland and the Holy Cross. Initially, Gamsakhurdia found it convenient to side with these new hardliners, since their romanticism and their pathos all but fitted perfectly into the dream world and persecution mania in which he himself dwelt. However, an unholy marriage such as this was never fated to last.

By 1987, the more sophisticated outlets of the Soviet media, such as *Izvestia* and the television programme *Novy Vremya*, had started delivering alarming reports about how social conditions in Georgia were getting out of hand. Within the space of only a few years, a massive surge of mobster activities were reported, linked especially to cells of 'hooligans' who installed unofficial road blocks along the highways, checking identity documents and noting names and addresses. In itself this seemed a mere pastime — admittedly morbid but little more than that. In reality, however, it was much worse. Any driver could expect any day — or night, preferably — a visit from a group of mostly armed young people who came to collect money. As time went on, simple extortion made way for looting, assault, rape and, in an increasing number of cases, murder.

In the eyes of Soviet journalists and commentators 'excesses' like these were a result of the economic misery spreading throughout the USSR as a whole — and although the crime rate in Georgia was one of the worst within the Soviet Union, it was far from the only member state facing such a problem. Still, the fact that the authorities failed to take action and restore order was a shame if not a disgrace. But publicly voicing the question why the authorities were not doing anything was crossing the line for perestroika. So nothing was done — apart from frequent appointments of committees who sat together around a bottle of vodka or two, invariably bound to concur that on the one hand things were serious indeed, but on the other were not as serious as was so often suggested.

And so, in early 1990, at the apogee of East-West detente and 'Gorby hysteria' throughout the Western world, Georgia claimed an estimated membership of 60,000 — mostly youths — who belonged to over a hundred underground armed groups, whose ranks varied from a few dozen to thousands. The two largest by far were the Mkhedrioni, whose ranks soon swelled to 17,000, and Tengiz Kitovani's National Guard, rapidly approaching 10,000 of the faithful. Like a *deus ex machina*, these were the precise forces that set the scene and then generated the Gamsakhurdia phenomenon — and all this right under the eyes of the Soviets and the KGB, until considered omnipotent, from whose scrutiny not even a fly would pass unnoticed.

It was not until the end of the year that Gamsakhurdia's constant pushing got him appointed head of the Georgian Supreme Soviet. A man who had been a local police chief in one of the provincial towns was to tell me later how the power structure, which had been always stitched together by corruption and nepotism, had now utterly come apart at the seams.

"The strangest telexes came in, from organisations I had never heard of. I had to collect this sum of money from factory director X, I had to arrest civil servant Y — he was to be 'picked up.' Other individuals, real felons, had to be released without further explanation. My own officers disappeared one by one without trace. One of them was found riddled with bullets on the edge of the town one morning — he never hurt a fly in his whole life and was always scrupulous in writing out parking tickets and collecting fines. Blokes in badly fitting uniforms or without any uniform at all would walk in and out of the station, mostly drunk or stoned or both — I was under the strong impression, to say the least, that people were dealing drugs under my very nose."

It would be forgiveable if one thought the situation could hardly get worse — but of course it did. By the end of 1990, there took place the inevitable: the coalition of the war lords fell apart. Tseretseli and Chanturia, who never held much regard for Gamsakhurdia in the first place, had previously stayed in the shadows but now openly pushed themselves into the spotlight as the opposition. By the turn of the year, Ioseliani broke with Gamsakhurdia, only to be thrown into jail shortly afterwards — something Gamsakhurdia was able to carry off thanks to the support he still received from Kitovani. In return for the favour, Kitovani's private army was promoted to official interior armed forces after the break-up with Ioseliani.

In April 1991, the Georgian Soviet declared all ties with the Soviet Union void and proclaimed the republic, and in May, Gamsakhurdia was elected head of state with 86 per cent of the votes. The old Soviet Assembly remained in place and was relabelled 'Parliament' — the same process whichwas to happen at a later stage in Azerbaijan and Armenia. It would seem the 'liberation' of Transcaucasia has seen the taking-over of power play a substantially more significant role than the process of democratisation.

On the streets of Tbilisi and elsewhere in the country, militias were now the new lords and masters, their ranks and numbers growing every day.

"You had to join — whether you liked it or not," remembered Sandro, a 27-year-old student at the Language Institute. "People responded to the calls to join up, not out of boredom like they did during the 1980s, but out of the need to preserve your life — as bit like in the old days when people joined the Komsomol 'to keep you out of trouble.' As a militia member, you had double protection: your own gang looked after you and other gangs feared you for it. You could go shopping in 'special' shops controlled by your own group — any shop that wasn't under control of a militia stayed open for long. Wherever you bought a sandwich on the street for, say 100 roubles, you could bet your life on it that 50 went in as a cut to the Mkhedrioni, Kitovani's men, the Panthers, the White Eagles [miltary drifters who were later incorporated into the Georgian army] or any one from the scores of other other groups."

What in fact happened is that the state had essentially merged with the underworld. Kidnappings for ransom were part of the daily routine — moreover, the line dividing arrest and kidnap was now obliterated. As for the prisons, these were the very places where the sublimation of this strange, schizoic world took place. Often someone who was behind bars one day could be spotted the next in guard's uniform or even behind the director's desk. While most cells were filled to overflowing with inmates, there were always a few that housed a fortunate sole individual or two. Booze, drugs and other goods were freely for sale and were openly consumed. Everyone knew that two, three, maybe four thousand dollars gave you the key to quietly walk out through prison gates. What everyone didn't know was whether or not you'd gunned down before reaching the corner of the street. Murder and extortion, needless to say, were commonplace.

Against this backdrop, Gamsakhurdia the patriot was to cheer at the Moscow putsch in 1991 and to loudly proclaim his unconditional loyalty to those who took over. It was an act of despair, since it had become all too clear that this hallucinating demagogue had lost touch with his powerbase and was forced to turn north of the border to appeal for support from a gang of thugs who may have belonged in a 1950s B-movie but certainly not at the top of one of the world's most powerful states. The fact that he managed to hold out for so long was due to the fact that no one had any notion who or indeed what what should take his place. As it was, it looked like all the (Georgian) world and his mother had announced their intention to take over, insisting they were saving the fatherland in the process. As the Russian putsch went under, Rustaveli Avenue in Tbilisi became the scene of at least ten demonstrations a day, most of them simultaneously.

The chaotic situation saw Gamsakhurdia lose the last of his departing sense of reality. Antone who did not blindly follow his whims was branded a "bandit" or a "Kremlin agent." The United States was synomymous for Nazi Germany and the superpower's Foreign Secretary James Baker was nicknamed Von Ribbentrop. Shortly after the final death throes of the Soviet Union, Gamsakhurdia ordered Kitovani to deploy his Guards in a bid to sweep the centre of Tbilisi clean of all "provocateurs." Kitovani refused and, soon after, he and his 10,000 men in arms left for the mountains up north, but letting everyone know they would return when they saw their moment.

After Kitovani's departure, Gamsakhurdia found himself left with only a few hundred armed men, whom he wasted no time in promoting to the grand title of 'Presidential Guard'. On September 2nd, his troops attempted to do what Kitovani had refused to do, to 'sweep' Rustaveli Avenue. They set about their task with grim efficiency. Shots were fired into the crowds that had gathered there, the dead and wounded fell to the ground. However, it was not only the crowd that suffered, but the ranks of the Presidential Guard as well — for this time the crowd fired back.

Things now began to move at lightning speed. On September 4th, the last to hold out in support for Gamsakhurdia and who still enjoyed some respect from the people, Tengiz Sigua, resigned as prime minister and immediately fled the city to join Kitovani in his mountain hide-out. The following day, Gamsakhurdia proclaimed a state of emergency. On September 14th, escorted by a brigade armed to the teeth, Kitovani and Sigua arrived in the courtyard of the Parliament Building, the former headquarters of the nation's Soviet — a Stalinist temple of overblown proportions at the end of Rustaveli Avenue, built by German prisoners of war and where the president had entrenched himself with his faithful. The intention of both men was to force Gamsakhurdia into a compromise. But they got no further than the courtyard since the president declared he had more important things on his mind.

On September 16th, Gia and Irina Chanturia attempted to flee to Moscow. Their plane had just taken off and was already on its way north when the airport radioed and ordered it back. The pilot stated it was impossible to land with the tanks still full of fuel, but the reply came back that if he did not comply, the plane would be shot down. Immediately on landing, the plane weas boarded by youths with machine-guns and the couple along with their party secretary were carted off.

This was only the beginning of a massive wave of arrests throughout the country. Although the pattern was by now utterly arbitrary, nevertheless the entire opposition leadership found themselves within a matter of days either behind bars, abroad or in heavily barricaded party headquarters. The German journalist Christian Schmidt Hauer, who had ventured into Tbilisi reporting for *Die Zeit*, gave a vivid description of the situation in the city centre:

> "The presidential palace has been barricaded with buses. The first outpost of the opposition is situated 50 metres ahead: these are the monarchists who have taken the same school under constant observation by Gamsakhurdia and Kitovani as their stronghold. Two hundred metres further on stand the concrete barricades of the National Democrats, the front of whose building is decorated with a Madonna and a loudspeaker from which grating calls resound. Again, 150 metres on, heaps of rusty pipes have been piled up in front of the National Independence Party headquarters — this being the former Marxist-Leninist Institute. Throughout the day, this triumph boulevard swarms with thousands all yelling their own slogans. At night, guards camp out everywhere and crawl among themselves as if in a Wallenstein camp . . ."

In the following months, however, friend and foe alike were surprised as to what then happened. What exactly happened was that nothing happened — except for a brave attempt by Shevardnadze to mediate — which was stillborn from the outset as the would-be mediator topped Gamsakhurdia's lengthening list of "Satan's servants and traitors." In October, Mkhedrioni units occupied large parts of the city. Some weeks later, Kitovani's troops occupied almost the entire part of the city north of the river, including the railway and its stations. The end was drawing nigh with Gamsakhurdia unwilling to even hear the word "compromise."

The ring around Gamsakhurdia's Parliament Building stronghold was completed on December 22nd when Kitovani occupied the Government House (the old Marxist-Leninist Institute) and the neighbouring main post office at the other end of Rustaveli Avenue, the city hall by the Parliament Building and the overlooking hilltop of Mtatsminda where the main television tower stands. Gamsakhurdia was trapped like a rat. On Boxing Day, Kitovani's men stormed the avenue and occupied the Hotel Tbilisi, from which position they were eyeball to eyeball with the Presidential Guard diagonally across the street.

What was so bizarre about the whole situation was in the middle of all this that the masses of pro- and anti-Gamsakhurdia demonstrators camped out in front of the Parliament building had not taken one step back throughout all this armed conflict for even an instant — anything up to 2,000 of them. To complete the surrealness of it all, the events of the following days unfolded before the eyes of thousands of spectators, who from time to time fled into the side streets to avoid being caught in crossfire only to be back on the spot twenty minutes later. It was as though they were watching a football match, in the process showing a real contempt for death in the face of the snipers of both sides who were terrorising the area.

On the morning of December 27th, Tbilisi found itself licking its wounds quite literally, with 54 killed and 187 more or less seriously wounded. During the days between Christmas and New Year one ultimatum chased another. On December 28th, defence state secretary Nodar Giorgadze, who had undertaken an attempt to mediate on his own initiative, was dragged off the street by Gamsakhurdia's men and taken by force into his fortress. On New Year's Eve, Ioseliani and Kitovani's men joined forces and attempted to storm the Parliament Building, but were forced to beat an ignominious retreat on being confronted by a furious — and well-armed — crowd of Gamsakhurdia's supporters outside.

On January 2nd, Sigua, Kitovani and Ioseliani's next step was to install a 'military council' with the intention of taking over power 'formally'. Next day, the Mkhedrioni moved in to disperse the crowd of Gamsakhurdia's supporters in front of the Parliament Building. Two demonstrators were killed and a Mkhedrioni commander was lynched by the mob. Since Christmas alone the death toll now stood at over two hundred. It was time for a resolution. On January 6th at 3.30 in the morning, Gamsakhurdia called a meeting with a few hundred of his followers in the basement to tell them their struggle was hopeless. He advised them to leave the premises and announced he intended to do the same. An hour later, three buses, accompanied by three armoured cars carrying white flags, left the city for the nearby border with Armenia. Safely over, the Armenian government debated for a week over what to do with him: should they send him to France or the Russian Federation? It is reported that they even considered sending him back across the Georgian border.

In fact, the 'blind visionary' found his final destination in Grozny, as guest of the leader of a country he had been the only head of state to recognise: the independent republic of Chechenia, headed by Jokhar Dudayev. By New Year's Eve 1993, he had died. Precisely when, where and how is subject to some controversy. Perhaps in his place of exile, perhaps in Mingrelia. Perhaps suicide according to the authorities, perhaps murder according to his family, perhaps cancer of the bladder (a trait of his family) according to his peers. What was certain was that he had perished, and with him his flawed blueprint for his country.

Gamsakhurdia's downfall and exit was followed in turn by a crackdown on the very people who had helped topple him. The experiment had failed: a mono-ethnic, ultra-nationalist Georgia under the leadership of romantic knights on white horses. The gods had fallen and their Valhalla lay ruined. The men in grey suits were poised to return, just like in Camus' *La Peste*.

But the damage had been done — and is effects were deep-rooted. For, not unlike the Armenians and the Azerbaijanis, two Caucasian tribes waited in the wings, prepared to blow up Gamsakhurdia's dream altogether. It was thus that the terrible wars over South Ossetia and Abkhazia came to pass.

11
War in the mini-empire

There are two Batumis: the sprawling city area on the other side of the railway station where the railtrack from Tbilisi ends, and the coastal strip west of the port where the villas and big hotels are situated. The largest, the Medea Hotel, is filled with refugees from Abkhazia, as is one wing of the pompous Intourist Hotel, built in Stalinist style.

Batumi is the capital of Ajaria, the only remaining autonomous state of Georgia which distinguishes itself from the rest of the 'mini-empire' by its Muslim majority as well as by the fact that during the 18th century and for some periods subsequent once formed part of the Ottoman Empire. The same happens to be true for nearby Samtskhe which, however, has not been provided with autonomous status in later times. In neither area, however, did the the virus of separatism appear to be in the air.

"We are Georgians, I say," stressed Irakli, the young press spokesman for Ajaria's head of state Aslan Abashidze, "and I daresay we're better Georgians than those who set the rules in Tbilisi at the moment!"

His chief Abashidze was himself shortly afterwards to outline to me the ambitious plans he had in store for his autonomous state: expansion of the port, the establishment of a free-trade zone, overall protection of the banking sector and a fully open investment regime. "You'll see how by the end of this century Batumi will be the Gibraltar of the Black Sea!" he declared. "Look for yourself, even now nobody has to worry here. Here in Batumi you can walk the streets in the evening with two, three thousand dollars in your pocket and nobody, I say nobody, will even point a finger at you!"

The last remark proved to be true — absolutely. Batumi has always been my ideal stop-over to and from the way home. Even if the city had its worries (although nowhere near the levels faced by the rest of Georgia) over electricity supplies and how the population could make ends meet, Ajaria remained an oasis of peace in a country where turbulence had become routine. "There are quite a lot of . . . let us say, certain individuals who would love to have their tanks roll through the streets of Batumi," Abashidze would say. "But they won't have their way — we won't give in to provocation!"

Abashidze's persistence has nonetheless equipped him with a number of no less persistent political opponents in the street. In May 1991, for example, when he was in the middle of a meeting in his own office, a terrorist group burst into the building and opened fire randomly at those in the chamber. Two were killed and the president was seriously wounded but survived. Two weeks after the event, seven kilos of high explosives were found and neutralised near his apartment on the port boulevard.

Abashidze's political opponents, who claim only loose ties with Tbilisi, were united in the Republican Party which occupies a scattering of seats in the local assembly. In March 1993 it looked for a moment as if things might get out of hand as on the 15th a bomb went off in front of the house of the Republican leader Davit Berdzenishvili — followed, two days later, by the kidnapping of his fellow activist Tamaz Diasamidze. The perpetrators were captured and sentenced, but this did not stop a mob from gathering which, on the 28th, stormed the party building and smashed up its interior.

But this was hardly the limit of the dangers Abashidze had to take into account. A year after these events, the head of the local police at the time, Ali Bakuridze, discovered a plot by one of the most prestigious families in the area, the Asanidzes, to stage a coup against Abashidze.

"Behind the Republicans hide the Russians," the more or less official comment in Abashidze's red carpet lobby could be heard, "whereas behind the Asanidze one could detect, let us say, certain elements who want to turn Georgia into a right-wing totalitarian state."

As it was, Bakuridze himself came to fall into disgrace and take a one-way ticket to Moscow in spring 1995 for unexplained reasons. Whatever the case, such episodes — minor in comparison to the dramatic events taking place at the same time in the rest of Georgia — failed to undermine Ajaria's status as an oasis of calm — whether the "certain elements" hinted at by Abashidze liked it or not.

The same, however, could certainly not be said of Georgia's two other cut-off regions. In South Ossetia, the struggle was comparatively brief if severe. The rift started in 1987 with petitions from South Ossetians to the Kremlin for 'reunification' with their brethren across the border in North Ossetia. In 1989 the word 'border correction' makes way for 'independence' and by autumn 1990 the South Ossetians had elected their own local parliament while the local Soviet assembly still remained intact. After a lengthy silence, the Kremlin eventually promised to install a committee to study the case, in the meantime, all decisions taken in both Tbilisi and the South Ossetian capital Tskhinvali over the issue were declared 'void'. In Tbilisi, however, the reaction of the Georgian government proved to be more substantial although hardly any wiser: South Ossetia's autonomy was henceforth 'suspended'.

Whether this was coincidence or not, things getting out of hand in South Ossetia neatly coincided with the rise in Georgia of Kitovani, Ioseliani and Gamsakhurdia and the decline of the grip of the authorities in general. On Christmas 1990, two of Gamsakhurdia's bodyguards were assassinated there. On January 6th the Georgian Soviet voted — in fact, ordered to do so by Gamsakhurdia — in favour of the "absolute abolition" of South Ossetia's autonomous status.

"We knew that this was a somewhat less than wise thing to do," one of the deputies was to tell me later. "But his mind was already rather wandering by that time. During the vote, there were armed guards at the doors, their gun barrels turned inward."

Meanwhile, in Tskhinvali far more had been more going on than people were led to believe.

"Days before the vote, warnings had come to us that bad things were going to happen," a Georgian from Ossetia, eking out a miserable existence in a draughty refugee centre in Tbilisi, told me. "Word came that the Red Army was moving into the area. If nothing else, they were going to create a blood bath that would dwarf the events of 1989 in Tbilisi. We somehow managed to get weapons ourselves. As the tanks moved into town, there was complete pandemonium. It was hard to distinguish friend from foe. The local mafiosi used the occasion to get even — this I know for sure. Since it was clear that the invaders had no idea of the way around town we became more and more convinced that they were Russians. It was only later that we overheard them talking to each other in Georgian. We watched them looting houses and shops. It was then it began to dawn on us that they were from Tbilisi . . . a thought we had confirmed later when they slunk off in the evening. The Red Army would never slink off."

Officially, twenty killed and about a hundred injured were reported a day after the onslaught.

"That's impossible!" claim Ossete and Georgian survivors alike. "That day and during the following days at least fifty farms in the area were attacked and their occupants massacred."

It is conjectured that the plan was to occupy Tskhinvali and use it as a base to systematically 'cleanse' the whole region. But few ethnic Ossetes inhabited the autonomous capital in those days, and the invaders had not counted on such united resistance by the rest of the population. The message was clear: Gamsakhurdia's intervention in Ossetia was unwelcome, period.

The Ossetes, however, proved themselves little grateful for the initial support granted to them by their Georgian compatriots. On arriving in Tbilisi a few weeks later, the leader of the South Ossetian Unity Movement Torez Gulumbekov bluntly informed government officials that the "Ossetian Nation" had decided to "reunite its territory" and that he had come to negotiate "a solution to the problem of ethnic Georgians who still lived in the area." The result was that he was thrown in jail where he remained until after Gamsakhurdia's downfall.

Soon after the attacks and the subsequent talks both sides dug themselves in and the towns and settlements on both sides of the line were harried by regular exchanges of artillery bombardments. The provisional government which had taken over in Tskhinvali after Gulumbekov's detention at first imprisoned every ethnic Georgian politician and official it could lay its hands on, eventually packing them up and dispatching them across the border in the company of thousands of their lesser compatriots. As they saw it, they were simply doing exactly the same as Gamsakhurdia would have done to them had he been given the chance.

Over the first few months of 1992, Gia Karkarishvili, a crony of Kitovani's who was his 'junior defence minister', made several attempts to breach the Ossetian lines using military force. On April 26th, the Russian garrison of 6,000 interior troops was evacuated from South Ossetia — much to the consternation of the governments of the since returned Gulumbekov, since only 300 men were left behind with strict orders not to shoot unless they were attacked themselves and to refrain from any interference in local conflicts.

This move gave the Georgian armed forces the perfect chance to recover their positions — or at least this is what they thought. In the afternoon of May 14th — mere hours after a friendly visit by Shevardnadze to Tskhinvali that morning — Karkarishvili's men entered the village of Pris, set all 72 houses ablaze, mostly with the inhabitants still in them, and shot at anyone trying to escape. On May 26th, a convoy of lorries carrying refugees leaving the capital heading north came under fire in an ambush, which left 36 killed and 18 seriously wounded.

Naturally, there were the odd international interludes. Earlier, on May 22nd, Tskhinvali had a strange guest in the form of the Belgian politician Marc Eyskens, there on behalf of the ubiquitous Conference for Security and Co-operation in Europe — the same organisation whose representatives were to blunder their way through Azerbaijan in later days. Eysens talked, listened, had lunch, talked, listened, had dinner, and then was back on his way. The dust had barely settled when the guns started firing again. On May 28th, a ceasefire was declared — said to be the result of 'mediation' by a Russian parliamentary delegation who had visited Tbilisi and Tskhinvali two days earlier. The following day, Tskhinvali was subjected to the worst ever shelling since the beginning of the siege.

Meanwhile, Tskhinvali was packed with Ossetes whose villages and settlements surrounding the capital had been cleansed and whose dwellings were now occupied by Georgians who had fled Tskhinvali in their turn. More than a few 'silent barters' were concluded as Georgians who lived too near the frontline occupied the farms abandoned by Ossetians who in their turn squatted houses in Tskhinvali previously occupied by Georgians.

Early that summer, the number of the slain on the Ossetian side alone had risen to over 800 and the number of seriously injured over 2,000, while 150 Ossetes were still in Georgian detention centres and at least one more thousand missing. All negotiation attempts were now to end in an endless series of multi-interpretable deals and 'misunderstandings' — and in fresh violence as well. As it was, none of the parties knew what they wanted — except for that third party: the Kremlin. But then, in Russia they had time and patience enough to wait until South Ossetia fell into their hands like a ripe apple.

The deadlock dragged on like this until spring 1993, when Shevardnadze accepted a Russian sponsored 'peace proposal' by which Russian troops were to supervise maintaining the status quo until a political compromise between the conflicting parties could be implemented.

"The Russians have, to put it bluntly, taken the area for themselves," confided MPs in Tbilisi. "And this makes it perfectly clear who was originally behind the double murder of Gamsakhurdia's men that started off the whole thing."

In summer 1996 the ruins of the former Jewish quarter of Tskhinvali, where the most dramatic fighting in 1992 had taken place, had already been covered with weeds for a long time. The self-elected parliament was a year away from the end of its first term, as was its president Ludvig Chibirov, the former rector of the town's university. Tskhinvali still had the look of a rambling provincial town than a sovereign republic's capital. The only building more than three storeys high was the 'government house' where a number of ministries were clumped together, the neighbouring building houses the parliament, the offices of the head of state and prime minister, and the foreign ministry. Most of the offices were locked and those which were open showed rows of empty desks.

That summer afternoon, around the time the head of state had promised me an interview, a luxurious four-wheel drive car with a Russian number plate entered the parking lot. After a brief discussion, this 'Russian delegation' then left for Vladikavkaz, the North Ossetian capital, carrying Chibirov along with them.

One OSCE official who happened to be there along with me, muttered: "So I don't think there's any doubt who's really in charge here."

"Incorporation into the Russian Federation is the wish of every living soul here," a presidential adviser speaking on behalf of his superior assured me, "even though reality will in all likelihood require us to end up in some federative relationship with Georgia. But we will only agree to that provided not only Shevardnadze but the international community as well fully guarantees us home rule. Heads of state come and go, and who can reassure us that one day a second Gamsakhurdia isn't going to step forward?"

As for the Russians, the Ossetian crisis was amplified by yet another, highly inconvenient dimension after October 1992, when, sparked by a string of incidents, street-fighting broke out in Vladikavkaz between Ossetes and Ingush. The Ingush are an Islamic Caucasian mountain people who, after the downfall of the USSR, broke away from their cousins the Chechens, with whom they were united under the banner of Chechen-Ingushetia, and joined the new Russian Federation as a separate unit. Ever since, they have been claiming as their homeland the North Ossetian capital of Vladikavkaz (or parts of it at least) and its eastern hinterland, where many Ingush are concentrated.

Needless to say, the Ingush are not very numerous: in 1943 they were accused by Stalin, along with among others such as the Chechens, of sympathy for the German invaders and en masse deported to Central Asia. As opposed to other mountain peoples, the Ingush managed to adapt rather well to their new environment and under Nikita Khruschev's subsequent 'rehabilitation' less than half of their number returned to the Caucasus. The Ingush feel themselves the pariahs of the New Russia — they have no real homeland but at the same time are denied the right to settle down elsewhere in the Russian Federation.

The clashes in Vladikavkaz soon got out of control as rumours rapidly spread that the Ossetes were busy "exterminating the Ingush." Despite the previous rift with Ingushetia, in Grozny the Chechen leader Dudayev appealed for help on behlaf of his Islamic brother nation in distress, and by the end of October an unruly but heavily armed fighting force crossed the border under the banner of the Confederation of Caucasian Mountain Nations, led by the Circassian Mussa Shanibov. In order to foil any attempt at a siege or, conceivably, a direct attack on Vladikavkaz, a Russian parachute unit landed at the edge of the city on Saturday October 31st, dispersing the attackers and disarming a part of them. The days that followed were days of sweet revenge for the Ossetes as, with the assistance of police units (and, according to the Ingush, of the Russian military), they butchered hundreds of Ingush and drove thousands more from the city. Once more the Oriental Christians had made a doubtful display of force — after the Lebanese Maronite, the Serb and the Armenian, the Ossete too could now boast of having made a stand against the 'Islamic threat' by the most radical means. And by the time the sky was clear of the last trace of gunsmoke in North Ossetia, it had to be admitted in Tbilisi, albeit reluctantly, that the chances now of ever recovering South Ossetia on its side of the border were looking a trifle bleak. Ominously, however, all was not deadlock and the warlords and their legions in arms were soon to get a new playground for their crusades.

The drama of Abkhazia is significantly older than the times it started making front page headlines. The Abkhazians have been Caucasians as far back in time as human memory goes. Like their neighbours to the north, the Circassians, they claim to be descendants from both the Scyths and the Amazons. In the early Middle Ages the Abkhazian kingdom was at its apogee, extending over all of the central Caucasus, it included present north-west Azerbaijan. Eventually the Abkhazians were pushed back east by the Alans, the present day Ossetes.

After the withdrawal in 1810 by Ottoman troops of the Caucasian Black Sea coast, the area was was occupied by the Russians. During the Turco-Russian war that raged in the early 19th century, the Abkhazians had hesitantly taken sides with the Russians. On the eve of peace they requested the formation of a Russian protectorate — which was duly granted. Until 1829, the political status of Abkhazia remained uncertain as long as the Sublime Porte continued to claim its erstwhile territory. A new war was averted for the time being by the Treaty of Adrianopole which granted the Russians control over the entire eastern Black Sea coast except for Batumi.

Russian rule triggered off fresh revolts, which made the Russians decide to chase over a hundred thousand Abkhazians across the Turkish border over the next decade and some three hundred thousand of them after the establishment of their authority over the country's inland areas. Then, in 1840, a series of uprisings in the North-Western Caucasus broke out conducted by the Ubykh leader Hajji Berzek, which spread rapidly and were to last until 1845. The final attempt to get rid of the Russians took place between 1857 and 1864, ending with a peace treaty signed with General Heiman, acting on behalf of the Russian commander-in-chief Prince Mikhail Vorontsov. The treaty coincided with the same mass ethnic cleansings that had ravaged the other North Caucasian nations five years earlier. It is estimated that between 1859 and 1867 between 1.5 and 2 million people were deported from the West and Central Caucasus after which Cossack and Russian colonists were brought in to occupy the empty villages and settlements. It was then that loyal Georgian landowners who had been deprived of their properties by the Russians earlier and had failed to regain them, were compensated for their losses in Abkhazia.

As for present-day Abkhazia, according to the 1989 census, it numbered just over half a million inhabitants, almost half of whom were ethnic Georgians/Mingrelians and the remainder a mixture of Russians, Greeks and Armenians. Abkhazians numbered less than 100,000 in their own land. The country had been an independent Soviet republic until, by a decree of Stalin in 1931, it was forced to join Georgia as an autonomous unit.

By early 1978, violence had broken out in the streets of Sukhumi after it was reported that Abkhazian delegates in the Supreme Soviet in Moscow had urged the ailing Brezhnev to reincorporate Abkhazia into the Russian Federation. Not much is on record about the riots, since officially they never took place — testament to the ever-amazing ease by which Soviet chroniclers decided that whatever conflicted with party interests simply never happened. Eyewitnesses to the Sukhumi disturbances to this day claim that the police took action only against Georgians, leaving the Abkhazians and Russians free to run riot. Whatever the case, the incident remained without political consequences.

In 1991, during the conflict with South Ossetia, Abkhazia had remained on the sidelines. In spring 1992, when in all the former Soviet domains the future status of the defunct Red Army's military facilities and materiel was under formal discussion, Shevardnadze agreed with the Abkhazian leadership that they were to supervise all armed units on their territory, although ultimate responsibility for the country's joint defence would remain in the hands of the defence minister in Tbilisi. Unfortunately, that minister happened to be Tengiz Kitovani, who considered his role to be somewhat more than purely ceremonial and administrative.

A revolt then took place in the north of Mingrelia, where the corridor between Gali and Zugdidi was occupied by the 'Zviadists', supporters of the deposed Gamsakhurdia. They had kidnapped Shevardnadze's envoy Sandro Kavsadze (later to be chairman of the State Committee for Human Rights), and the situation gave Kitovani precisely the pretext he required to make his move. What was about to happen makes accusations made later that he negotiated secretly with the Zviadists behind Shevardnadze's back — especially with Gamsakhurdia's old crony Loti Kobalia, who was now the president in exile's military supreme commander — not entirely stripped of logic.

Little had been done about Kavsadze's kidnapping. Attempts to free the hostage foundered because of Shevardnadze's refusal to make concessions — which he nonetheless did by proclaiming, on August 4th, a general amnesty in Georgia excluding those sentenced for murder. Indeed, on the one day all political prisoners were free men again. The hostage, hwoever, still remained under lock and key.

On the evening of August 11th, the Georgian interior minister Roman Gensadze and Shevardnadze's personal adviser and confidant Davit Salaridze arrived in Zugdidi. Together with their host, the governor of the province Otar Patsatsia (later rewarded by Shevardnadze for his loyalty with the post of prime minister after Tengiz Sigua's dismissal), they drove to a house which belonged to one of Gamsakhurdia's 'personal friends and counsellors'. Once they had entered, they heard vehicles outside. Shots were fired and suddenly they realised that their armed escort was under attack by around hundred militiamen — Chechens, as the three were to later claim. Resistance proved futile, and within a short time the delegation was bundled into an army vehicle which took them to a settlement near Gali where Vakhtang Kobalia was waiting for them. The crucial point of whether or not Gamsakhurdia himself was present is something over which the various accounts disagree.

It could be argued that the events sparked by these two senseless abductions made a solid contribution to what could well have become the most serious international stand-off since the Cuban Crisis of 1963. On August 14th, Kitovani was ordered to march on Gali with a thousand or so armed national guards with the aim of liberating the prisoners — by force if need be. But he never reached his target, since the hostages were released shortly afterwards unharmed. But there was no stopping this patriotic hero, whose career had started as a street-gang leader, then plotter against the state, ending up as the country's defence minister. He made a bee-line for for Sukhumi at the head of not one but three thousand paramilitary troops, armed to the teeth and supported by tanks and heavy artillery. Fierce resistance by local interior troops could not prevent Kitovani's National Guard from taking control of the city within 24 hours. Massacre, abduction and looting followed.

Shevardnadze was plunged into a state of grave embarrasment, to say the least, and he immediately had security chief Ioseliani and prime-minister Sigua flown over to Sukhumi to straighten things out. On August 17th, both parties agreed to a ceasefire, including a commitment to withdraw the Guards from the city within 24 hours. Instead, Kitovani stormed the local Parliament Building early next morning, sending cabinet ministers and people's representatives fleeing — literally and figuratively speaking — through the back door further up the coast to Gudauta, where independence was proclaimed and a government formed. Meanwhile, Moscow had started the evacuation of all Russian citizens trapped in Sukhumi — a operation which was put in jeopardy when on August 20th fighting flared up again between Kitovani's Guards who were terrorising the area and re-entering Abkhazian troops — the latter supported by Cossacks, other (North) Caucasians and even a unit of Turkish volunteers who had hastily moved in.

This time it was not only Shevardnadze who faced extreme embarrassment. The same can be said of Boris Yeltsin, who found himself caught in the cross-fire of a major political row at home. Among the hawks were vice prime-minister George Khiza, foreign minister Andrei Kozyrev and Parliament's factotum Sergey Baburin, whose extremist views veered significantly close to those of the notorious ultra-nationalist MP Zhirinovsky. Whilst publicly shedding crocodile's tears over the Armenians in Azerbaijan and the Abkhazians and Ossetes in Georgia, these politicians were out for one thing only: to provoke an all-out regional conflict in Transcaucasia with the final aim of rolling the Russian border forward again to the banks of the River Arax.

In reality, the spectre of total war in Transcaucasia was far less imaginary than it would seem — certainly when compared with how the situation was viewed in the West, or rather *not* viewed due to total indifference. Nevertheless, further along the coast, the Ukraine was witnessing an ever more heated row that escalated over status of the Crimea and control of the Black Sea fleet. Kiev had already made repeated warnings to the Kremlin that in the event of direct armed intervention in Georgia it would occupy the Crimea and come to Georgia's aid — in fact, units of the Ukrainian National Defence Force had already fought on the Georgians' side since the first fighting in Sukhumi.

The plan as set out by the Russian warmongers was simple: occupy the road linking Tbilisi to Vladikavkaz, have marines land in both Poti and Baku and from there march on and reoccupy Abkhazia, the former Soviet base near Ganja, in Azerbaijan, and the autonomous Nakhchivan. The most unequivocal broadside came from Ankara, who pointed to the treaty signed in the aftermath of the Second World War and ratified by the Warsaw Pact, NATO and the United Nations, which guaranteed an open border between Nakhchivan and Turkey as well as the region's integrity. Briefly stated: taking Nakhchivan by force would mean war between Russia and Turkey since any action taken within its existing borders without Ankara's prior consent violated the agreement. Thus, Turgut Özal's message to Moscow and Yerevan was clear: hands off.

It is conceivable that Yeltsin and defence minister Grachov might have ventured on a military campaign against the Ukraine. But waging war on

Turkey and thereby on NATO would surely have meant the end of both the CIS and the Russian Federation — even if the Americans had avoided becoming embroiled in the conflict, torn as they would have been between supporting the Turks, as they were legally bound, and cherishing their old-time sentiments towards the Armenians — and this the pair realised all too well. Just how American pressure made Yeltsin call off a mass intervention is not known. However, it is not difficult to conclude that any such intervention would have taken the situation in Abkhazia from bad to worse.

Averting a Russian invasion hardly meant that Abkhazia's troubles were over. In late September, four thousand heavily armed troops consisting of Abkhazian, Caucasian, Turkish, Arab and Iranian volunteers moved against the occupied city of Gagra, on the coast near the border with Russia. On October 3rd, the city fell, despite fierce resistance by the same Gia Karkarishvili who had been responsible for the chaos in Tskhinvali — after his promotion to defence minister as Kitovani's successor, he was sacked again and ended up exiled in Moscow, crippled for life after being shot by snipers. During the fighting, some 300 of Karkarishvili's men were reported killed.

The same day that Gagra fell, the Abkhazians began shelling Sukhumi, which was to become a daily routine all winter for those who were left behind, as they would be for such other localities as Adzinbzha, Kindgi, Tamysh and Chartveli, which were situated on the other side of the Georgian-Abkhazian frontline — both sides were busy bombarding each other. One of the Georgian side's favourite targets was Eshera, where Russian troops were still stationed and the site, according to the Russians, of an important military research and development laboratory still in operation. On November 2nd, unexpectedly heavy shelling destroyed all the supply systems of power and drinking water in Sukhumi. This was a winter to be forever etched in the inhabitants' memories.

"As I see it, it wouldn't have been too difficult to repair the systems," recalls one woman who had sent her children to Tbilisi but herself remained until the bitter end. "But it simply wasn't done. We were told that we were in a state of liberty and legitimately lived on Georgian territory. But there wasn't a hint of the Georgian government anywhere. The only thing visible to us were the stuck-up, pathetic parades of the militias belonging to Ioseliani and Kitovani.

"The shops were overflowing with stolen stuff: furniture, luxury goods, medicine and food parcels with the Red Cross labels still on them. Everything, including bread, was exorbitantly expensive. Anyone who wanted to get out to anywhere safer had to pay heaps of money to get through the roadblocks — anyone who went and simply tried his luck was sent back just as simply. Nothing was done to defend the city — nothing.

Those brave fighters were always the first to dive into the basements the second the first shots were heard. Each week students and other youngsters were recruited, most of them by force, and sent off to the front line. They were told they wouldn't have to fight, only to stand guard . . . but as far as I know, less than half of them ever came back, pure cannon fodder."

Meanwhile, the ever enigmatic Caucasian Mountain Confederation had garnered so much support that they now reckoned themselves powerful enough to break through the Georgian lines. A first attempt on January 5th was to fail. A second on March 2nd saw the town of Labra (Ochantir) fall into the Abkhazians' hands, together with a number of strategic positions to the north east of the district of Sukhumi, which made the city itself a sitting duck.

That winter, the 'neo-imperialistic' dream of Yeltsin's opponents drew as close to reality as it was ever to come. As the fighting escalated, the risk of the Russians becoming involved in the conflict directly and up to their ears was very real indeed — a risk they took with every thought for the calamitous consequences, according to the vast majority of the Georgian public, a vociferous minority headed by Shevardnadze insisting the contrary.

The events now fell into place fast and furious. On December 3rd, a Georgian foray out of Sukhumi resulted in the temporary recapture of Labra and Tamysh. Three days later, on December 6th, Russian commanders threatened Sukhumi with air raids. On December 14th, a Russian helicopter loaded with 'relief goods' was shot down near Charkveli. Shortly afterwards, Grachov appointed General Victor Solokin 'Supreme Commander of West Transcaucasia'. The move was political rather than military: Solokin, after all, was no less than the Butcher of Tbilisi under whose command Soviet troops had committed their atrocities in the Georgian capital in April 1989.

By the end of December, the Abkhazian leader Zurab Achba launched a recruitment drive among those Russians who had been hounded from their homes by the Georgians. During the month of January, a shady political game began to be played in and around the battle arena. On January 12th, Kitovani met Grachov in secret. Two weeks later, Shevardnadze and a Russian delegation agreed in Tbilisi that January 1st 1996 would be the final deadline to end all Russian military presence on Georgian territory. On February 20th, residential areas of Sukhumi were strafed by Russian aircraft, leaving dozens killed and hundreds wounded. Off the Russian port of Sochi, Georgian fishing boats were seized by Russian coastguards.

The same day, Grachov publicly declared that both Ajaria and Abkhazia "are zones of strategic interest" for Russia and flatly denied the existence of any agreement with respect to the withdrawal of Russian troops. As for the air raids on Sukhumi, he ludicrously claimed that the aircraft in question were in fact Georgian planes with fake Russian markings painted on them.

In Tbilisi, a political storm broke out.

"I was beside myself," Irina Chanturia-Sarishvili was to recall. "But at the same time I felt satisfied in one way or another when I heard Shevardnadze admit: 'It seems the opposition's opinion concerning the role played by the Russians in the conflict is far from unfounded.' In fact, it looked for a while that some comprehension of the facts behind the Abkhazian conflict had finally got into his thick skull, that it was a string of deliberate Russian provocations leading to them trampling all over Georgia, just as they had twice already done in the past. Unfortunately, this insight of his proved to be short-lived."

As it would appear. On February 24th, the Georgian Parliament voted with an overrwhelming majority in favour of a resolution calling for immediate withdrawal of "all foreign military personnel" from Georgian territory. At first, Shevardnadze declared himself "sympathetic." Subsequently, he spoke of his "regret" over the latest events of recent months. But the resolution was to remain a signed sheet of paper, nothing more.

Three days later Grachov, accompanied like a movie star by a train of reporters and cameramen, went on a whistle-stop tour of Batumi and Sukhumi.

In Batumi, people still vividly remember the spectacle: "He was wandering around with a group of officers and every time he spotted a camera or a microphone he'd blare out that no one in the whole wide world would ever dare interfere with the movements of the Russian Army. We were under the strong impression that these gentlemen were far from sober."

"At that moment, we were as close as we ever were to a solution," members of Shevardnadze's entourage were to claim later, "since the Abkhazian side was prepared to stop its attacks on Sukhumi in exchange for special status within the Georgian republic. The displaced persons on both sides would have been allowed to return to their homes. A joint Georgian-Abkhazian force would supervise the peace operation. After that, the original agreement of 1992 would be implemented."

So everyone appeared to be satisfied. Except, of course, for Kitovani and Ioseliani who feared that this turn of events would deprive them of the pretext they had long nurtured to justify the existence of their respective armed units, which in Tbilisi and large parts of the rest of the country had taken control of the streets and, most importantly, the black market. For their part, the Russians, ever wary they would be ousted from the scene, were most interested in continuation of the conflict until they themselves were in a position to move in as keepers of the peace — at gunpoint.

To show he meant business with his various declarations, on February 24th, Grachov had the Russian planes raid Sukhumi on a daily basis between March 11th-16th. Initially, he claimed as he had done before that the aircraft were "repainted" Georgian planes. Later, he was to state that the bombardments were "in retaliation" for the earlier shooting-down of a Russian SU27 fighter plane. Meanwhile, Kitovani's dubious role in the Russian provocations had split the Georgian party in Sukhumi. On December 9th 1992, he transferred those troops he considered loyal into his personal armed force, and informed Kitovani, who was still minister of defence, that he would take or leave the latter's orders as he so desired. By the end of February, fighting broke out between the armies of both warlords. Russian forces attempted to intervene but were came under fire from the other two sides for their pains. Shortly afterwards, Kitovani was fired by Shevardnadze, and Karkarishvili to be granted his post. Political disruption had its own impact.

Sukhumi had become a place where no one could live any longer. "Everybody was fighting against everybody else," survivors recalled. "Families were split as they took different sides. We almost longed for the Russians to occupy the city. But anyone saying that thought aloud wasn't going to stay alive for long."

The final blow to the stricken city and its people was not long in coming.

On May 6th, the same day of Kitovani's dismissal and Karkarishvili's promotion, Russian aircraft bombarded Sukhumi once more, in retaliation, so it was said, for a "Georgian air raid" on Eshera four days earlier during which, it was claimed, a Georgian SU25 had been shot down. On May 10th, without the government's knowledge (or so the government insisted), a unit of less than a hundred Mkhedrioni attacked Russian barracks near Kutaisi. They were repelled with extreme force, leaving behind as they fled the scene six 'knights' killed and ten others carried off wounded.

Meanwhile, in Sukhumi pandemonium continued its reign. Hunger and shortages of everything affected every individual by now including the troops, for whom there was nothing left to loot any more. To make matters worse, Kobalia's troops, who had stood apart so far, now intervened and cut off the roads and railway from Sukhumi to the south east. It was not until July 27th, this time under the UN Security Council's supervision, that a ceasefire between all the sides involved was agreed on. Effectively, the withdrawal of armed units and dismantling of military installations on both sides of the frontline could be observed in the days that followed, while convoys carrying food and medicine were directed into a Sukhumi wracked by starvation and epidemics.

The truce was barely two days old when a new offensive was launched from an unexpected quarter. On July 29th Kobalia suddenly occupied Senaki, followed by Abasha and Khobi. After this, the rebel troops turned east and pushed across the mountains into the southern parts of South Ossetia to take up position in the suburbs of Tskhinvali. On October 2nd, the Zviadists (still fired by the memory still fresh of their founder, barely deceased less than a year) seized their chance and, following Kobalia's initiative, simultaneously moved east and west. That day, Poti fell into their hands, depriving Shevardnadze of his sole access to the Black Sea. The following day Khoni and Vali fell, bringing Kobalia within shooting distance of Kutaisi. He chose not to attack the city, however, pushing instead further eastwards to take Kvemo-Kartli and Javakheti, south-west of Tbilisi. In a final flourish to his master-plan, he swooped back into Abkhazia and occupied Gali, the only slice of Abkhazia that had been spared the war and where Abkhazians and Mingrelians/Georgians had continued, if uneasily, to live side by side. Shevardnadze's republic had been sliced into two.

The situation was sobering: Tbilisi and a surrounding strip of about 20 miles formed the only territory where the president had any say left. The conquests of the Gamsakhurdists appear to have been accomplished without as much of a shot, and by the end of September, almost a week after the rebels' subsqent "forced withdrawal," Poti was as sleepy and quiet as it had ever been since the downfall of the Soviet Union, with not a ship in the port, not a car in the street.

Was there any danger?

"Absolutely not," insisted the acting head of police who received me at the port. "There's no fuel around and, in any case, what's there for any merchant vessel to come here for? The rebels turned up — hardly a shot was fired because the Mkhedrioni and other irregular groups had abandoned the town the day before. The rebels came to my office and told me that from now on they represented the lawful authorities. I told them to do as they pleased since I'm just a policeman and don't have anything to do with politics. Then they opened up the municipal safe and realised it was empty, so they then started looting the liquor stores. That was nothing new — Kitovani and Ioseliani's lot really hadn't done much else when *they* were here."

By evening, the liberators of the nation were to a man tanked up on booze and so it went on for three weeks after which they departed as casuallly as they had moved in.

Zugdidi, however, offered quite a different view. Here, most government buildings had been turned into smoking ruins and shells. On the evening of my visit, the prime-minister Otar Patsatsia had come to his native town to see for himself what was left of its governing council and to appoint a new prefect, Colonel Adamia, a jolly old man in his 1960s who invited me to join him in a cup of coffee the next morning.

"Consider what has happened as a family quarrel," he said, dressed up in a grey-silver uniform glittering with all his old Soviet decorations. "I helped stop the Nazis in the mountains not far from here, sir — now that was war! It's not what you've seen here . . . We had a little chat with a few of the commanders of those lads, and then most of them came afterwards and handed in their weapons. We've given each of them a transfer and a letter of safe conduct and now they are free to go where they please. You can see it for yourself: Georgia won't go under that easily, I assure you."

A month later, Kobalia's men surrendered en masse and their hardliners had fled abroad. 'Loti' himself was apprehended in Kiev the following year and extradited to Georgia where he stood trial. In Abkhazia, events were to take a much more tragic turn. Early in the morning of September 16th, the Abkhazian and other Caucasian forces embarked on their final attack on the city. From that point on, it was every man woman and child for themselves and *sauve qui peut*.

This proved not to be easy at all, since all the roads were blocked and so was the port by gunboats. Only the airport was still functioning, so the only way out that remained was by air.

"The airport's hall was a mass of pushing, shoving, sometimes fighting people," remembers a young woman who tried to get a place on a plane — in vain. "And incredibly that turned out to be my good luck. I did have a ticket but three, four, maybe five times more tickets had been sold than there were places available. So I didn't get on. Later I found out that the plane I was supposed to have been on was been shot down."

The incident involving the shooting down of two civilian Tupolev 24 planes carrying refugees to Georgia proper has long been the subject of controversy. If the Georgian claims are true and the number of casualties amounted to less than a hundred, then the planes must have been more than half empty, a supposition which under the circumstances is highly unlikely.

An entirely different version was given by one of the main players on the other side of the Abkhazian scene: Ali Aliev. A Daghestani Lak from Makhachkala, a retired Soviet navy officer and secretary general of the Confederation of Caucasian Mountain Nations, Aliev dusted off his uniform once more in order to liberate the Caucasus "from Sukhumi to Derbent" and set off for Gudauta — alone in his car straight through four civil war zones. On arrival, he was asked to take command of the Confederation batallions.

"I said all right, but only if I could go with them myself into battle instead of sitting in some office. I drew up an elite unit of fighters with the courage of lions to take Sukhumi. That was my most glorious hour! In the dead of night, we loaded up a number of missiles brought over from Afghanistan — USA-made Stingers — onto boats and sailed out to a strategic spot. I personally fired the missiles [at the planes]. What you've heard so far of the incident is correct. What is *not* correct is the claim the planes were carrying passengers. We saw the craft come down and spotted boxes crammed with arms and ammunition in the wreckage that floated in our direction."

Ever since, Aliev has been known as the 'Pirate from Daghestan' on both sides of the Caucasus. "Sure, there's a price on my head in Georgia and the Russians would love to see me hang as well. Let them come and get me — but they'd never dare!"

Some say Aliev was just boasting. But the fact remains that no one else has claimed direct responsibility for the act. Whatever the case, given Shevardnadze's precarious position in Tbilisi, the fall of Sukhumi was only a matter of time — a time that swiftly approached. The hour everybody was waiting for came finally on September 27th, a week after the last ultimatum imposed on the Georgian armed forces had expired. The fearless head of state had himself flown into the Abkhazian capital a number of occasions, and there were times when he was lucky to get out with his life as he dodged the Grads.

"It really did look as if there was no escape," he recalled. "A number of times I honestly thought I wasn't going to get out of there alive. Everybody wanted an end to it all, but nobody dared make the move. Nobody dared go to the Russian commander, who was the only one in town in possession of a telephone that worked, and say: 'Please tell the enemy we surrender unconditionally.'"

It seemed as though the spirit of Gamsakhurdia ruled over Sukhumi from his grave.

The taking of the city, the countless acts of revenge taken on the remaining inhabitants by Abkhazians and their fellow fighters, the mass forcing out of refugees straight into the battlefield of Mingrelia where disorder and danger ruled, was the media scoop of the year and for a while drove even the drama of Yugoslavia from the front pages. But there was no way for the quarter of a million Georgians fleeing Abkhazia to pass through Mingrelia. Whole convoys of refugees were turned back by both warring sides — Kitovani and Ioseliani's men branded them as "cowardly traitors" and the fall of Sukhumi as "propaganda." Did they refuse to believe what had happened or did they genuinely not know? It was impossible to tell either way. In the confusion that raged all around, the only remaining escape route for the exhausted and starving families was the road to Svanetiaa, over the more than 6,000 foot high Kodori Pass. Storms and exhaustion tormented this 'Journey of the Desperate' and at least two thousand refugees were not to survive.

On October 8th, a tired and disillusioned Shevardnadze walked into Yeltsin's office to sort things out — the Russian premier barely able to contain his joy at the turn of events. A week later, Shevardnadze returned to address a Georgian Parliament overwhelmed with impotent rage at the terms on offer: Georgia was to become a member of the CIS and Russian troops were to occupy all the main roads and railroads connecting Tbilisi with the coast.

On November 8th the Russian navy landed in Poti to join the small Russian army garrison already there. One of the commanders told me a day after his arrival: "We haven't heard a single shot. We've arrested a few dozens of men in arms but we haven't been able to establish which group they belong to. Apart from that, this place is a ghost town — it's certainly not a town in a state of war."

Within a month Kobalia's regiments had either surrendered of vanished into thin air. According to the subsequent treaty signed by Georgia and Russia on October 26th 1993, "all vital connections" would be placed under Russian military supervision — including the railways and highways between Tbilisi and Baku, between Tbilisi and Yerevan . . . and between Yerevan and Baku, without so much as asking the Azeris' permission. That would have come down to a blatant military occupation of the entire former Transcaucasian Soviet border with the exception of Talysh.

Back in Baku, prime-minister Surat Husseynov spoke out — something he rarely did — "in favour of complete implementation of the agreement." President Aliev too did something he rarely did. He hesitated. And then refused. Meanwhile, the Abkhazian government, now headed by rebel leader Vladislav Ardzinba, had taken refuge in Sukhumi, along with the Confederation of Mountain Nations. A ceasefire was agreed that included maintaining the status quo. And so Mother Russia kept guard. Peace was signed. And the war continued.

In the final week of November the Abkhazians and their Caucasian brethren attacked on all fronts. Gali and Kodori fell and by the end of the month not only all of eastern Abkhazia but also the western marches of Svanetia had fallen into separatist hands. Amidst all the misery, one tiny bright spot had shone for the government in Tbilisi: the offensive had broken the last shred of resistance by Kobalia's forces. The enemy had finished Shevardnadze's job for him.

In early February, in the press hall of the government house which also served as a temporary shelter for Parliament (since the real parliamentary buildings were still gutted ruins after Gamskhurdia's siege), Shevardnadze appeared with an icily grinning Yeltsin at his side in yet another display of solidarity.

"Of course I've gone a long way," Shevardnadze was to tell me later, "And the opposition are perfectly justified in accusing me of firing a shot in the dark — although they really should stop calling me a traitor and all that. In fact, I'm ready to take an even greater step forward and turn Georgia into a federation after the German example. But whatever the case, total secession of Abkhazia remains unacceptable for me, and if that's going to happen then I'll fight it by whatever means — including force if I have to."

That day, February 10th, at about the precise time we were talking, Abkhazia's self-declared Parliament had declared its republic "sovereign and fully independent" in sharp contrast to the "declaration of mutual understanding" they had agreed to with Georgia in Geneva six weeks earlier. There then followed an internal struggle within the Abkhazian leadership between those who favoured incorporation into the Russian Federation and those who argued for some form of compromise with Tbilisi. Initially, the Confederation's leadership supported the pro-Russian faction, but subsequently tended more and more towards the reconciliatory faction as tensions grew between the Kremlin and Dudayev. At the time of the invasion of Chechenia in late December, the Confederation immediately declared its support for the beleaguered Chechen leader and, shortly after, the same fighting force of Chechen, Circassian, Ingush and Abkhazian warriors who had forced the 'mini-empire' of Georgia to its knees marched on Chechenia in order to teach Big Brother a lesson.

Throughout 1994, it was all quiet on on the Abkhazian front as, despite regular shoot-outs and skirmishes, large-scale violence was not resorted to. In the first half of 1995, repeated efforts were made to repatriate the Mingrelians/Georgians who had fled Abkhazia — beginning with the District of Gali where, despite the heavy fighting, a few dozen villages had managed to be preserved by their Georgian inhabitants. The climate for repatriaton, however, proved hostile in the most literal sense — between January 17th-22nd, Abkhazian armed units had carried out a series of raids on the villages of Shesheleti, Totoboya and Tagiloni in the Gali region, the remaining pocket of Abkhazia where Georgians lingered on. The scenario had been the usual one: murder, rape, abduction, looting. The observers of the CIS and the UN looked on — and looked awkward — and observed that there was nothing they could do with regard to these events nor others yet to happen.

For two more years, Russian troops continued to be stationed in

Georgia in order to "keep peace." In the course of their duties, they killed dozens of Georgian citizens on the streets for no apparent reason, wounded hundreds more and harassed and robbed thousands. As for the refugees trying to return to their homes, they were stopped, stripped of their belongings and sent back (sometimes by abduction) by their self-same former colonial protectors who had been despatched to the area to aid them and facilitate their resettlement.

Time and time again, it seemed that the UN spokeswoman in Tblisi was programmed to produce the same reply to such allegations: "We know of no recent incidents, our observers are doing their jobs unhindered, everything is OK."

In July 1997, as one more half year mandate of the Russian troops was on the point of expiring, the Georgian parliament at last reached tyhe conclusion that everything was not OK and refused to authorised another half year extension.

"From now on," wrote editor-in-chief Zaza Gachechiladze in his newspaper *The Georgian Times*, "the Russian military in Georgia should be considered trespassers."

In fact, this was exactly what they had been from the first moment on. According to the CIS treaty, troops operating under the CIS banner may be deployed only with the consensus of all CIS member states. When the issue of sending CIS troops came to a vote in 1992, Azerbaijan voted against, making the ensuing "decision" and "mandates" legally void. Moreover, only Russian troops were deployed whereas, according to the rules, no single state may provide more than 49 per cent of the force comprising such a mission.

Not unlike the Upper Karabakh conflict, searching for true motives and reasons behind the conflicts over South Ossetia and Abkhazia means having to wade through an ocean of sloganeering, allegations, counter-allegations and trite 'expert' analysis. If there is one thing that brings these three conflicts together under one indicator, it must surely be the desire of Russian political forces to block the natural outlet along which Caspian oil would flow ultimately towards the Mediterranean — or at least make it such a risky venture that oil prices would stay at $15-plus per barrel.

Ironically, this is not entirely out of keeping with the interests of the Western oil multinationals, who have to keep stock values high — any dramatic decrease would send costs of their banking credits soaring. Which, in all, indicates that below the understandable outbursts of emotion there is a clear pattern underpinning the conflicts in the Southern Caucasus which various parties would rather passed unnoticed.

12

Clearing up the mess with Shevardnadze

"*I*t was the year 1937. From Mamati and its surrounding villages anyone in authority or simply respected had started disappearing. Every day there were rumours that yet another 'people's enemy' had been apprehended. The chairman of the farmers' council, the director of the collective farm, the agricultural engineer, supervisers of the farming co-operatives, all were stigmatised as embezzlers, Trotskyites, nationalist heretics.

"Then one day, my father disappeared. He had been a member of the Party since 1924 and was in charge of the secondary school that opened in our village. The village looked up to him as a brilliant mind that commanded respect. My mother became withdrawn and refused to answer any of our burning questions. Outside the house, I felt a chilling alienation around me . . ."

The passage comes from the book *The Future Belongs to Freedom*. Its author is Eduard Shevardnadze. Elsewhere, he writes: "I believed in Stalin." The nation believed in Stalin. Unfortunately, Stalin did not believe in the nation. Then the nation believed in Khruschev. But Khruschev could hardly care less about the nation. Then when Brezhnev, Andropov and Chernenko turned up, nobody believed in them any more. Shevardnadze's "most faithful friend and confidant," Mikhail Sergeyovich Gorbachev, believed the nation believed in him. But his belief was unfounded.

Elsewhere in his mini-memoir, Shevardnadze writes that he was "shocked" by 1989's Bloody April in Tbilisi. This is most likely to be true since it would be hard to assume that Ligachov and his associates had briefed the Georgian fully over the measures to be taken with the capital's 'hooligans' and 'anti-Soviet activists'.

As Shevardnadze drily puts it: "The slogans of 'truth' and 'glasnost' were stifled then discarded by a mechanism incapable of adapting to them."

Mamati is the village in Guria, south-west Georgia, where Eduard Shevardnadze was born on January 25th 1928. Since March 1992 its most famous son had stood at the helm of the rudderless ship of Georgia, and which, as friend and foe alike were forced to admit, he prevented from sinking.

Spring 1995 in Tbilisi was sunny and happy. For a while, the crowds along Rustaveli Avenue could once more lose themselves in the heady spirit of bygone days. At the universities, the usual listlessness, so characteristic of Georgian young people of the time, had been taken over by a ripple of excitement: exams were drawing to a close.

On Chavchavadze Avenue, in broad daylight, the sound of shots were heard. Glass shattered, voices shouted. Less than a minute later, a Volga with no numberplates drove away from the scene at top speed, leaving a shop assistant lying bleeding in a fashion boutique, with broken glass and clothes strewn all over the floor. Later, the shop assistant was back on his feet — apart from some cuts he appeared to be all right, nothing serious. Two plainclothes policemen finally turned up. Nothing appeared to have been taken, it was reported. No, attacks like this are chilling 'warnings' or 'reminders'.

Anyone in Georgia, Armenia or Azerbaijan who is in retail business has to pay the mafia for 'protection' — against the same mafia. In Baku, shopkeepers told me that it all goes rather smoothly there, since they only have one mafia to deal with. In Tbilisi, however, there is more than one mafia — and each comes to claim its dues.

Despite such an alarming fact, it looked that in 1995 the fight against crime in Georgia had not been without some success: the rate of murders, burglaries and other violent crimes was down and most of the criminal organisations at local level, known as 'brotherhoods', were said to have been disbanded or else to have eliminated one another in gang wars. This had had been the fate of gangs like the Culinaria and the Wild Boys in Tbilisi. These hooligan gangs were formed during the Soviet 1980s by youths, usually from well-to-do families, who found their inspiration in the make-believe gangster world depicted in movies like *Once Upon a Time in America*. Each time they got arrested, they were back on the street again within days. All they wanted was a buzz or whatever mischief they could get up to as long as it helped get them away, even momentarily, from the suffocating grip of the horror that was petty-bourgeois, grey-suited Communism.

But the demise of the gangs in Georgia did not mean that terror had yet disappeared from the streets of Tbilisi. Since the end of 1994, police desperately sought a group of 'Jack the Rippers' who committed ritual murders on passers-by after dark. One of their most horrific acts was in early July 1995 when a mother and her son were mercilessly butchered: the child had been hanged from a tree nearby while the mother was then raped and her throat slit.

It was on December 20th 1990 that Eduard Shevardnadze — the amiable Soviet foreign minister and, after Gorbachev, the most popular Soviet politician in the outside world — announced his surprise resignation, "in protest against dictatorship gaining ground" in the USSR. After his return to Tbilisi, that dictatorship no longer had a ground to stand on in any case. But in Georgia, that ground had been taken by the forces of organised crime, under the dubious 'salutary committee' of Ioseliani and Kitovani. Former cabinet leader Sigua, one of Gamsakhurdia's good old boys who had joined forces with the two firebrands, had got his old job back but his reputation had suffered irreparably in the meantime.

Still, it was Sigua who managed to convince both coup plotters that nobody in the outside world would take them seriously so long as they failed to find a driving personality who would save Georgia from the violent abyss of the Somalia syndrome of the 'stateless state' and put its flag back on the world map. And as they well knew, there was only one person who could do that: Shevardnadze.

Of course he got the job. But although the saviour of Georgia went on to lose the war over Abkhazia — never a good move for the ratings — it is curious, to go by the opinion polls carried out at regular intervals by both government and opposition, that he was given less blame for this than might be expected. In fact, all all times, even in the most difficult circumstances, the head of state kept a comfortable lead in terms of popularity in comparison to other politicians — even if sometimes Gia Chanturia came pretty close.

By the mid-1990s, however, at the same time election campaigns were going on, it looked as though Shevardnadze's star had begun to wane. In the cafes and at home, people were expressing mostly disrespectful disappointment in their head of state. The main cause was not so much the war but rather his perpetual tendency to compromise with Yeltsin and, paticularly, his political support for his Russian counterpart during the invasion of Chechenia. Another joint press conference on February 1994 by the two leaders in Tbilisi, simultaneously broadcast on television, featured an argumentative Shevardnadze and a unperturbed Yeltsin who smiled like a Cheshire cat.

It made a deep impression on the public whilst heavily annoying them at the same time. "Did you see that Russian?" came the indignant shouts at the journalists' cafe, a shabby establishment in the Old City where the customers aren't usually good examples of energetic movement. "Grinning from ear to ear — that sod's got his way everywhere! We're right back at square one."

Now whether Shevardnadze really had any choice in signing Georgia up to the CIS and allowing Russian troops onto Georgian territory, or else face the course of his country being set directly into the abyss, is a question most Georgians refuse to answer, even if deep in their hearts they know the reality of the situation. But this has never stopped them from cultivating hard feelings over what they perceive as the president's "capitulation" — Georgians tend to let their damaged pride prevail over common-sense in such matters.

"Shevardnadze?!" barked an army officer on leave, who with a few chums was busy consuming impressive piles of (cheap) Georgian champagne under the hot Tbilisi summer sun in 1995. "Believe you me, that's no president, that's a Russian marionette!"

But what would he have done in his place?

"Anything! Do a deal with the Abkhazians, the Ossetes. Split the entire country for all I care. But a single Russian soldier on our territory — over my dead body!"

But that's precisely what Gamsakhurdia tried to do and look what happened there.

"If you don't understand, you don't understand Georgia!" came the reply.

As an elderly university professor was later to observe: "Naturally I'm familiar with reactions like that. We've got more than our fair share of Don Quixotes over here."

According to subsequent opinion polls, in those days little more than 15 per cent of the public held a positive view of the head of state and his cabinet ministers. As for Parliament, only seven per cent approved of it and its actions. In both cases, half the remainder gave a negative response while the rest had had no opinion. Tellingly, no one suggested a possible alternative. The average Georgian (then a tiny minority in society between a mega-rich upper layer and the starving working masses dumped in the gutter) could merely shrug.

Hardly a favorable atmosphere, therefore, for the general and presidential elections which were to take place in October 1995 — provided, that is, Parliament managed to approve a new constitution which would turn Georgia into a federation along German lines in an attempt to join with the lost territories of Abkhazia and South Ossetia.

For the time being, Shevardnadze would neither confirm nor deny his candidacy for the presidency. Only in the late summer did he announce he would run — which ended in an easy victory for Shevardnadze himself as well as his party, which gained an absolute majority in the new parliament.

But for all the grumbling and groaning, it has to be acknowledged that anyone who took an objective look at Tbilisi during the summer of 1995 had to admit that the complaints were somewhat less than reasonable. People could — at least during the day — walk the streets in relative safely, they went to socialise once more, spending their money on ice creams, coffees and bottles of Coca-Cola (the global soft drink giant was quick to set up a factory in Georgia and does good business there despite the fact that Georgia's traditional fruit cocktails are admiteedly far tastier). In all, the low opinion the general public seems to have for Georgia's politics seems to be less damaging to political progress than the physical danger attached to being active in politics — a phenomenon of which Georgia has a long and colourful tradition, but which seems to have got slightly out of hand since independence, as the series of political murders committed from there on has reached quite impressive statistics.

For example, on April 20th 1994, interior secretary of state Gia Gulua came under a hail of machine-guns when still in his car outside his home. In the attack Gulua, his fiancee, driver and bodyguard were all killed. Later that year, on December 10th the same thing happened to Gia and Irina Chanturia when in their car — Gia perished while Irina escaped alive with serious injuries. In Moscow, on January 25th 1995, the former vice minister of defence and Butcher of Tskhinvali, Gia Karkarashvili, and his former secretary of state Gaatu Datuashvili were sprayed with gunfire as they stepped out of the military academy. Although his companion died of his wounds, Karkarashvili survived but, as mentioned previously, was to spend the rest of his life as an invalid.

Far more numerous were the attempts that failed to hit their targets, such as the bombs at the homes of the centre left political leader Jumbar Patiashvili on February 27th and the monarchist politician Timur Giorgioliani on November 3rd 1995. In both cases, it turned out that no one was at home. That same year on August 23rd, it was Shevardnadze himself who narrowly escaped death when a bomb exploded in the car waiting for him in the courtyard of the presidential office. A number of MPs present at the parking lot were severely injured, but the president, in a visible state of shock, got off with superficial cuts. Within the hour, armoured vehicles rumbled through the streets of Tbilisi and took up position by the ministries and national television station.

But nothing happened, and a few hours later Shevardnadze appeared, bruised and in his underwear, in front of the television cameras to assure the nation: "As long as I'm alive, let there be no doubt that from November onwards Georgia will be ruled by a democratically elected parliament and not by the mafia . . ."

Mafia? It's only a word, really.

It soon began to look as if the man behind the attempt on Shevardnadze was no less than his own national security minister, Igor Giorgadze, who had flown overnight to Moscow immediately following the attack. Bids at extradition, just as in the case of Mutalibov, led to nothing, easy as it is for a reasonable sum to buy into the Russian system and thus, as a citizen of the Russian Federation, rest secure against extradition to any foreign power.

Meanwhile, the real mafia had more than enough cause to worry and betrayed more than enough grounds therefore on which their involvement in the attack could be deduced. Kitovani was slammed in jail on charges of murder, racketeering, looting and other crimes. As for his fellow conspirator Ioseliani, for the moment he was better off — he continued to sit comfortably in his seat in Parliament while his Mkhedrioni were rehabilitated under the guise of a cultural humanitarian organisation. They claimed they had surrendered their weapons "voluntarily."

"Well, at least that's what *they* claim,"observed the UNHCR's representative Geldolph Everts, who in the meantime had been transferred from Yerevan to Tbilisi. "But as far as I know, confiscation of their arms by police turned out to be a complete fiasco. So they were given the okay to hand their arms over to the army, and the details of that are still subject to some controversy."

"It's my personal belief that not even ten per cent of the Mkhedrioni's weapons have been handed in," Shevardnadze's adviser Peter Mamradze was to acknowledge little later. "But their paramilitary display has vanished off the streets — and in this country that's already quite an accomplishment in itself."

It was all change in many ways. The Mkhedrioni instantly had an already notorious successor in the shape of the Agheti Wolves, a movement from the area of the same name which had moulded itself along the lines of the militias of the American extreme right. On January 25th 1995, they came out into the open for the first time with a bomb attack on the main headquarters of the Russian troops near Tbilisi, followed on April 9th by an attack on the residence of the Russian ambassador and the Russian military delegation's office in the capital.

So far, no victims had been claimed by the attacks of the Agheti Wolves. That changed on June 8th as a unit opened fire on a joint Russian-Georgian checkpoint in the north of the country, killing a Georgian officer, David Arabidze. As for the terrorists, they escaped by almost miraculous means. This most recent attack created some confusion within the opposition.

"Confusion?" commented the leader of the centre-right Georgian Unity Party, Nodar Natadze. "In my opinion, I have not the slightest doubt as to who is really behind the Agheti Wolves. The mere fact that after any assassination or assassination attempt no name of any suspect is ever made public, let alone arrests made, is proof enough for me that a very substantial part of the political violence in this country is the handiwork of the 'Gravnye Rasverdoplavyenye Armiy' — the Kremlin's own secret army which has an unlimited agenda and unlimited cash and arms. Why do the perpetrators carry out these acts time and again unhindered? Why, out of a whole group of Russian soldiers, is it precisely a Georgian officer who is shot dead? I keep demanding answers to all those questions and I never get them!"

Despite the gathering controversy, the Georgian government did try to constrain political crime along with 'ordinary' crime — even if the word 'political' in this context was interpreted rather one-sidedly. Kitovani had been incarcerated in early 1995, after together with a few hundred armed followers he had tried to cross the border from Abkhazia in attempt to launch a 'reconquista'. The attempt failed and ended in a blood-bath, thereby serving its real purpose: to frustrate the laborious negotiations and therefore undermine Shevardnadze's position.

The most provocative event in spring 1995, however, was the Dokvadze/Gelbakhiani 'trial', which was concluded with death sentences passed against two terrorists, Irakli Dokvadze and Peter Gelbakhiani. They were the perpetrators of a bomb attack in June 1992 made against Ioseliani. Their target had escaped unhurt, but five bystanders lost their lives and twenty more lay injured. Both bombers had been arrested six months later by Interpol in Baku and immediately extradited. Likewise, in the autumn of 1994, Loti Kobalia was arrested in the Ukraine and dispatched back to Georgia with little fuss. He was charged, among other things, with conspiracy, multiple murder and armed insurrection against the state. Beyond doubt a capital verdict was in store for him as well. However, the offical line is that no executions have taken place in Georgia since Shevardnadze's ascendancy since he generously signed every request for clemency (pressure groups claim otherwise). In 1997, Parliament had prepared the necessary legislation to abolish capital punishment altogether.

Whether some officials were a bit too zealous in marginalising any emergence of 'neo-Zviadism' or intended to abuse their positions to settle personal scores, a number of arrests of partisans, real or assumed, loyal to the fallen head of state did cause many an eyebrow to be raised. Among those apprehended were Tamaz Kikachkheishvili, who had been at the head of the nationalist 'Round Table' when it was under Gamsakhurdia's control, but had taken his distance from him long before the president's downfall, Clara Shorman, the local representative of Helsinki Watch, Eteri Mgabalishvili, leader of the St Ilia Society, and the poet activist Nodar Zalaghonia. At the same time, the offices of the Round Table's most prominent publications, *Iberia Spektri* and *Sakartvelos Samreko*, were raided at regular intervals. The so-called Pan-Georgian Association for Human Rights, a pressure group with close ties with the Round Table, spoke in those days of a hundred or so political prisoners, packed up with other detainees in overcrowded jails where sixty people living in a room meant for eight was reported to be far from exceptional.

Between January 1994 and May 1995, the number of unnatural deaths in prisons and detention centres was up to 150. Outside the prison walls, hundreds of complaints were filed against the forces maintaining law and order during the summer of 1995, the worst cases among them being the murder by police of a suspected car thief in Kuirta on the road to Chkhinvali and the near murder of the correspondent of Russian TV channel Ostankino, who was taken to hospital with serious injuries but survived "through sheer luck" in the words of the surgeons on duty. No charges have followed up the allegations, leaving the motives behind the spate of deaths unclear.

To the surprise of many, the government did react and address itself to the causes behind the worsening image of its forces. During the autumn, hundreds of policemen of all ranks were fired and dozens thrown in jail. As for political developments, there was even more hope glimmering on the horizon.

The new consitution, signed by Shevardnadze the day after the car bomb had almost exploded in his face, made a federation of Georgia, and included a high level of home rule for Ajaria, South Ossetia and Abkhazia: all decisions made by their local parliaments would be respected by the national assembly except those concerning defence and foreign affairs. Only the head of state could use his right of veto, which in its turn, however, would be subject to appeal at the high court.

Only Ajaria went along with the new system without too many objections. The Abkhazian separatists rejected the new consitution outright even before the ink had dried. The South Ossetian regime at first also refused any form of reintegration and infromed the president that "reunification" with North Ossetia in the Russian Federation was their only aim. However, it soon became clear that the North Ossetians, who meanwhile had joined the Confederation of Caucasian Mountain Nations despite their continuing battle with the Ingush, would not hear of this and by the end of 1995 had even expressed their intention of opening an 'embassy' in the Georgian capital. In spring 1997, a compromise with South Ossetia seemed imminent.

In Abkhazia, things were to get even more complicated. Initially, the Abkhazians had continued to enjoy Moscow's support but all this had changed dramatically as in spring 1995 the Abkhazian leader Vladislav

Ardzinba announced a general mobilisation throughout the area, this time against the Russians, supporting resistance in Chechenia against the Russian invaders. Meanwhile, he turned to Tbilisi in a reconciliatory move and even managed to agree to the return of at least a section of the quarter of a million refugees waiting to go back home to Abkhazia. This proved more than Moscow was willing to tolerate. The border with Abkhazia was sealed off and 'punitive expeditions' were carried out against both newly-returned Georgians and Abkhazians loyal to Ardzinba. Houses were ransacked and burnt and whole families massacred before the very eyes of the Russian 'peacekeepers'. The main culprits were Abkhazia's 'interior minister' Agrba and another local leader, by name Shamba, who openly advocated Abkhazia's incorporation into the Russian Federation.

From that point on, the situation steadily worsened in Abkhazia. Most people had to live without electricity, and food distribution had become all but completely disrupted. Apart from a few exceptions, such as the protection by Russian troops of the villagers of Kvemo Bargebi against the ganags of murderous looters, the Russians generally behaved as occupiers rather than peacekeepers and, in most cases, did nothing to stop the rapidly expanding wave of murder and destruction.

There's an old Caucasian saying that goes: "Let's look back in honesty and speak our minds frankly." The basic cause of the rapid accumulation of crises in Georgia is international diplomacy. Just as in Azerbaijan, the Organisation for Security and Co-operation in Europe in particular has self-indulgently revelled in one act of idiocy after another. After the example of the European Union, the OSCE has proved itself to be little more a safety net for politicians in trouble. For the countless victims of armed conflicts, its interventions usually mean a confinement, no more, of their misery. One simply sees to it that the guns fall silent, the bloodstained images disappear from the front pages and that one keeps one's lavishly paid job. This is no criticism but simply a statement of the facts.

The Georgian displaced peoples from the seceded areas were far from being the only victims languishing in the general state of misery throughout the country. During the winter of 1994-95 the pyramid scam had hit Georgia, and thousands of families were ruined by cynical businessmen who lured them into investment schemes that promised as much as 15-25 per cent return on their cash per month. Even foreigners, among them quite respectable UNHCR employees, had fallen into the trap. For most of the local victims, however, the losses meant the end of their last means of survival — most had sold whatever antiques or other valuable objects they could lay their hands on in order to create a cash reserve.

About half of these Georgian financial vampires were put behind bars by the summer of 1995. But most of the stolen cash — estimated at well over $30 million — remained hidden abroad, as did the other half of the fraudsters. The hide-out of one, Koba Devidze, whose firm Ocrus Tassi had stolen about $3 million from its small investors, was even publicly known: together with a German accomplice he had bought a chain of restaurants in Karlsruhe, Germany, in the process laundering his stolen money unhindered by the local authorities. Among the other slippery-fingered individuals on the run were Devidze's partners Gia Galoglishvili and Ramaz Chitia, SASCO's director Kadagishvili, Monarch director Lagradze and A&Co director Batiashvili, along with amounts of anything between $1-3 million. Apart from Germany, Austria, Italy and Benelux were postulated as their possible hide-outs.

Gamsakhurdia's former political power-base by 1996 had all but died out after the last trials had ended with mainly light sentences. Crack-downs and arrests had become rare. Although demand was now minimal and sales figures low, publications of the Zviadists were back on the streets again for sale as were their failed mentor's books. After a few stiff drinks too many, an individual could sometimes be provoked into raising his fist against another tippler who had insulted the ex-president — but most times it would end with a meek apology. "The man was no good, but he was chosen by the people and the Russians did him in" — or so goes popular wisdom. Of course, Gamsakhurdia's "Four Thousand Years of Humiliation" are not over yet, but expecting a Georgian to take the barricade on an empty stomach is really asking too much.

The question remains where all this will leave Georgia in decades to come. Not unlike Azerbaijan, the remaining parts of the county are far from prosperous but at least no one is starving and the economy is doing substantially better than even the most pessimistic balance-sheet predictions. As for the breakaway Abkhazian and Ossetian communities, solutions seemed far more within reach at the time of writing than in Azerbaijan. The ultimate publicity gimmick which embarrassed both Russian and Western observers was the surprise visit of Ardzinba to Tblisi in the summer of 1997 during which, in front of a wall of television cameras, he and Shevardnadze fell into each others' arms. The conclusion has to be that if the nations of the Caucasus want to organise peace, they can only achieve success if they do it by defying all others and blocking all foreign interference. It is this interference lies at the very bottom of the outbreak of conflicts, muzzling the media with evasive statements and straightforward obstruction while encouraging shadowy powers behind the scenes to take control of the stage. Which they did, swiftly, and in a most profitable way, as the concluding chapter of this book will illustrate.

13

The Caucasus connection

I f, in Baku, Tbilisi or Yerevan, you venture in the morning into any one of their concrete 'micro-rayons' (as these dormitory cities are called in Soviet jargon), you'll see syringe needles littering the doorways and gutters. Entering these areas after dark is hardly recommended: a stab in the back, a bullet through the head, for no reason at all, is a real risk and incidents like these keep happening in a quite unceremonial way.

Planners, sociologists, security specialists, everyone in fact from the professor in his ivory tower down to the policeman on the street who can do no more than watch it happen and report it, will be all too ready to confirm it: these concrete deserts with which the world's national and provincial cities have been surrounded during the last decades (and still going up in so many other countries) are the slums of the 21st century. Here, the rule of the jungle is law, for cash anything and everything's for sale, bretrayal lurks on every corner and authority is hard to find.

In Baku, almost four times the size of Tbilisi and once the USSR's fifth largest city, aside from the mico-rayons, real Third World slums can be found — shanty towns that date from the times of the oil boom and which have defied and outlasted the Soviet Union without too much resistance. Spread throughout the city from its heart to its outskirts, their most striking features are the half-savage children, piles of garbage, rusting car wrecks and eyes peering from every corner and every door.

In Baku as well as in Yerevan and Tbilisi, social disruption has been worsened by the influx of tens of thousands of refugee families who have squatted empty apartments, or live rough in barns, garages or corrugated iron containers. Just as in the refugee camps in the countryside, civil solidarity with the refugees here is minimal. "Filth, that's what they are!" complain townspeople in Baku. "The word 'bath' is alien to them and they lower the standards of our streets with their sheep and goats!"

And so the refugee runs around as though on a treadmill: twice the victim of a war for which he never asked and the meaning of which he fails to grasp. Not understanding, not understood and robbed of his final sense of social limits.

Ever since the outbreaks of the secessionist wars in Azerbaijan and Georgia, it is the refugees who have become the easiest prey for the mafia — as cheap couriers ($100 for a job or sometimes less will do) for expensive drugs and as sales market for cheap ones. It may very well be true, as local authorities staunchly claimed throughout the early 1990s, that in each of the three Transcaucasian republics turnover of the local narcotics markets has been limited to "a few million dollars" only. But whatever the revenue, they were foreced to admit early on that the rise in number of drug consumers in the area has taken on alarming proportions. In Azerbaijan, for example, 1,855 arrests were made for possession, trade and/or transport of drugs, against 1305 in 1992. 1132 of those 1855 arrests were for possession of drugs for one's own consumption, 380 cases were for growing or preparation for one's own consumption and in only 216 cases had narcotics been prepared or cultivated in order to sell them.

Statistics are nice as long as they reflect the facts as they are, a situation hardly likely in a country where until not so long ago statistic material was only designed to be used in a selective way and for no other purpose than propaganda.

So, by the end of 1994 only around four thousand individuals were registered as 'drug users' in Azerbaijan, and even then, after taking a closer look, experts could only conclude that not even a quarter of them could be really considered as drug addicts. Nonetheless, those registered represented the tiniest fraction of those whose daily life up to one level or another qualifies as beingdetermined by narcotics in Azerbaijan and whose number must be considered well over a hundred thousand.

The limited development and widescale destruction of purchasing power in Azerbaijan has resulted in a restricted market for heroin and cocaine for the tiny moneyed upper layer of society there. Meanwhile, an equally limited street trade in marijuana and hashish was developing: the products, of local, Iranian or Afghan origin, used to cost about a dollar fifty per gramme on the street in 1993. For the less materially privileged there was ephedrine, which can be easily prepared in any back room since the plant that provides the raw material for it grows about everywhere.

The most popular drug, however, in the Transcaucasian slums and concrete dormitory cities is *tirzhak*, a derivate from a plant of the same name that can be found in abundance growing on the plains of central and southern Azerbaijan as well as in northern Iran. The leaves are either dried and smoked (which gives an effect similar to that of marijuana but at least five times stronger) or powdered, put into solution and injected. This latter form of consumption in particular is highly addictive and causes disruption of the nervous system and, in the longer term, paralysis.

In Georgia, where by tradition drug consumption has always been less taboo than in the Islamic republics, according to a report by the United Nations Development Programme issued in June 1995 (the expertise of which is in any case somewhat doubtful), the number of drug consumers could be estimated at anything between "some tens of thousands up to a hundred and fifty thousand." In spring 1995, international and mostly US dominated bodies claiming to be engaged in the combat of drugs repeatedly accused Georgia of allowing drugs barons to hold high positions in government — without, however, providing any factual back-up, an omission which made the accusations appear ludicrous while casting doubts on the original motives for the attacks.

The true reason behind the accusations would appear to be of political rather than ethical motivation. In 1994, a Georgian parliamentary commission had proposed a law that would allow private licence-holders to produce and/or sell a range of narcotics that included opium and opium products. This was provided the quality of their products met standards to be set by the government. In spring 1995, it looked as if there was an overall majority in the Georgian Parliament, including both government and opposition 'fractions', that would be in favour of such legislation. Unfortunately, pressure from the West prevented from being realised what would doubtless have been both a unique experiment and a relief to drug addicts living in misery on the streets of Georgia.

But problems involving drugs, including the activities of extremely well organised syndicates, is not exactly novel in the former West and Central Asian Soviet republics. Nor is up-to-date scientific research, something actually started in earnest during the early 1960s. One of the first conclusions to be made was that the policy dating from the times of the Russian tsars and continued by Stalin and Khruschev had taken a heavy toll. From the early years of Communism onwards, Moscow had adopted the treacherous habit of appointing heads of important local families and clans as local party leaders and state officials, in order to impress the local population and to lead them to believe that the new order represented some form of real authority. Soon, however, it became clear that the upper-class appointees, converted to proletarism as they were, simply did with their new jobs what they had always done: fill their pockets and put themselves above the law.

One of the results of this maintaining of clan structures is that the drugs business has remained well structured and virtually untouchable right from the start. For example, harvests of narcotics seized in Azerbaijan by the end of the 1980s ran to many tons on an annual basis, but the number of arrests carried out in connection with them remained limited to a few dozen — and then, these were the only hired hands while as a rule the big boys remained safely behind the scenes.

It was in the same period that the Kremlin for the first time started to get an inkling of the true dimensions of the problem, eventually forcing Gorbachev to order the implementation of 'Operation Opium Flower'. The initiative was not seriously intended to eliminate any drugs syndicates but to gain a realistic insight in the size of production of narcotics within the borders of the USSR.

Dr Anzor Gabiani, a sociologist in the service of the Georgian interior ministry, was the only scientific researcher given permission to join the team which was otherwise made up of KGB officials. In his books and interviews, Gabiani relates how, in 1987, in Eastern Kazakhstan hundreds of thousands of acres of opium were mapped out. In other republics of the southern Soviet Union, the situation proved to be little better, including Kirgizstan where opium was cultivated on a legal basis for the preparation of morphine and other medical necessities but where half or more of the harvest disappeared, elaborated or not, into the black market.

Gabiani's experiences in Uzbekistan were even more hallucinatory. "In 1987, we arrived in Tashkent," he remembers. "Remember, this was a delegation consisting of KGB heavyweights, but we were bluntly informed by the local authorities that they were in no position to allow us out of the capital, as they could not 'guarantee our personal security' as they quaintly put it."

It took until next year for the Uzbeks to give way, and Gabiani was astounded at what he saw. "Every tiny farm house had a few square metres of weed cultivation in its back garden. That is nothing special in itself: they have been doing that for at least a thousand years primarily for their own consumption. What was alarming was the sight of hundreds of cultivation areas stretching further than the eye could see, surrounded by fences and watchtowers manned by guards with heavy automatic guns and other weapons — we even spotted rocket launchers among them."

The whole story throws some intriguing light on the history of the Soviet Union as well as on conditions in the Western world during the same period. Throughout those days, we were suppsoed to believe that the USSR was a super-totalitarian state where nothing could ever escape the whim and control of the all-powerful authorities. But did all those white-collar cowboys working for the CIS, MI5, DGSE themselves really not know any better, or do we conclude that half the world's population has been duped by their propaganda machine for more than three generations? Anyone hoping for a genuine answer will have to wait for a long time to come.

In reality, the first drugs scandal in the USSR broke out as early as 1965 with the confiscation of about a hundred kilos of morphine in the Kazakh district of Ust Kamingorsk, destined for the black market. In 1973, the first large-scale drugs syndicate was disbanded. It had consisted of Armenians, Georgians, Uzbeks, Kazakhs and Chinese. They had operated for more than a decade from Chimkent, in Kazakhstan. Because of its vastness and inaccessibility, the country is an ideal hide-out for smugglers in general while for drugs smugglers in particular, the attraction also lies in the arid steppes that offer quite favourable conditions for opium cultivation.

In Transcaucasia, although less dramatically, the fading of the Kremlin's power led to clans becoming openly what they had always been in any case: a state within the state. The arrest of the Talysh 'capo' Yavuz Mirzahassanov in 1993 in no way meant that his organisation had been disbanded. And it didn't stop there: in May of the following year, Mirzahassanov's private militia led by his sons stormed the prison where he was being held in Lerikh, not far from the Iranian border. In a fight straight out of the Wild West that lasted half the day, eight prison guards were critically wounded and two of the attackers, including one of the brothers, lost their lives. Little doubt exists that these events never once even remotely affected the normal running of the family's drugs business.

In Georgia, the government had some success in combating the drugs trade in those areas where it had got out of hand. Apart from Svanetia and northern Kakheti, one such areas was western Kartli, where not so long ago Stalin had uttered his first cries in his cradle but which a century and a half later had become a symbol for corruption, disorder and festering criminality. What happened in Gori and its surrounding areas at dawn on January 22nd 1994 came like a bolt from the blue, when over a hundred policemen conducted by Col. Jemal Danashia, the head of the interior ministry drugs squad, burst into the homes of suspected drugs dealers. Among the detainees was the regional drugs baron Avtandil Buziashvili and an army commander, Lt. Col. Lariashvili, who ran a distribution network within the armed forces. It looked like a blow of some significance. But after a few months, the opposition caused a row in Parliament by demanding an explanation as to why the greater majority of the defendants had been long been walking the streets as free men since the police raid.

In both Azerbaijan and Georgia, as well as Armenia where information on crime-fighting statistics is as unforthcoming as it used to be, in the fine Soviet tradition of hushing-up, organised and covert forms of crime showed an increase during the 1990s, whereas 'petty crime' had gradually declined. In Georgia, for example, reported murders and assaults decreased from 8,735 in 1993 to 5,683 in 1994. No one could doubt that other less violent, less prominent crimes were continuing their relentless rise, being now all the more dangerous for it in political terms.

*

Ganja, Azerbaijan's second city, at first glance appears a lazy provincial town which was momentarily roused from its slumbers only when a young man by the name of Surat Husseynov started his crusade from there against the government of President Abulfaz Elchibey, in late spring 1993. Then, mass demonstrations gathered at regular intervals in the central square. The town echoed with the crowd's cheers, punctuated by bouts of boos and hissing. When Husseynov marched on Baku with his boys, not to return for a long time, the city almost at once fell back into its traditional sleepiness.

At least, that's the impression it wanted give. Because there's a lot more to Ganja. The main bazaar there, which appears the very epitome of gentility to those who know no better, is not a place recommended to visit.

"Please don't go there, I beg you!" insisted a man at the hotel who spoke some German. "If you need something, please ask me or one of the hotel staff instead, and it'll be taken care of. And even here, don't listen to any offers to change money, buy antiques, gold or jewellery. *Keine gute Leute, mein Herr. Viele gute Aseris sind hier, aber leider auch schlechte Leute . . . bitte!*"

It's a strange fact, but I have experienced it on many occasions, that the more criminal and dangerous a place, the friendlier the ordinary people living there. A policeman explained me later that the hissed *"pakupaat?"* ("buy?") was vey often not for a sale of 'objets d'art'. In the streets and the bazaar of Ganja a gramme of uncut opium costs less than a dollar against between five and six in Moscow. In Ganja, the wholesale price for serious traders drops to less than $300 per kilo. One individual who amassed an impressive fortune through this, between late 1991 and late 1994, was the same Surat Husseynov who, in summer 1993, had taken the to barricades to defend the fatherland.

In both activities, it would appear that Husseynov did not act on his own. According to a report, published on the eve of the Russian invasion in Chechenia by the Russian criminologist Anton Surikov, Husseynov used to operate in those days along with Beslan Gantemirov, Ruslan Labazanov and Omar Avturkanov. The names of these individuals and their treacherous role in the bloody events to follow were to become known throughout the world, but Surikov had already made the disclosure that they had close links with Doku Zavgayev, the last Communist leader in Chechenia under Gorbachev, and with Ruslan Hezbollatov, the Russian Federal Parliament's Speaker and Yeltsin's arch rival, also a Chechen.

Their political aim: to undermine the independence movement in Chechenia and bring the nation back inside the Russian Federation. Their reward: control over the profitable arms and drugs trade connection between Transcaucasia and Russia. It has even been suggested that the whole 'connection' was under the indirect or even direct control of Paul

Grachov, the Russian ex-minister of defence and Butcher of Grozny, who in spring 1993 and at various later occasions is reported to have been spotted in Ganja in the company of Surat Husseynov.

Certainly, it can be argued that such a web of relationships casts the Russian invasion of Chechenia in a different light. It can be argued that adding up all the facts and figures leads to only one possible conclusion: that this was no more and no less a common-or-garden mafia war in which the West politely applauded the way the Kremlin settled a score with a man who hardly had a clean record himself, and who would settle for little less than putting himself at the head of the north-south drugs trade-route at the other's expense.

That man was Jokhar Dudayev, member of a lesser *teip*, or clan, from the High Caucasus, who initially enjoyed the support of Sultan Qelish-khanov, head of the all-powerful Chechen Melkhy clan. Qelishkhanov became Dudayev's security chief until they split after a quarrel — which signalled the beginning of the end for Chechenia's 'experiment' in independence.

The story Surikov has to tell is a real eye-opener, at least for those who know how to filter facts from allegations and over-affirmative, unsustainable claims. His blunt assertion, for example, that 'the' drugs mafia in the former Soviet Union is completely 'dominated' by 'the Chechen group' (as if there were no all-Russian drug mafias) echoes the statements of others seeking justification for 'policing' Chechenia in the very way that was to happen. Of course, one should not let any of this detract from the fact that the drug mafias, Chechen or otherwise, throughout the Russian Federation and its neighbouring states lack political dimensions.

Georgia is a case in point: according to Surikov and other experts, by the mid 1990s the country was responsible for at least half the transit of opium and opium products between Central Asia and Europe (although, in Surikov's case, the absence again of figures or even rough estimates casts some doubt on the basis of the allegation), but those trade lines that did exist were definitely controlled by people with political aspirations.

In 1993-94, unscheduled flights would land at regular intervals at the airport of Kutaisi, the second largest city in Georgia, which in those days was under the tight control of Ioseliani's Mkhedrioni. From there, loads varying from a few hundred kilos to a tonne or more went either straight or via the Russian army base to the port of Poti, from where they were shipped to the Crimea right under the noses of the Russian navy officers based there. The Crimea has a long history as a hotbed of Black Sea piracy. Post-Soviet Russian and Ukrainian sources have even suggested that one of the reasons for Britain playing hero over there in the days of Florence Nightingale was the protection of its own lucrative opium trade. Again, no details are given, which in no way detracts from such a fascinating chain of thought.

How exactly the Transcaucasian conglomerate of drug smuggling fits together and how in turn it slots into the jigsaw of world narcotics was still pretty much guesswork when in 1995 the newly-created Interpol departments in the three republics embarked on their first investigations. Speculation was rife, aside from the connections already mentioned, about the 'Armenian Connection' between the Bekaa Valley in Lebanon and drugs syndicates in Rostov, Kislovosk and Sebastopol and the prominent role the Dashnaks played in them (see above), but little more information was on offer than reports about the revival of old feuds — such as rivalry with supporters of the leader of the redundant Lebanese military rebels, ex-General Michel Aoun, who since 1990 from his villa in the south of France, where he lived in exile, allegedly maintained close ties with the Marseilles underworld. Whatever the case, even if the most conservative inventory was made of all the 'connections', it should be clear by now that their tentacles have spread far beyond the borders of the former USSR, and this didn't exactly happen yesterday.

One such border, opened in 1987, is Sarp on the Black Sea coast between Hopa on the Turkish side and Batumi in Georgia. In the early 1990s, the border post was a chaotic place to be. Buses and lorries had to queue for 24 hours or more in order to get the necessary paperwork cleared, and it was only after the opening of a second border post in 1996 near Akhaltsikhe (outside Ajaria to the east) was the pressure relieved.

Now every country has (at least) two societies. Each of these has its own economy, its own social relationships, its own laws and means of implementing them. What is goes on in one society is clearly visible in the form of published rules, facts and statistics, whereas in the other rules tend to stay unwritten and facts and figures are rare to say the least. Since every country across the world offers 'layered' societies in one form or another, neither the Transcaucasian republics nor Turkey are exceptions to this rule.

People learn to live with both these worlds — as if bilingual. For example, I was at the Dutch embassy in Ankara when a man burst in panting. He blurted out that "they" were on his heels and if he was forced off the premises he wouldn't make it alive to the next street corner. This was just another colourful episode confirming the decades-long flow of reports and stories about the Turkish underworld and its hot-lines to top political circles. In the embassy, the man's story barely raised an eyebrow: Greenmantle revisited . . .

Upholders of the law, however, who declare themselves honest and refuse to have anything to do with the schemes of those wanting to undermine public order can be found anywhere, even in Hopa. One of them is Enver, a short, balding and, most of all, friendly and brave man who has been repeatedly offered the carrot of a high-flying career as home office official in Ankara. He always refused, and in 1994 he had even considered giving it all up to spend a few years doing business — upfront business, that is, according to the book unlike the practices of all those pirates his efforts had helped put behind bars — so he could enjoy a comfortable retirement. However, he stayed on the job.

By the end of 1992 the first arrest in Turkey of post-Soviet drugs couriers had already taken place, as in Ankara a group of Uzbeks were apprehended in possession of a ton and a half of uncut opium. As they were to admit under interrogation, they had managed to take consignment through Turkmenistan, Azerbaijan and Georgia unhindered. The arrest triggered off a tightening of the Black Sea border post between Batumi and Hopa by the Turkish authorities. Enver was ordered to rigorously check anything that came through — lorries in particular — and was give the authority to stop and search anything that aroused his suspicion.

Despite receiving a tip-off from Tbilisi, the policeman could hardly contain his astonishment when, on New Year's Eve 1992 — surely his finest hour — he discovered hidden under two Turkish lorries, which had entered from Iran through Ganja and Tbilisi, uncut morphine with a street value of well over $15 million. Ever since, the number of arrests in both Georgia and Turkey has risen into the hundreds — although this must mean that the number of couriers slipping through the net is well into the thousands.

Initially, many couriers tried to leave Georgia through the port of Batumi in order to reach Turkey or other Mediterranean countries by sea. However, transit cargo in Batumi has also become subject to tighter control which has led to the arrests of a large number of couriers representing a broad international spectrum. In February 1994, for example, a Nigerian was caught on his way to Bulgaria carrying 220 grammes of uncut opium originating from Tajikistan.

Since then, the 'safest' route for drugs couriers across the border has been over the inaccessible mountain ridges (the 'Lesser Caucasus') in the hinterland to the south-east, and from there towards Kars and Artvin on the Turkish side. From there, the merchandise is smuggled to Europe principally through the ports of Marseilles, Barcelona and Antwerp.

On top of all this, however, Transcaucasia has become far more than a mere transfer station for long-distance drugs trafficking, rendered attractive for its strategic position. Apart from the cultivation in Azerbaijan of opiuum and marijuana mentioned earlier, Georgia in particular has started producing cocaine in recent years — for the moment, not more than a few score tons of raw material, but with an ominous quality, according to local security officials, that fully matches its Peruvian, Bolivian and Colombian competitors.

What happens with the revenues generated by this contemporary version of the ancient and medieval slave trade is not hard to guess. As with the Russian Federation and the other former Soviet republics, the three Transcaucasian states cannot afford to be over-selective in terms of investments. The public treasuries are empty and, as long as they remain so, every penny counts, no matter its colour. Widespread corruption and bureacratic lethargy do the rest. The result is that, ever since the gradual collapse of the 'Realm of Evil' at the end of the 1980s, each community is forced to cope with what is generally referred to the 'Lost Generation'.

Not the older generation, of whose ranks many learnt nothing and are likely to stay that way. No, these are the new generation, people now in their twenties and thirties who have to learn things the hard way if they are ever to do so. While they are at it, these communities are forced to battle the potential emergence of an immense 'Sicily', where civilisation merely serves as a cover for an unprecedented underworld order that knows no bounds. Perversely, this is as much as result of the 'New World Order', introduced to the market by US-driven 'Reaganomics', which itself was based more on random sloganeering than business sense.

Interpol officials in the three Transcaucasian capitals openly acknowledge such dangers and accept that for the present at least they are hardly in a position to deal with the huge rise in crime. Indeed, as Peter Mamradze, adviser to Shevardnadze, added in spring 1995: "When you take into account that each year in New York alone drugs worth anything up to $20 billion are sold, or that in the City of London some $80 billion is laundered yearly, can you in all honesty expect us — considering the state we're in — to wave a magic wand and create a drugs-free zone here?'

We know already that the danger created by the drug connection in and through Transcaucasia is created not so much by the physical connection itself than by its political dimension. As was the case with the US during the 1950s, '60s and '70s in Latin America, those who today wield power in the Kremlin actively cultivate the loyal cliques of power-brokers in their former satellite states. Thus we see conmen on the run in Chechenia promoted as complete gangs to form a 'democratically'-minded opposition, lavished with cash and arms, while political and material support no less generous is handed to former Communist power syndicates in the Central Asian republics, blatantly ignoring of their criminal sidelines.

This is the structure that allows and encourages such individuals as 'General' Dostom, a shady warlord in Afghanistan of Uzbek origin heavily involved in the Afghan civil war, to maintain a personal mini-empire in the north east of Afghanistan, bordering Tajikistan and Uzbekistan, supported openly by the Uzbek head of state Islam Karimov, who in turn enjoys the Kremlin's full and generous support.

It must be admitted that the Western World is no position to protest, even if it wanted to. The various dictatorships of recent decades were all notable for the public and private treasuries that were just as generously filled with illicit revenues from arms and drugs deals. And, even if the accusations against someone like Paul Grachov are proved in time, his misdeeds must surely fade in comparison to gangster generals like Mont, Videla and Pinochet. Franco and Papadopoulos, for their part, have already become part of history. Whether or not short-term civic decency will find a chance of prevailing in the Central and West Asian republics of the ex-Soviet Union boils down to looking to the future with hope and expectation. What is certain, however, is that a significant, new dimension has been added to the world of organised crime and its multinational facets, twisting it all around, namely that crime itself is just another dimension of socio-political rupture and disruption.

Concluding a book on the Southern Caucasus, it would therefore seem, is a harder task than writing it. Five years of picking my way through reports on massacres, political intrigue, shady business deals, risking physical danger, enduring back in Europe endless debates with armchair experts, witnessing the love for this unique part of the world shared by a growing number of my compatriots in the West, all this has resulted in an immense enrichment of mental experience and tolerance. As I fly in a rickety plane from Baku to Tblisi, the majestic peaks of the Caucasus below are dwarfed before my eyes. But still they remain the calm rock for those dwelling on its slopes who refuse to calm themselves so long as there are those who refuse to let them do so.

*

References

Afanasyan, Serge, *L'Arménie, l'Azerbaidjan et la Géorgie de l'indépendence à l'instauration du pouvoir soviétique 1917-1923*, L'Harmattan, Paris, 1982.

Aliyev, Elgar, *Nagorno-Karabakh — istoriye, fakty, rabitiya*, Elm, Baku, 1989.

Allen, W. E. D. & P. Muratov, *Caucasian battlefields*, Cambridge University Press, Cambridge, 1953.

Alstadt, Audrey L., *The Azerbaijani Turks — power and identity under Russian rule*, Hoover Institution Press, Stanford, 1992.

Ashorbely, Sara, *Gazudarstvo Shirvanshahov*, Elm, Baku, 1983.

Atkin, M., *Russia and Iran 1780-1828*, Minnesota University Press, Minneapolis, 1980.

Baddeley, F. C., *The Russian conquest of the Caucasus*, Longman, 1903 [Curzon, 1999].

Bakikhanov, Abbas-Kuly Aga, *Gulstan Iram*, ed. Z. M. Bunyatov, Zam, Baku, 1993.

Bihl, W., *Die Kaukazuspolitik der Mittelmaechte*, Kommission für Geschichte Oesterreichs, Vienna, 1975.

Daskuranzhy, Movses, *The history of the Caucasian Albanians*, London Oriental Series, London, 1961.

Donabédian, patrick & Claude Moutafian, *Le Karabakh*, GDM, Paris, 1989.

Dumas, Alexandre, *Le Caucase*, François Bourin, Paris, 1990.

Eberhard, Elke, *Osmanische Politik gegen die Safaviden im 16. Jahrhundert*, Freiburg, 1970.

Environmental condition and nature producing activity in the Republic of Azerbaijan, State Committee of the Azerbaijan Republic on Nature Protection, Baku, 1993.

Gerretson, C., *De geschiedenis der 'Koninklijke'*, I:VI, Bosch & Keuning, baarn, 1972.

Gougouchvili, S. & N., D. & O. Zourabichvili, *La Géorgie*, Presses Universitaires de France, Paris, 1972.

Gunter, Michael M., *Transnational Armenian Activism*, RISCT Conflict Studies No. 229, London, 1990.

Homayounpour, P., *L'affaire Azerbaidjan*, Payot, Lausanne, 1967.

Kazemzadeh, Firuz, *The struggle for Transcaucaucasia*, Oxford, 1951.
Keun, Odette, *Au pays du toissin d'or*, Flammarion, Paris, 1923.

Lordkipanidze, Mariam, *Georgia in the 11th-12th centuries*, Ganatleba, Tbilisi, 1987.

Mahmudov, Yagub, *Vzaymoyotnoshenya gazudarstvo Akkoyonlu y Sefevidov s Zapadnoyevopeyisksmy Stranamy*, Yzdatelsto Bakinskovo Universitiyeta, Baku, 1991.
Malville, Georges de, *La tragédie arménienne de 1915*, Lanore, Paris, n.d.
Minorsky, V., *Studies in Caucasian history*, Taylor's Foreign Press, London, 1953.

Pasdermadjian, H., *Histoire de l'Arménie*, Libraire Orientale, Paris, 1986.
Podlesskikh, Gyorgy & Andrei Tyereshonok, *Vory v zakony*, Vyeche, Moscow, 1995.

Sumbatoglu Sumbatzadeh, Alisoybat, *Azerbeidzhansty etnogenez y formirovanye naroda*, Elm, Baku, 1993.
Suny, R. G., *Transcaucasia — nationalism and social change*, Ann Arbour, Michigan, 1983.
Suny, R. G., *The making of the Georgian nation*, Indiana University Press, Bloomington, 1988.
Swietochowski, Tadeusz, *Russian Azerbaijan 1905-1920*, Cambridge University Press, Cambridge, 1985.

Ter Nimassian, Anahide, *La république arménienne 1918-1920*, Complexe, Brussels, 1989.
Trevor, K. B., *Essay on the history and culture of Caucasian Albania*, London, 1959.

van der Leeuw, Charles, *Storm over de Kaukasus*, Babylon, Amsterdam, 1997.
Velichky, Vasily Lvovich, *Kavkaz*, St Petersburg, 1904 [Elm, Baku 1990].

Wolf, R. W., *The saga of the Nobel family and the Russian oil industry*, Stanford University Press, London, 1976.
Woods, J. E., *The Aqqoyunlu — clan, confederation, empire*, Chicago, 1976.

Yunussova, Leila, *Torgovaya expansiya Anglyi v basseinyi Kaspiya v pervoy plovnye XVIII veka*, Elm, Baku, 1988.

Index

Index

Index

Index